Science and Racket Sports II

OTHER TITLES FROM E & FN SPON

Science and Racket Sports II

Edited by

A. Lees
Centre for Sport and Exercise Sciences,
Liverpool John Moores University, UK

I. Maynard
School of Sports Studies,
Chichester Institute of Higher Education, UK

M. Hughes
The Centre for Notational Analysis,
University of Wales Institute, Cardiff, UK

and

T. Reilly
Centre for Sport and Exercise Sciences,
Liverpool John Moores University, UK

E & FN Spon
An imprint of Routledge

London and New York

First published 1998
by E & FN Spon, an imprint of Routledge
11 New Fetter Lane, London EC4P 4EE

Simultaneously published in the USA and Canada
by Routledge
29 West 35th Street, New York, NY 10001

Printed and bound in Great Britain by
St Edmundsbury Press, Bury St Edmunds, Suffolk

Publisher's Note
This book has been produced from camera-ready copy
provided by the individual contributors.

British Library Cataloguing in Publication Data
A catalogue record for this book is available
from the British Library

ISBN 0 419 23030 0

Second World Congress of Science and Racket Sports and the Fifth International Table Tennis Federation Sports Science Congress
22–25 April 1997

held at The National Sports Centre, Lillishall, Shropshire, UK

Organising Committee
Mike Hughes
Adrian Lees
Gail McCulloch
Ian Maynard (Chair)

Scientific Committee
Mike Hughes
Adrian Lees (Chair)
Ian Maynard,
Thomas Reilly

Organising Secretariat
Julia Roebuck

CONTENTS

PREFACE

The conference incorporating both the Second World Congress of Science and Racket Sports and the Fifth International Table Tennis Federation Sports Science Congress was held at the National Sports Centre, Lilleshall, Shropshire, UK from April 22 – 25 1997. The combination of the two conferences was timely and coincided with the 44th World Table Tennis Championships held at Manchester, UK in the week following.

The World Congress of Science and Racket Sports was the second in its series (the first being held at Runcorn, UK in 1993) and has a four-yearly cycle. It is a part of the academic programmes initiated by the World Commission of Sports Biomechanics which, over the last three decades, has promoted applied sports science congresses on swimming, football, golf, and winter sports. The broad aim of these is to bring together scientists whose research work is concerned with particular sports and practitioners in these sports who are interested in obtaining current information about scientific aspects.

The International Table Tennis Federation (ITTF) holds its Sports Science Congress biannually and this was the fifth in its series (previous congresses being held at Dortmund, Chiba, Gothenberg and Tianjin). It has the aim of promoting and disseminating scientific research specifically within the game of table tennis.

The aims of each congress are thus broadly similar and so when the opportunity arose to combine the two congresses the amalgamation was welcomed by both groups. Joint organising and scientific committees were established and their members worked together to promote the aims of both organisations. The scientific programme consisted of a series of keynote lectures, podium communications, poster presentations and workshops. These were complemented by practical demonstrations in badminton, tennis, table tennis, and squash. The result was a well attended congress with participants from every continent who were able to interact across the scientific disciplines and across the various racket sports.

The organisers are indebted to the ITTF whose sponsorship of the combined event ensured its success. The organisers are also grateful for the co-operation and support given by the host country's governing bodies, the Badminton Association of England, the English Table Tennis Association, the Lawn Tennis Association, and the Squash Rackets Association.

Adrian Lees (Chair)
Ian Maynard
Mike Hughes
Thomas Reilly

INTRODUCTION

This volume contains papers presented at the Second World Congress of Science and Racket Sports and the Fifth International Table Tennis Federation Sports Science Congress held at the National Sports Centre, Lilleshall, Shropshire, UK from April 22 – 25 1997. Each manuscript has been subject to peer review by at least two expert referees and editorial judgement before being accepted for publication. This review process has ensured that there is consistency and a high level of scientific quality across all papers.

The volume contains 40 papers covering all four racket sports, although most address issues which have application across all racket disciplines. The papers are organised into six scientific parts, each part representing a theme of the congress and in most cases is introduced by one of the keynote lectures. One of the aims of the Congress was to make the work of scientists more accessible to those working and coaching within the racket sports. To this end authors were asked to address the practical implications of their work. Details of these are contained in each paper, but an overview of the key findings is presented below. It is hoped that this overview enhances the value of the volume to practitioners by giving direction to those papers which may be of relevance to them. It is also hoped that such a development is a practical outcome of an underlying theme of the congress, which was to provide a link between scientist and practitioner.

Part one is concerned with the physiological characteristics of racket sports players and the demands of the sport, focusing particularly on squash and tennis. Two papers are concerned with the game of squash at elite level. Sharp in his keynote paper identifies the demands of play in terms of speed of movement, duration of play and work-rest intervals, and the corresponding physiological characteristics demonstrated by players at this level. The efficacy of training regimens is considered in detail and suggestions for appropriate fitness training given. The theme of players' physiological characteristics is continued by Brown *et al.* who demonstrate the increased capability for oxygen uptake in senior as opposed to elite junior players and identify this as a major consideration in the transition from elite junior to the senior game. They recommend the re-introduction of intermediate (under 21 and under 23) training squads to ease this transition. The training effect associated with playing tennis is considered in three of the papers. Bernardi *et al.* found a training effect for tennis players of medium ability providing they engaged in base-line play that prolonged their game. Ferrauti *et al.* show that senior league tennis players exhibit increased energy expenditure and lipid metabolism that could induce long term physiological adaptations. Sanchis Moysi *et al.* report that elite tennis players show enhanced muscle mass and bone mineral density in the playing arm. These studies therefore suggest that the game of tennis should be promoted for its beneficial effects on the fitness of participants.

Part two is concerned with the nutritional requirements of racket sports and is introduced with the keynote lecture by MacLaren. He compares the energy expenditure of the four major racket sports and the role of carbohydrate consumption for providing this energy. Strategies are given to promote the rapid restoration of muscle glycogen by means of carbohydrate consumption. The problems of dehydration are considered and the efficacy of carbohydrate-electrolyte drinks discussed. Strategies are recommended for hydration before, during and immediately after the match. To complete the review, recommendations are given for protein and mineral consumption. The theme of dehydration is continued by McCarthy *et al.* who report fluid losses in junior tennis players of 2-3% of body mass, and Brown and Winter who report fluid loss in competitive squash players of up to 2.5 l.h^{-1} which amounts to 3-4% of body mass. Both sets of authors comment on rehydration strategies. Ferrauti and Weber describe the ergogenic effects of caffeine on tennis performance. They found that consuming a caffeine loaded drink (equivalent to that contained in a coke drink) had in general no effect on energy metabolism but they reported some transient effects at the onset of exercise and an indication that the female players in their study derived more benefit from this substance than male players. The effects of carbohydrate loading on shot accuracy in squash were investigated by Graydon *et al.* who report improved performance in a carbohydrate loaded group. It is clear that nutritional control is a vital aspect of all racket sport play. There are issues relating to correct nutritional preparation for play, the deleterious effect of dehydration and the beneficial effects of nutritional substances, which all racket players should be aware of.

Part three is concerned with preparation for playing racket sports. A comprehensive coverage of the factors associated with correct conditioning for play are given in the keynote paper by Chandler. From a consideration of the demands of the sport, the general principles of designing exercise programmes are given. The role of periodisation in preparation for play is considered as is the need to maintain fitness over a long playing season. Suggestions are given for planning the conditioning programme which moves from general athletic fitness to sport specific fitness. Testing fitness within the context of the game is an issue addressed by Bawden and Maynard. They report a table-tennis specific fitness test which appears to have some practical advantages compared to standard tests of fitness. Todd *et al.* have an interest in the efficacy of training routines as a preparation for competitive play in squash. They report that a specific boast, drop and drive routine exceeds the intensity of an average game and is recommended as an overload training routine. Modern racket play takes place throughout the world and players are frequently required to travel long distance for competition. Reilly *et al.* in their keynote paper, consider the problems of travel fatigue and those problems associated with crossing time zones. The recommendations for coping with these disruptions and minimising their effect are of practical use to all racket players.

Part four is concerned with psychology of racket sports and covers a range of applications. Singer, in his keynote paper, considers the role of anticipation and decision making in racket play. He identifies key factors underlying these phenomena such as the use of visual cues and visual search patters used by players. He also considers the role of perception and the extent that these skills may be trainable. Further information on how highly skilled tennis players search their visual field during play are given by Williams *et al.* who conclude that reliable assessments of visual search strategies can be obtained from players in a practical setting. Also in tennis, Smith and Jones use a qualitative research paradigm to establish the levels of anxiety experienced by players of different skill levels and the effects that anxiety has on their core playing skills. They found that better players were more likely to perceive their anxiety as facilitative than less able players. A range of psychological investigations has been conducted in table tennis. Lapszo reports on a device which simulates table tennis play and enables anticipation skills as well as a range of other psycho-motor characteristics to be evaluated and trained. Potter and Anderson use performance profiling with junior table tennis players as a basis to support psychological interventions. Samulski and Lima investigate the efficacy of cognitive self-regulation techniques to help players face critical situations in competition, finding that they were more effective than other (e.g. motor) techniques used by players. Falby uses technical rehearsal and imagery techniques to promote relaxed movements in play with skilled table tennis players. The relaxation was monitored by measuring levels of muscle activity and this combination of techniques proved viable and helpful to players. Robertson *et al.* investigate the link between individuals with Type A behaviour patterns and their participation in squash. They report a prevalence of Type A behaviour amongst the higher ability players, but there was no link found with a higher cardiac risk as measured by blood lipid profiles. Mahoney and Todd report on the baseline psychological skills possessed by elite junior players and use this to form the basis of a psychological skills training programme. In badminton, Hudson reports on the efficacy of intervention in young players to manage their arousal levels and to help players understand their arousal discrepancy and its likely effect on their performance and continued participation in the game. It is apparent that there are numerous directions which sports psychology can take to both understand the mechanisms and characteristics of racket play, and to offer practical help to players. The techniques described in these papers will have applications across all racket sports.

Part five is concerned with the medical, biomechanical and technological aspects of racket sports. Racket players who make frequent overhead movements such as serving in tennis or smashing in badminton, may suffer from a sense of discomfort or pain and inhibited performance which is generally termed Thoracic Outlet Syndrome. Clarys *et al.* report on the presence of a muscular arch between the upper arm and the ribcage known as the Arch of Langer. This is found in about 10% of the population and is thought to be an explanatory mechanism for the syndrome. Although speed of serve in tennis is thought to be an important factor, Mantis *et al.* claim that it does not appear to be a decisive factor in the ranking of Greek junior tennis players. Speed measurements can be easily made by radar gun and provide helpful feedback to players and coaches, but needs to be combined with additional information in order to explain levels of achievement. Pizzinato *et al.* describe the use of an 'expert system' to investigate the decision making process in tennis. The system can provide players with feedback concerning the processes they go through so as to help them understand any mistakes they may make. The techniques used in performing the forehand shots in table tennis are described by Kasai and Mori who found that their approach helped to identify weaknesses in technical performance of players. The effect of manipulating mass and diameter of the table tennis ball is reported by Xiaopeng. He found that the speed and spin of the larger and heavier balls were significantly lower than that of the standard ball, thus suggesting that its adoption would affect on the way the game is played. A detailed study of the physical characteristics of players' movements and the equipment they use can help to understand some of the factors enhancing and limiting performance in racket sports.

Part six is concerned with the techniques of notational analysis and their application to racket sports. Notational analysis provides the means for quantifying players' movements during competition and can be used for assessing the technical or physiological demands of the game, evaluating the effects of environmental and equipment factors on performance, modelling player behaviour and inferring tactics used by players. The keynote paper by Hughes describes these uses through various examples from squash and tennis. Further applications follow in the papers presented. In squash, McGarry *et al.* attempt to model the movement interaction between two players on court as a dynamical system, thereby giving insight into their current and likely future actions. Hughes and Robertson present a template for elite squash players so as to help in the development of a tactical model for this game. Murray *et al.* give feedback from notational analysis to squash players in order to investigate whether this information can improve performance, and their preliminary results suggest this is a fruitful avenue for intervention. In tennis, O'Donoghue and Liddle investigate the effect of surface on the length of rallies at the French and Wimbledon tournaments. They report significantly longer rallies on clay rather than grass, thus confirming that the slower clay courts lead to longer rally lengths. The same authors also investigate tactical plays used in the ladies singles event on clay and on grass surfaces. They report differences in tactics used with the serve and the initiation of a move towards the net which were attributed to the type of surface. Hughes and Moore investigate the extent that tennis players moved around the ball so as to hit it on their preferred side and the effect that this has on the outcome of rallies. Their preliminary results suggest that moving to play a shot on the preferred side did place added pressure on the player often leading to the loss of a point. Taylor and Hughes found that patterns of play for British under-18 players differed from those of the same age from another country. The authors suggest this might be a factor inhibiting British players in their transition to the senior game. Table tennis has received less attention from notational analysts, but Wilson and Barnes report on the development of a valid and objective analysis system for that game. The availability of an instrument for quantifying table tennis play will undoubtedly encourage others to research into this game. Two reports focus on badminton. Blomqvist *et al.* report that Finnish primary school children demonstrate a similar technical understanding of the game to that of older children but their progress is inhibited by their lack of technical ability. Finally, Liddle and O'Donoghue compare rally lengths and rest intervals between mens' and ladies' tournament badminton. Their findings suggest that these differed significantly between the two events. This led the authors to suggest that there should be a differential training programme for men and women players and that a positive strategy should be employed to take full advantage of the inter-rally rest periods.

The papers presented in this volume are a testimony to the quality of applied research currently undertaken in the area of racket sports. It is clear from the continuing success of these racket specific congresses that there is a sustained and expanding interest in the application of scientific principles to racket sport performance. It is hoped that the work presented in this volume will stimulate further investigations and that some of these will be presented at the Sixth International Table Tennis Federation Sports Science Congress in 1999, or the Third World Congress of Science and Racket Sports in 2001.

Adrian Lees (Chair)

Part One

Physiology of Racket Sports

1 Physiological demands and fitness for squash

N.C.C. Sharp
Department of Sport Sciences, Brunel University, Middlesex, UK

1 Introduction

This year (1997), which sees England as World Men's Senior and Junior Squash Team champions, a Scottish player, Peter Nicol, in the final of the British Open Championship and ranked three in the world, and seven England women players in the world top 12, is a good time to review briefly some of the physical demands of squash. 'Total Fitness' for squash includes nine items, all of which must be optimised, to provide:- 1) the best racket techniques and court movement skills; 2) the best equipment; - rackets and balls, shoes and clothing; 3) the best on-court tactics at different stages of the rally, game, match, and tournament; 4) an appropriate psychological approach; 5) excellent sports medicine, including physiotherapy and podiatry; 6) appropriate nutrition, including fluid intake; 7) elite physiological and fitness preparation; 8) the best team selection; 9) top class team management.

This review considers investigations into fitness levels of squash players, some demands of the game and of anaerobic interval shadow-training, together with a brief consideration of training modes for squash.

Studies have been made on tennis (Reilly and Palmer, 1995; Elliott et al., 1985), badminton (Hughes, M.G., 1995; Coad et al., 1979, Mikkelsen, 1979) and squash (Blanksby et al., 1980; Noakes et al., 1982; Montpetit, 1990; Reilly, 1990; Brown and Winter, 1995; Buckley et al., 1993; Lynch et al., 1992; Winter et al., 1995; Mellor et al., 1995 and Mahoney and Sharp, 1995), but there is still a remarkable amount of information needed before comprehensive knowledge of any of the racket sports can be claimed. Here the focus will be on squash rackets, including some previously unpublished data from the author and his postgraduate group's work with England men's, women's, junior's and boy's national squads, and the Scottish women's squad, between 1975 and 1992.

Science and Racket Sports II, edited by A. Lees, I. Maynard, M. Hughes and T. Reilly. Published in 1998 by E & FN Spon, 11 New Fetter Lane, London EC4P 4EE, UK.   ISBN: 0 419 23030 0

2 The Demands of the Game

Physical fitness for squash also consists of a cluster of items; 1) Cardio-respiratory fitness ('aerobic fitness'); 2) Muscle endurance - a combination of the ability to deliver appropriate anaerobic and aerobic power together with the equally important ability to recover. This is often termed 'local muscle endurance - or, somewhat inaccurately, 'anaerobic endurance'; 3) Muscle strength - more important in tennis than the other racket sports, but nevertheless, for squash players it is particularly important to have a strong abdomen and lower back with reasonable leg strength, and a grip strength that is not below threshold levels; 4) Muscle speed - an important component of power in all the racket sports, particularly off-the-mark speed of movement, and racket speed; 5) Flexibility - especially of quadriceps and hamstrings, mainly to help prevent injury; 6) Low percentage body fat (7-12% for men, and 18-27% for women, at elite levels).

2.1 Duration
Major competition squash matches have been timed to run from minima of 6 min 37 s (Kenyon v Nadi, 1992) or 6 min 48 s (Mrs D. Murray v Ms C. Rees 1979), both matches 27-0, up to a maximum of 2 h 45 min (Jahangir v Awad, 9-10, 9-5, 9-7, 9-2. 1983) - with a first game lasting 71 min. One rally may last one stroke and 1.5 s, or 400 strokes and 10 min (Hunt v Awad, 1982). More usually - for training purposes - rallies can be categorised into three main groups, those lasting up to 5 s, those between 6-20 s (the majority), and a small but important number which lasts upwards of 20, but not usually longer than 60 s (Figure 1). There is approximately 7 s between rallies, which are played at a stroke rate of up to 40 strokes per minute, i.e. 20 per player. The author has numerated games between senior men players of national/international standard resulting in a mean of 1722 (573 - 4128) shots in 82 (48 - 172) rallies per match, which compares well with the findings of Hughes and McGarry (1988) at 1651 shots in 89.2 rallies per match. Such surveys have means which are of limited value due to their very large standard deviations.

2.2 Mechanics
The Physics Department of Birmingham University, utilising a sonic timing system, has timed national standard players on the forehand drive (Dunlop 'yellow spot' ball, temperature 52oC) at upwards of 70 $m.s^{-1}$ (157 mph) and club players at around 40 $m.s^{-1}$ (89 mph), (Wilson and Sharp, unpublished observation, University of Birmingham, 1980). Due to the coefficient of restitution of the competition squash ball being set at around 20%, the front-wall rebound speeds are of the order of 14 and 8 $m.s^{-1}$ (31 and 18 mph) respectively. This disparity between hitting velocity, and rebound velocity off the front wall, confuses beginners, who thus tend to over-run the ball. These squash ball velocities compare with the tennis serve 63.6 $m.s^{-1}$ (142.3 mph, Mark Philippoussis), fast bowling 44.6 $m.s^{-1}$ (100 mph, Jeff Thomson), golf 75.8 $m.s^{-1}$ (170 mph), and pelota, 83.9 $m.s^{-1}$ (188 mph) - (Guinness Records, 1996). For comparison, a cheetah runs at 29 $m.s^{-1}$ (64 mph, Sharp 1997).

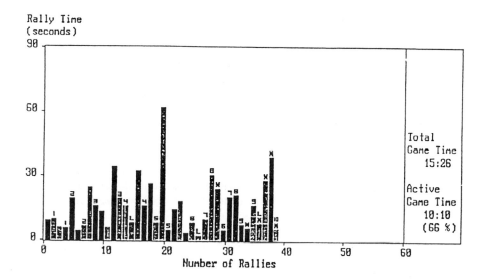

Figure 1. Examples of different lengths of rally during an international match
(European Men's Squash championship, England vs Sweden).

2.3 Physiological data during play

The heart rate rises in the first few minutes of play to 80-90% of maximum, which is maintained throughout the match (Blanksby et al., 1973; Beaudin et al., 1978; Brown and Winter, 1995). Body temperature may rise by 2°C in the first 40 min, thereafter more slowly, and male players lose may sweat at a rate of up to 2.0 l.h^{-1}, and women at approximately 60% of this rate (Blanksby et al., 1980). Systolic blood pressure rises by up to 30% in the first 5 min, but thereafter falls linearly to pre-match levels after 30-40 min. Diastolic blood pressure tends to fall by about 10 mm Hg or more, according to standard, throughout the same period (Blanksby et al., 1980; Brown and Winter, 1995).

Oxygen consumption during the game ranges from 2.0 to 3.5 l.min^{-1} (up to about 32 ml.kg^{-1}.min^{-1} for women, 40 ml.kg^{-1}.min^{-1} for men), with energy expenditures of 10 to 18 kcal (42 - 75 kJ).min^{-1}. Lactic acid levels, after 30-40 min play, range from 3.5 to >10.0 mmol.l^{-1} (for men, less for women) and may be reduced during play by exploitation of suitable tactics involving 'time shots'. Lactate levels may also be minimised by 4 to 12 weeks of suitably phased interval 'shadow-training' or 'ghosting' (*vide infra*). Such interval-training regimen are surprisingly specific in their application to individual players. In players of all standards, a poorer tactical sense may surface as an apparent lack of physical fitness, e.g. if one player is allowed to dominate the court movement pattern, fmrcing over-exertion in the other.

3 Physiological Parameters of Players

Top class male players tend to have maximum oxygen uptakes in the mid-60's and upwards (ml.kg^{-1}.min^{-1}), high anaerobic thresholds (60 to >80% $\dot{V}O_2$ max) and body fat percentages between 7 and 12%. On the Wingate anaerobic test they tend to have leg peak powers of 12.5-13.5 W.kg^{-1}, a 'fatigue index' of between -10 and -15 W.s^{-1}, and a 'recovery index' (measuring work done in kJ on a repeat test 4 min later, expressed as a percentage of that achieved on the first test) of 95-98%. They tend to have hand-grip strengths of 450-600 N (Sharp and Allan, unpublished observations, University of Birmingham, 1975-87; Sharp, Koutedakis and Hughes, unpublished observations, Northwick Park, 1987-1992). A grip strength threshold of about 400-450 N for men and 300-350 N for women is considered desirable, to prevent the racket twisting in the hand on an off-centre hard-hit shot, as assessed from high-speed film data (Sharp and Joshi, unpublished observations, University of Birmingham, 1978). 'Late-game' errors are often considered to be due to lapses in concentration, but forearm muscle fatigue may be an important element.

Female players tend to have a $\dot{V}O_{2max}$ in the low to mid-50's (ml.kg^{-1}.min^{-1}), with similarly high anaerobic thresholds to men, and body fat percentages in the 18 to 27% range. Their anaerobic leg peak power tend to be around 7.5-8.0 W.kg^{-1}, and their 'fatigue indices' tend to be between -8 and -15 W/s, with 'recovery indices' of 94-100%, and grip strengths of 300-450 N. Within limits, the amount of force required to hold a racket tends to vary inversely with the diameter of the grip (Wilson and Sharp, unpublished observations, University of Birmingham, 1975-82). So the anecdotal view of a thicker grip helping to alleviate recurrence of the lateral epicondylitis of 'tennis/squash elbow' may have some basis in fact, if the amount of force required to grip it is less.

On time-lapse cinephotographic analysis, Sharp and Joshi (unpublished observations, 1978) noted that players of county-standard and upwards tended to deviate markedly through the 'T' on moving from the front to the rear (or vice-versa) of the court; club and recreational players tended to have a more random movement pattern on traversing the court longitudinally. Hughes, M. (1995) and Hughes and Franks (1994) have greatly extended knowledge of playing patterns, and time and motion analysis of squash.

Players of both sexes tend to have 5 to 15% better-than-average simple and complex reaction times. They also have good dynamic balance on stabilometry testing, with upwards of 20 s out of 30 s on settings of 5 degrees from the horizontal (Sharp and Allan, 1975-87, unpublished observations, University of Birmingham; Sharp, Koutedakis and Hughes, unpublished observations, Northwick Park, 1987-92).

4 Investigation of Shadow Training

Hammond, Taylor and Sharp (unpublished observations, University of Birmingham, 1984) investigated levels of blood lactate attained during squash matches of county and international level. A match between two good English county men players showed (Table 1a) fairly typical levels of blood lactate, up to 6.5 mmol.l^{-1} in the winner and 4.7 mmol.l^{-1} in his opponent. The match between an English and a Welsh international player (Table 1b) shows several features: note that it was not until the end of the third game, after some 53 min play, that the lactate levels rose to around 4 mmol.l^{-1}. In the fourth game, player A had to win to stay in the match, but player B, - due to inferior fitness and technical levels, - knew that this was his main chance to win the match. Player B maintained the higher work-rate, but lost the game 9-10, and also came off worse biochemically, by elevating his blood lactate to 9.2 mmol.l^{-1}, compared to his opponent's 5.7 mmol.l^{-1}. In the fifth game, player B tried to get back into the match physically, by slowing the game up with time shots, lobs, a minimum of volleying and a maximum of kills. He succeeded physiologically, but lost the game 5-9. It was noteworthy that he reduced his blood lactate by 3.5 mmol.l^{-1}, which lends credence to the adage that one should not be merciful to a tiring opponent - who may well recover given time, with lowered lactate and renewed vigour and confidence.

Table 1a. Blood lactate levels in male county players during match-play

Sample	Game Score	Blood Lactates (mmol.l^{-1}) Subject	
		A	B
Resting		0.9	1.9
Game 1	9 - 3	3.8	3.4
Game 2	9 - 6	6.5	3.8
Game 3	9 - 6	6.8	4.7
Post Test		2.9	2.1

Table 1b. Blood lactate levels in male international players during match-play

Sample	Game Score	Blood Lactates (mmol.l^{-1}) Subject	
		A	B
Resting		1.1	1.8
Game 1	10 - 9	1.3	2.9
Game 2	8 - 10	3.8	3.7
Game 3	2 - 9	4.3	4.0
Game 4	10 - 9	5.8	9.2
Game 5	9 - 5	4.8	5.7
Post Test		2.7	3.7

The second major point in a series of such investigations of lactate during matches was to provide data on the range of blood lactates to be expected - and therefore the range to be aimed at in training. It was noteworthy that contemporary football players showed similar levels of blood lactate, e.g. German teams had levels of blood lactate of the order of 5.7+1.3 mmol.l^{-1} (1st half) and 6.1±2.7 mmol.l^{-1} (2nd half) with a first half range of 2.2 - 6.8 mmol.l^{-1}, and 2nd half range of 2.2 - 12.4 mmol.l^{-1} (Burger, Leipzig, personal communication, 1984).

Hammond (1984) investigated aspects of shadow training or 'ghosting', to see if they approximated to match play in 14 subjects of good club to international level. The main interval regimen chosen was 45 s of work, with an equal rest (Table 2). Two other regimens, 30 s work 60 s rest, and 60 s work 30 s rest were also investigated on five subjects each (Table 3). All ghosting was done in single sets of 10 repetitions. The work consisted of a given movement pattern at approximately 90% maximum effort, with 'active' rests, in the form of an on-court jog/walk of about 50% work-rate. Results showed the levels of blood lactate in the training approximated well to those produced during match play. In other words, the shadow training is an effective anaerobic glycolytic training stimulus. There was no significant difference between the three training regimens in terms of blood lactate accumulation, although marked differences occurred between the responses of the individual players. For motivational reasons, the 30: 60 work:rest, or 45:45 regimens are preferable.

Table 2. Blood lactates (mmol.l^{-1}) in 45:45 s anaerobic shadow training regime

Subjects	Rest	Lactates:Intervals		
		3	7	10
1	1.42	6.78	10.40	13.80
2	1.30	5.41	8.53	11.60
3	1.20	7.00	10.06	11.16
4	1.86	5.58	6.56	5.10
5	1.64	8.64	9.95	11.16
6	1.30	6.92	7.43	7.78
7	1.83	9.62	11.64	12.83
8	1.97	6.89	7.44	9.95
9	1.70	13.96	18.47	18.65
10	1.64	5.57	8.86	10.83
11	1.97	6.89	7.44	9.95
12	1.75	8.21	9.52	10.72
13	2.31	7.88	13.34	14.21
14	2.18	7.88	7.44	10.28

Seven of the above 14 male players underwent 12 weeks of a standardised predominantly anaerobic training programme for an hour twice weekly, which the other seven players did not do. All 14 performed a 45 s work: 45 s rest 10-repitition maximal anaerobic on-court shuttle test before and after the 12 weeks training: results are displayed in Table 4. The training group showed a significant drop in blood lactate, compared to the controls. In a similar experiment on elite slalom kayak paddlers, Baker (1987) showed that such training could target type 2 muscle fibres. In nine subjects, pre- and post-training biopsies (m. latissimus dorsi) showed the mean type 1 fibre area to be 1984±328 µm2 before, and 2082±372 µ2 after, and type 2 fibre areas to be 3057±827 µ2 before and 4972±1200 µm2 after, indicating that the glycolytic training had indeed targeted the type 2 fibres.

With the squash players, it is important to note the very marked individual differences. In the experimental training group (Table 4), the training for player 1 was ineffective not being aimed enough at lactate removal; for player 2, it was also ineffective, possibly through not sufficiently stimulating glycolytic enzyme induction. This illustrates an important point regarding the training of squash squads, and possibly those in other racket sports. Their common factors for excellence are their

Table 3. Blood lactates (mmol.l^{-1}) in 30:60 s and 60:30 s anaerobic shadow training regimes

30 s work : 60 s rest

Subjects	Lactates:Intervals (mmol.l^{-1})			
	Rest	3	7	10
1	4.60	9.63	10.50	13.35
2	1.64	5.70	6.43	8.90
4	1.31	3.52	1.24	1.63
11	1.75	6.00	6.93	9.14
14	1.92	6.78	5.64	5.25

60 s work : 30 s rest

Subjects	Lactates:Intervals (mmol.l^{-1})			
	Rest	3	7	10
1	1.91	11.40	16.20	15.10
2	1.86	6.24	7.00	13.56
4	1.91	3.72	3.95	4.69
11	1.67	6.00	7.10	7.33
14	2.15	7.22	8.42	10.56

Table 4. Blood lactates from anaerobic shadow tests on experimental training group (top) and control training group (bottom). Post-training levels were significantly lower in the experimental group (P=0.05), but not in the control group

Subjects	Blood Lactate (mmol.l^{-1})	
	Pre-training	Post-training
1	18.6	18.3
2	7.7	8.6
3	11.6	5.6
4	12.8	7.5
5	11.2	9.3
6	10.3	8.8
7	10.7	9.6

Subjects	Blood Lactate (mmol.l^{-1})	
	Pre-training	Post-training
1	13.8	13.2
2	11.6	11.0
3	5.1	6.5
4	9.9	10.4
5	14.2	13.8
6	11.2	12.3
7	10.8	9.3

racket skills, movement ability and tactical sense, together with a good psychological approach. These attributes may accompany a physique, body composition and fibre profile ranging from a sprinter to a marathoner. So unlike, for example, a sprint squad, a marathon squad or a rowing eight - who tend to be relative physiological clones - squash players at national level need individual assessment and training programmes.

5 Fitness Programmes

Several squash texts contain comprehensive tried-and-tested training programmes, for example those by McKenzie (1992), Stevenson (1990), Taylor (1985) and McKay (1977), and the SRA booklet (Sharp, 1986; Chapman and Sharp, 1994). A good pre-season physical training programme will incorporate five elements:- aerobic training, glycotic training, phosphagen (speed) training, strength/power training, and flexibility.

5.1 Aerobic/cardiorespiratory training
This involves a wide variety of modes of training, from aerobic interval on-court work (working for 5 to 10 repetitions of 2-4 min each, with 1-2 min rests) to 20- to 40-min outdoor running or fartlek sessions, performed from two to four times weekly, depending on stage in the training macro-cycle. Skipping at 120 skips/min in one to five 7.5 min sets, with 5 min rests, is an effective alternative training mode.

5.2 Lactate/glycolytic training (for anaerobic power, endurance and recovery)
This involves 6 to 20 repetitions of on-court near-maximal 'ghosting' interval work of 30-45 s, with similar periods of an active (jogging) 'rest': usually training is completed in one set, but possibly two, and the work:rest ratios may alter as the macro-cycle progresses. Fast skipping (180 skips/min) in a set of three to ten 30-45 s repetitions is a useful change.

5.3 Phosphagen (CP)/speed training
This involves on-court interval regimens of possibly 10-15 repetitions of 5 to 10 s maximal speed activity, with 1 min (or more) active rest. Some of items 2) and 3) are often incorporated into various regimens of on-court pressure training, as in former England National Coach Paul Wright's 'interval pressure sessions', 'speed bursts', 'lactate ghosts', 'pyramid ghosts', 'length pyramids' and 'enduro ghosts', as the author has noted when working with him (1990-1995).

5.4 A basic general strength/power training programme
As with most sports, the strength component is primarily needed to improve muscle power, the product of force x velocity. For strength, the weights or loads should be of the order of upwards of 85% of single repetition maximum (SRM), with steady movements, in sets of 4-8. For the speed component, 50 - 65% SRM should be utilised, in sets of 10 to 15, carried out with dynamic movements. These can be done with free or fixed weight systems.

Training exercises with free weights should include: cleans (for posterior deltoid, triceps, gluteus medius, quadriceps, erector spinae, gastrocnemeus, soleus), back squats (for quadriceps, sartorius, iliopsoas, gluteus medius, hip adductors, erector spinae), split squats (for hip adductors), biceps curls (for brachialis, biceps), wrist curls (for wrist flexors), wrist rolls (for finger and wrist flexors), lateral raises (for deltoids, supraspinatus), military presses behind neck (for deltoids, supraspinatus, triceps), trunk curls (for abdominals) along with (unloaded) back hyperextensions. Equivalents of the above exercises may also be done on general fixed weight apparatus such as the "multi-gym", or on dedicated apparatus stations of well-known equipment brands. Ideally, such strength/power work should also include gradually introduced plyometrics (Behm, 1992), such as squat jumps, split jumps, and alternate leg bounds; together with medicine ball press throws, and twist tosses for the upper body. For further information, see Hazeldine (1990).

5.5 Flexibility
Slow stretching exercises for calf muscles, hamstrings, quadriceps, hip adductors and hip flexors with lying side-bends, together with gradually more vigorous arm circling, stride jumps, and progressive head and trunk twisting and side bending (as mobilising exercises) would form a good warm-up programme. It would also constitute flexibility training on a daily basis.

It is important that the physical programme should have an appropriate in-season maintenance component (Koutedakis et al., 1992), and an appropriate series of phased meso- and macro-cycles to peak for the highlighted tournaments (Wollstein, 1993). The programme will, of course, be fully complemented with solo and pairs practices, practice and conditioned games, and games against opponents selected to probe particular technical, tactical or physical weaknesses. Squash players are not alone among athletes in too often wishing to train their strengths rather than their weaknesses, whether in skills or physical attributes, and whether on or off the court. So their weaknesses should be identified (which is, in part, where field or laboratory fitness and strength tests may act diagnostically). Once identified, relative weaknesses may be specifically trained. Here again, further fitness and strength testing help to monitor the training effects.

6 Acknowledgements

The author offers E.M. Winter very many thanks for data and help - and for taking over where I left off with the squads and players. Warm thanks also, for much collective help in various ways over many years, to Tim Allan, Jonah Barrington MBE, Bernard Carpenter, the late Claire Chapman, Carleton Cooke, Alex Cowie, Haydn Davies, John Durnin, Mike Eggleton, Vivian Grisogono, Leo Faulmann, Matt Hammond, 'Bomber' Harris, Rex Hazeldine, Mike Hughes, Simon Humphreys, Bill Jarrett FRS, Suresh Joshi, the late Nazrullah Khan, Yiannis Koutedakis, Craig Mahoney, the late Ed Poore, Jane Poynder, Dorothy Sharp, Bill Slater OBE, Chris Stahl, Graham Stevenson, Tony Swift, John Taylor, Mark Taylor, Stan Tudor, Chris van Zyl, Billy Wilson, and Paul Wright.

7 References

Baker, S. (1987) Physiological aspects of slalom kayak/canoe racing. Unpublished Ph.D. thesis, University of Wales, Bangor.

Beaudin, P., Zapiec, C. and Montgomery, D. (1978) Heart rate and lactic acid concentration in squash players. **Research Quarterly for Exercise and Sport,** 49, 406-412.

Behm, D.G. (1992) Plyometric training for squash. **Journal of the National Strength and Conditioning Association.,** 14, (6) 26-28.

Blanksby, B.A., Elliott, B.C., and Bloomfield, J. (1973) Telemetred heart rate responses in male squash players. **Medical Journal of Australia,** 2, 477-481.

Blanksby, B.A., Eliott, B.C, Davis, K.H. and Mercer, M.D. (1980) Blood pressure and rectal temperature responses of middle-aged sedentary, middle-aged active and 'A' grade competitve male squash players. **British Journal of Sports Medicine,** 14, 133-138.

Brown, D. and Winter, E.M. (1995) Heart rate response in squash during competitive match-play. **Journal of Sports Sciences,** 14, 68-69.

Buckley, J.D., Scroop, G.C. and Catcheside, P.G. (1993) Lactate disposal in resting trained and untrained forearm skeletal muscle during high intensity leg exercise. **Journal of Applied Physiology and Occupational Physiology,** 76, 360-366.

Chapman, C. and Sharp, N.C.C. (1994) **WSRA 12-Week Training Programme for Squash Players.** Booklet published by SRA, London.

Coad, D., Rasmussen, B. and Mikkelsen, F. (1979) Physical demands of recreational badminton, in **Science in Racquet Sports** (ed. J. Terauds) Academic Publishers, Del Mar,California, pp. 43-54.

Elliott,B., Dawson, B. and Pyke, F. (1985) The energetics of singles tennis. **Journal of Human Movement Studies,** 11, 11- 20.

Guinness Book of Records (1996), 42nd edition, (ed. P. Matthews). Guinness Publishing, London.

Hammond, M.O. (1984) An investigation into anaerobic aspects of the game of squash rackets. **MA Dissertation,** Department of PE and Sports Science, University of Birmingham.

Hazeldine, R. (1990) **Strength Training for Sport.** Crowood Press, Marlborough.

Hughes, M. (1995) Computerised notation of racket sports, in **Science and Racket Sports,** (eds T. Reilly, M. Hughes and A. Lees), E. and F.N. Spon, London, pp. 249-257.

Hughes, M. and McGarry,T. (1988) Computerised notational analysis of squash. **Proceedings of Conference on Sports Science in Squash.** School of Health Sciences, Liverpool Polytechnic, pp.1-27.

Hughes, M. and Franks, I.M. (1994) Dynamic patterns of movement of squash players of different standards in winning and losing rallies. **Ergonomics,** 37, 23-29.

Hughes, M.G. (1995) Physiological demands of training in elite badminton players, in **Science and Racket Sports** (eds T. Reilly, M. Hughes and A. Lees), E. and F.N. Spon, London, pp. 32-37.

Koutedakis, Y., Boreham, C. and Sharp, N.C.C. (1992) Seasonal deterioration of selected physiological parameters in elite competitors. **International Journal of Sports Medicine,** 13, 548-551.

Lynch,T., Kinirons, M.T., O'Callaghan, D., Ismail, S., Brady, H.R. and Horgan, J.H. (1992) Metabolic changes during serial squash matches in older men. **Canadian Journal of Sports Science,** 17 (2), 110-113.

Mahoney, C. and Sharp, N.C.C. (1995) The physiological profiles of junior elite squash players, in **Science and Racket Sports** (eds T. Reilly, M. Hughes and A. Lees), E. and F.N. Spon, London, pp. 76-80.

McKay, H., (1977) **Complete Book of Squash.** Angus and Robertson, Publishers, London.

McKenzie, I. (1992) **The Squash Workshop.** The Crowood Press, Marlborough, Wiltshire.

Mellor, S., Hughes, M., Reilly, T., and Robertson, K. (1995) Physiological profiles of squash players of different standards, in **Science and Racket Sports** (eds T. Reilly, M. Hughes and A. Lees), E. and F.N. Spon, London, pp. 72-75.

Mikkelson, F. (1979) Physical demands and muscle adaptation in elite badminton players, in **Science in Racquet Sports** (ed. J. Terauds) Academic Publishers, Del Mar, California. pp. 55-67.

Montpetit, R. (1990) Applied physiology of squash. **Sports Medicine,** 10, 31-41.

Noakes, T.D., Cowling, J.R., Gevers, W., and Van Niekerk, J.P. de V. (1982) The metabolic response to squash including the influence of pre-exercise carbohydrate ingestion. **South African Medical Journal,** 62, 721-723.

Reilly, T. (1990) The racquet sports, in **Physiology of Sports** (eds T. Reilly, N. Secher, P. Snell and C. Williams), E. and F.N. Spon, London, pp.337-369.

Reilly, T. and Palmer, J. (1995) Investigation of exercise intensity in male singles lawn tennis, in **Science and Racket Sports** (eds T. Reilly, M. Hughes and A. Lees), E. and F.N. Spon, London, pp. 10-13.

Sharp, N.C.C. (1986). **Developing Endurance. Resource Pack 3,** National Coaching Foundation, Headingley, Leeds LS6 3QH.

Sharp, N.C.C. (1997) Timed running speed of cheetah (Acinonyx jubatus). **Journal of Zoology,** 241, 493- 494.

Stevenson, G. (1990) **How to Coach Squash.** Willow Books, London.

Taylor, J. (1985) **Squash.** Pelham Books, London.

Winter, E.M., Brewer, J., Brown, D. and Davis, J. (1995) Scaling maximum oxygen uptake for differences in body mass in elite junior male squash players. **Journal of Sports Sciences,** 13, 17-18.

Wollstein, J. (1993) Periodisation - an essential tool for modern day coaches. **Australian Squash Coach,** 1 (2), 20-23.

2 Maximum oxygen uptake in junior and senior elite squash players

D. Brown, D.A. Weigand and E.M. Winter
De Montfort University Bedford, Bedford, UK

1 Introduction

One of the major challenges in an athlete's career is the move from elite junior to senior levels of performance. Kennedy and Dimick (1987, cited by Parker, 1994) reported that in American inter-collegiate football and basketball, more than 60% of black athletes and almost 40% of white athletes anticipate professional careers, but only 2% of these college athletes actually attain a professional career. In squash, only about 20% of players who compete for England at junior international level subsequently compete for England at senior international level. In addition, many players who attain top ten rankings as juniors never make the same breakthrough at senior level. This highlights a transition phase in squash, as with many sports, where players from the elite junior category attempt to progress to senior levels of competition. The factors which distinguish between elite junior and senior competitors are poorly understood, but probably involve cultural, psychological and biological factors. With regards to playing performance, improvements in technical and tactical abilities are likely to occur and in addition this transition might also illustrate changes in physiological characteristics.

Squash matches at elite level can last up to 3 hours, and energy is supplied largely by aerobic mechanisms. Although activity during play is intermittent, Brown and Winter (1995) reported remarkably stable heart rate responses during competitive match-play which were equivalent to about 90% of an individual's maximum. Because of the aerobic demands of the game, a physiological characteristic that is probably associated with success in squash at elite level is a performer's maximum oxygen uptake ($\dot{V}O_2$ max) which is commonly used as an indicator of an individual's potential for endurance performance.

Physiological and performance variables are frequently influenced by body size (Winter and Nevill, 1996), and so if comparisons are to be made between groups then differences in body size need to be partitioned out. This partitioning is called scaling (Schmidt-Nielsen, 1984) and has become the subject of renewed interest in the physiology of exercise (Nevill et al., 1992; Jakeman et al., 1994; Nevill and Holder, 1994). The $\dot{V}O_2$ max is influenced by differences in the size of subjects and allometric

Science and Racket Sports II, edited by A. Lees, I. Maynard, M. Hughes and T. Reilly. Published in 1998 by E & FN Spon, 11 New Fetter Lane, London EC4P 4EE, UK. ISBN: 0 419 23030 0

modelling has been shown to be as an appropriate technique for partitioning out differences in body size thereby allowing comparisons between groups to be made (Nevill et al., 1992).

The purpose of this study was to use allometric modelling to investigate changes in $\dot{V}O_2$max in the transition from junior to senior play in elite level squash.

2 Methods

England national squad players provided written informed consent and were recruited for the study. The players were categorised into 4 groups : junior men (under 19 years of age), junior women (under 19 years of age), senior men (19 years of age and above), and senior women (19 years of age and above). Anthropometry followed the measurements recommended by Weiner and Lourie (1981) and included stature, body mass and skinfold thicknesses. Body mass was determined to the nearest 50 g using beam balance scales (Herbert and Sons, Edmonton, UK). Body fat was estimated from skinfold measurements taken at the biceps, triceps, subscapular and suprailiac sites, using the equation of Durnin and Womersley (1974). Subject details are reported in Table 1.

Table 1. Anthropometric characteristics of subjects. Values are Mean ± SEM

	Junior Men n=24	Junior Women n=13	Senior Men n=5	Senior Women n=7
Age (years)	17.7 ± 0.2	16.7 ± 0.3	24.9 ± 0.6	25.6 ± 1.7
Stature (cm)	180.7 ± 1.4	164.8 ± 1.6	179.7 ± 2.6	167.8 ± 1.5
Mass (kg)	72.6 ± 1.4	60.6 ± 1.2	73.5 ± 3.6	64.2 ± 1.3
Body fat (%)	14.4 ± 0.7	24.1 ± 1.1	10.2 ± 0.7	24.7 ± 1.2

Maximum oxygen uptake of the players was determined using an incremental test to volitional exhaustion on a motorised treadmill (Powerjog, Model MX2000, Birmingham, UK) and followed the British Association of Sport and Exercise Sciences guidelines (Hale et al., 1988). Expired air was collected and analysed by means of an on-line system (Covox Microlab, Exeter, UK), which was calibrated before and after testing using gases of known concentration and a syringe of known volume. Heart rate was measured throughout the test using a Polar heart monitor (Polar Electro OY, Kempele, Finland).

The following criteria were used to establish whether or not maximum oxygen uptake had been achieved:

1. a plateau in oxygen uptake to within 5 % with an increase in exercise intensity;
2. a final test heart rate value to within ± 10 beats.min^{-1} of theoretical age relatedmaximum;
3. a respiratory exchange ratio of 1.10 or above;
4. a post-exercise blood lactate concentration of 7 mmol.l^{-1} or more;
5. the performer's subjective appraisal of volitional exhaustion.

The $\dot{V}O_2$max was expressed relative to body mass as a power function ratio standard (PFR) with body mass raised to the power 0.67 (referred to as PFR67 ml.kg$^{-0.67}$.min^{-1}) and as the natural log of this measure (referred to as lnPFR67) so as to remove possible skew in the data. The suitability of an exponent of 0.67 was determined by log-log transformations and subsequent linear regression on the raw data.

A 2 × 2 (age × gender) MANOVA and univariate F tests were performed on the dependent variable ($\dot{V}O_2$max). Statistical significance was set at $P < 0.05$.

3 Results and Discussion

Table 2 displays the individual body mass exponents identified for each group based on regressions performed on the log transformed $\dot{V}O_2$max and body mass data. For each group the exponent ± the Standard Error of the Estimate (SEE) encompassed the theoretical exponent of 0.67 and so justified the use of the 0.67 exponent and supports evidence that measures such as $\dot{V}O_2$max are related to body mass raised to this power (Nevill at al., 1992; Nevill and Holder, 1994).

Table 2. Body mass exponents for each group of squash players

Group	Exponent	SEE
Junior Men	0.58	0.18
Junior Women	0.55	0.23
Senior Men	0.61	0.16
Senior Women	0.75	0.23

The $\dot{V}O_2$max values for each group are shown in Table 3. They are reported as absolute $\dot{V}O_2$max (l.min^{-1}), a power function ratio standard (ml.kg$^{-0.67}$.min^{-1}) and the natural log of this measure (ln ml.kg$^{-0.67}$.min^{-1}).

Table 3. Group $\dot{V}O_2$max results, values are Mean ± SEM

Group	$\dot{V}O_2$max		
	l.min^{-1}	ml.kg$^{-0.67}$.min^{-1}	ln ml.kg$^{-0.67}$.min^{-1}
Junior Men, n = 24	4.43 ± 0.08	252 ± 4	5.53 ± 0.014
Junior Women, n = 13	3.14 ± 0.06	201 ± 4	5.30 ± 0.020
Senior Men, n = 5	4.86 ± 0.16	274 ± 4	5.61 ± 0.014
Senior Women, n = 7	3.50 ± 0.12	215 ± 5	5.37 ± 0.023

For men and women, the PFR67 and lnPFR67 $\dot{V}O_2$max data were greater in the senior than the junior players (F= 11.82 and 11.58 respectively, P < 0.01). In both age categories $\dot{V}O_2$max was greater in the men than the women (F= 108.92 and 106.75 respectively, P < 0.01).

Maximal oxygen uptake ($\dot{V}O_2$max) is defined as the maximum rate at which an individual can take up and utilise oxygen while breathing air at sea level (Åstrand and Rodahl, 1986). Measurements of $\dot{V}O_2$max indicate aerobic potential and, to a lesser extent, training status.

Information about physiological profiles of elite squash players is limited and all previous studies that have reported $\dot{V}O_2$max have presented this measure as a simple ratio standard relative to body mass (ml.kg^{-1}.min^{-1}). For this reason comparisons between the results of this study with others have to be made cautiously. It is possible to estimate the power function ratio $\dot{V}O_2$max values in other studies from calculations based on the mean $\dot{V}O_2$max data (ml.kg^{-1}.min^{-1}) and body mass values that have been reported. Table 4 displays such estimations of power function ratio $\dot{V}O_2$max values from previous studies.

Table 4. Estimated power function ratio $\dot{V}O_2$max data from previous studies

Study	Level of players	$\dot{V}O_2$max (ml.kg$^{-0.67}$.min^{-1})
van Rensburg et al. (1982)	Top club male	245
Chin et al. (1995)	Elite male	250
Mahoney and Sharp (1994)	Elite junior male	211
Todd and Mahoney (1994)	Elite male	261

Mean $\dot{V}O_2$max values for the elite senior men in this study were higher than those reported for top club players (van Rensburg et al., 1982), elite Asian players (Chin et al., 1995) and elite Irish players (Todd and Mahoney, 1994). The mean $\dot{V}O_2$max values for the elite junior men were higher than those reported for elite Irish juniors (Mahoney and Sharp, 1994). There are no comparative data for elite female squash players. Recent work in our laboratories (unpublished findings) has suggested that scaled $\dot{V}O_2$max values of 300 - 310 ml.kg$^{-0.67}$.min^{-1} and 230 - 240 ml.kg$^{-0.67}$.min^{-1} characterise elite male and female endurance athletes, respectively.

Investigations into differences in the physiological characteristics of elite junior and senior athletes are few, and limit comparisons that can be made with results of the present study. Janiak et al. (1993) considered muscle force in elite junior and senior rowers and reported significant differences between juniors and seniors in mean torques of eight principal muscle groups. As illustrated in Table 4, $\dot{V}O_2$max data reported by Todd and Mahoney (1994) for elite Irish senior squash players are considerably higher than the data reported by Mahoney and Sharp (1994) for the elite Irish juniors, suggesting a difference in the physiological characteristics of elite Irish junior and senior players.

The results of this study suggest that in addition to those tactical and technical factors which probably influence the transition from elite junior to senior level in squash, there are differences in physiological characteristics of juniors and seniors. This is exemplified by significant differences in the scaled $\dot{V}O_2$max data.

As differences in the physiological characteristics of junior and senior players have been identified, there are implications for the training strategies junior players should adopt based on what is expected of them at senior level. It is important that the differences between junior and senior levels of competition are understood as the move up to senior level represents a critical stage in elite junior players' development.

Results of this study can be used to advise junior players of the physical changes that might help to improve their chances of success at senior level. They could also help to guide the formulation of appropriate training programmes which would include a focus on developing their capacity for endurance performance.

A consequence of this study has been the recommendation for the use of intermediate training squads (under 21 and under 23 year age groups). Intermediate training squads would be used to implement developmental training programmes and monitor the progress of the player in the transition from elite junior to senior levels of competition.

4 Conclusions

The results demonstrate that $\dot{V}O_2$max increases in both men and women from junior to senior level, and confirm the use of allometric modelling as an appropriate technique to compare groups.

The data from this study suggest that there is a change in the aerobic capabilities of the performer in the transition from elite junior to senior level in squash. This information could be used to guide the training strategies adopted by players.

The re-introduction of intermediate (under 21 and under 23 years) training squads could help ease the transition in elite level squash.

5 References

Åstrand, P.O. and Rodahl, K. (1986) 3rd ed. **Textbook of Work Physiology**. McGraw Hill, New York.

Brown, D. and Winter, E.M. (1995) Heart rate response in squash during competitive matchplay. **Journal of Sports Sciences**, 14, 68-69.

Durnin, J.V.G.A. and Womersley, J. (1974) Body fat assessed from total density and its estimation from skinfold thickness: measurements on 481 men and women aged 16 to 72 years. **British Journal of Nutrition**, 32, 169-179.

Chin, M., Steininger, K., Raymond, C.H., Clark, C.R. and Wong, A.S.K. (1995) Physiological profiles and sport specific fitness of Asian elite squash players. **British Journal of Sports Medicine**, 29, 158-164.

Hale, T., Armstrong, N., Hardman, A., Jakeman, P., Sharp, C. and Winter, E.M. (1988) **Position Statement on the Physiological Testing of the Elite Competitor**, 2nd ed., British Association of Sports Sciences, White Line Press, Leeds.

Jakeman, P.M., Winter, E.M. and Doust, J. (1994) A review of research in sports physiology. **Journal of Sports Sciences**, 12, 33-60.

Janiak, J., Wit, A. and Stupnicki, R. (1993) Static muscle force in athletes practising rowing. **Biology of Sport**, 10, 30-34.

Kennedy, S. and Dimick, K. (1987) Career maturity and professional sports expectations of college football and basketball players. **Journal of College Student Personnel**, 28, 293-297.

Mahoney, C.A. and Sharp, N.C.C. (1994) The physiological profile of elite junior squash players, in **Science and Racket Sports** (eds T. Reilly, M. Hughes and A. Lees), E. and F.N. Spon, London. pp. 76-80.

Nevill, A.M. and Holder, R.L. (1994) Modelling maximum oxygen uptake - a case study in non linear regression model formulation and comparison. **Applied Statistics**, 43, 653-66.

Nevill, A.M., Ramsbottom, R. and Williams, C. (1992) Scaling physiological measurements for individuals of different body size. **European Journal of Applied Physiology**, 65, 110-17.

Parker, K.B. (1994) "Has-beens" and "Wanna-Bes": Transition experiences of former major college football players. **The Sport Psychologist**, 8, 287-304.

Schmidt-Nielsen, K. (1984) **Scaling: Why is Animal Size so Important?**, Cambridge University Press, Cambridge.

Todd, M.K. and Mahoney, C.A. (1994) Determination of pre-season physiological characteristics of elite male squash players, in **Science and Racket Sports** (eds T. Reilly, M. Hughes and A. Lees), E and FN Spon, London. pp. 81-86.

van Rensburg, J.P., van der Linde, A., Ackermann, P.C., Kielblock, A.J. and Strydom, N.B. (1982) Physiological profile of squash players. **South African Journal for Research in Sport, Physical Education and Recreation**, 5, 25-56.

Weiner, J.S. and Lourie, J.A. (1981) **Practical Human Biology**, Academic Press, London.

Winter, E.M. and Nevill, A.M. (1996) Scaling: Adjusting for differences in body size, in **Kinanthropometry and Exercise Physiology Laboratory Manual: Tests, procedures and data** (eds R. Eston and T. Reilly), E. and F.N. Spon, London. pp. 321-335.

3 Cardiorespiratory adjustment in middle-level tennis players: are long term cardiovascular adjustments possible?

M. Bernardi[1,3], G. De Vito[2], M.E. Falvo[1], S. Marino[3] and F. Montellanico[1]

[1]Istituto di Fisiologia Umana, Università 'La Sapienza', Rome, Italy; [2]Scottish School of Sports Studies, Strathclyde University, Glasgow, UK and [3]Scuola di Specializzazione in Medicina dello Sport, Università 'La Sapienza', Rome, Italy

1 Introduction

According to the guidelines established by the American College of Sports Medicine (ACSM) in 1995, tennis can be considered an endurance activity where both the skill and the intensity of exercise are highly variable. Many factors have been considered to explain this variability (Reilly, 1990). Among these are the type of match - singles or doubles (Morgans et al., 1987), the gender of the players (Seliger et al., 1973), the surface of the court (Brouns, 1990) and the technical skill of the opponents (Groppel and Roeter, 1992). It is reasonable to suppose that the kind of play that a subject is in the habit of performing, or is forced to choose by the opponent, could also affect the intensity of the exercise.

The aim of the present research was to establish possible training effects of tennis taking into account differences in subjects' play. According to the principles of exercise prescription recommended by the ACSM (1995), in order either to develop or maintain cardiorespiratory fitness, the intensity of an exercise, in terms of oxygen uptake ($\dot{V}O_2$) and heart rate (HR), should be between 50 and 85% of the maximal oxygen uptake ($\dot{V}O_{2max}$) and between 60 and 90% of the maximal heart rate (HR_{max}). To accomplish this purpose we wanted to estimate for each subject, and possibly for different categories of players, the actual metabolic and cardiovascular load during tennis matches which were compared with maximal measurements obtained in laboratory exercise tests.

2 Material and Methods

2.1 Subjects
Special care was taken in selecting tennis players with different kinds of play. Seven middle-level (non-professional) healthy male subjects gave their informed consent and participated in the study. They were classified as C category players (regionally ranked). Their mean age was 28.1 ± 3 years, their mean height was 179.1 ± 6 cm and

Science and Racket Sports II, edited by A. Lees, I. Maynard, M. Hughes and T. Reilly. Published in 1998 by E & FN Spon, 11 New Fetter Lane, London EC4P 4EE, UK.   ISBN: 0 419 23030 0 their mean body mass was 73.9 ± 5.7 kg. All of them were very well trained. They used to add to the hours of tennis practised per week (at least 6 hours) at least three hours per week of endurance training. According to their style and tactics, three types of players were identified:

(1) players (2 subjects) who preferred to play from the baseline (baseline players);
(2) players (2 subjects) who played volleys often (attacking players);
(3) players (3 subjects) who played both attacking and baseline play (whole-court players).

This selection was carried out to accomplish the aim of the research: the evaluation of the effect of the type of play on the intensity of exercise. However, on the basis of the results in the tournaments of the previous year, the subjects were matched on skill and performance levels. The subjects were tested both in the laboratory and during actual matches.

2.2 Laboratory test

The subjects underwent a continuous incremental exercise test on a treadmill to assess $\dot{V}O_{2max}$ and ventilatory threshold (T_{vent}). The protocol consisted of a warm-up at a speed of 10 km·h^{-1}. When the heart rate and the $\dot{V}O_2$ reached a steady state value, the speed was increased each minute by 1 km·h^{-1}. At the speed of 16 km.h^{-1} the workload was increased each minute alternating the speed increment with a 2.5% increment of the slope. The heart rate was continuously recorded by means of a telemetric apparatus (Polar Sport-Tester). The expired pulmonary ventilation (VE), the $\dot{V}O_2$, the carbon dioxide production ($\dot{V}CO_2$) and the derived parameters were measured every 15 s using an automatic apparatus (Eos-Sprint-Jaeger, Höchberg). The $\dot{V}O_{2max}$ was considered to be that value of $\dot{V}O_2$ which did not change in spite of an increase of workload (< 2 ml.kg^{-1}.min^{-1}). The T_{vent} was assessed using both the ventilatory equivalent methods (Caiozzo et al., 1982) and the simplified V-slope method (Sue et al., 1988).

2.3 Field test

A telemetric device (K4, Cosmed, Rome) was used to measure VE, $\dot{V}O_2$, $\dot{V}CO_2$ and HR, during regular matches performed on a clay court. The measurements were monitored and recorded on-line during 15 matches (each subject played 2 matches, except for baseline player who was submitted to measurement three times). The duration of each rally (corresponding to the time in which the ball was in play) and the duration of the break between rallies were timed by different operators. The total time of the match, including the period of rest for the change of end, was set, corresponding to about 45 minutes for every test.

3 Results and Discussion

3.1 Laboratory tests
All subjects showed a very high aerobic power. In fact, $\dot{V}O_{2max}$ ranged between 60 and 69 (ml.kg⁻1.min⁻¹), and T_{vent} was between 81 to 85 per cent of the $\dot{V}O_{2max}$. In the following table (Table 1) the mean values of the measurements taken during the exercise test are given, grouping the subjects according to their type of play. Because of the small number of subjects and the narrow difference among them, the range is reported and the standard deviation is not given.

Our data are well above those reported by Docherty (1982) and by Copley (1980) for professional tennis players. In both studies, however, the $\dot{V}O_{2max}$ (44 and 50 ml.kg⁻¹. min⁻¹ respectively) was predicted on the basis of the heart rate. Data closer to ours have been reported by Gallozzi et al. (1992) and by Bergeron et al. (1991). The first authors studied semi-professional tennis players (B category, nationally ranked) finding mean $\dot{V}O_{2max}$ of 57.3 ± 3.1 ml.kg⁻¹.min⁻¹. Bergeron et al. (1991) found values of 58.5 ± 9.4 ml.kg⁻¹.min⁻¹ in Division I University team members

On the other hand, the present subjects had values ($\dot{V}O_{2max}$ equal to 65 ± 6 ml.kg⁻¹·min⁻¹) similar to those measured by Elliott et al. (1985) (mean $\dot{V}O_{2max}$ of 65.9 ± 6.3 ml.kg⁻¹.min⁻¹). In the latter study the subjects added long distance training runs to their specific tennis training .

Table 1. Mean cardiorespiratory values and ranges (in brackets) obtained during the laboratory tests (n = 7)

Category of play	HR_{max} (beats.min⁻¹)	$\dot{V}O_{2max}$ (ml·kg⁻¹.min⁻¹)	$\dot{V}O_{2max}$ (l.min⁻¹)	T_{vent} (%$\dot{V}O_{2max}$)
Attacking players	190 (186-194)	67 (65-69)	5.09 (4.94-5.24)	81 (80-82)
Baseline players	200 (203-197)	66 (63-69)	4.55 (4.45-4.65)	83.5 (83-84)
Whole-court players	192 (187-198)	62 (60-64)	4.62 (4-5.32)	83.3 (83-85)

The conclusion to this part of the study is that our values are very close to those measured on top level endurance athletes. Furthermore the very high values of T_{vent} confirm this statement. All these factors could reflect the effects of other physical exercises on the cardiorespiratory fitness of our subjects.

3.2 Field test: evaluation of the times of play
The mean duration of the rallies throughout the whole match ranged between 4.3 and 18.1 s (mean value equal to 8.3 ± 3.7 s). This parameter was used to quantify the prevalent kind of play observed during the match. In fact, when the player in control of the rally was an attacking player, the average duration of the rallies was 4.8 ± 0.4 s.

It ranged between 6 and 11 s (mean value equal to 8.2 ± 1.2 s), when the player in control of the rally was a whole-court player. It lasted on average 15.7 ± 3.5 s when the player in control of the rally was a baseline player. The difference in duration was statistically significant (P<0.05). On the basis of these results, each match was classified in one of the three above-mentioned types of play. There were 4 matches in group A (matches in which the player in control of the rally was an attacking player), 4 matches in group B (matches in which the player in control of the rally was a baseline player), 7 matches in group C (matches in which the player in control of the rally was a whole-court player). Regarding the duration of the rally, the literature (see for example Reilly, 1990) shows a wide range of data: from an average duration of about 4 s (Docherty, 1982) to values of 10 s (Elliott et al., 1985). It appears that the opponents' play determines these differences. In our study the duration of the rallies was correlated significantly with the duration of the time between the rallies (r= 0.70 P<0.05) and with the playing time as a percent of the total match-time including the rest for the change of end (r=0.80). It can be supposed that the players automatically chose a longer period of rest when the rallies lasted longer. In fact, the break between rallies, increased from 14.8 ± 0.5 s in group A, to 15.8 ± 1.7 s in group C, to 18.6 ± 1.5 s in group B, but the difference in duration between groups was non significant (P>0.05). The percentage of the playing time with respect to the total time of the match was 21% ± 5.5 for group A, 28.6% ± 4.2 for group C, and 38.5% ± 4.9 for group B. The difference in percentages between groups was significant (P<0.05).

Comparing these figures with those in the literature (Reilly, 1990), it seems that the observations taken during the matches of group B are well above the values found by other authors. This can be explained not only on the basis of the type of play (match between two baseline players) but also by the surface of the court (clay court).

3.3 Field test: metabolic and cardiac measurements
In all the matches there was a general trend towards an increase in VO_2 and HR as the game progressed with a decrease during the rest phase while changing end. This trend was noted in all the three groups.

A typical pattern of VO_2 and HR trend is shown in figure 1 for a match between baseline players. The line shows the VO_2 value measured at the T_{vent} (laboratory test).

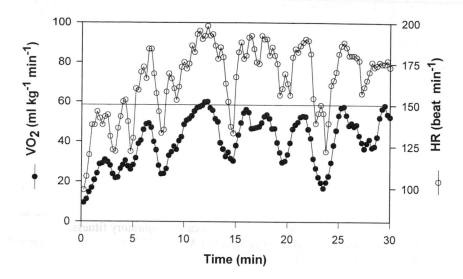

Figure 1. The $\dot{V}O_2$ and HR of a baseline player while playing against another
baseline player.

In the match shown in Fig. 1, the average duration of the rally and the percentage of
playing time were the highest observed: 18.1 s and 42 %, respectively. However, the
trend and the mean values of $\dot{V}O_2$ and HR found in the other matches categorised in
group B were similar. The $\dot{V}O_2$ values were close to and sometimes exceeded the
T_{vent} measured during the treadmill exercise test. The values of $\dot{V}CO_2$ (not shown in
the figure) also testify to the high intensity. The respiratory exchange ratio
($\dot{V}CO_2/\dot{V}O_2$) was often around 1.0. This kind of match must be definitively
considered as provoking endurance training effects on the cardiorespiratory fitness of
the player.

The analysis of all $\dot{V}O_2$ and HR data showed the same pattern found for the average
times of play. The average values of $\dot{V}O_2$ and HR varied widely depending on the
type of play in the match. Therefore these data were also grouped in accordance with
the three types of play (Table 2). For each type of play, the percentage of $\dot{V}O_2$ and
HR with respect to the maximal values measured during the treadmill exercise test are
also shown.

The $\dot{V}O_2$ and HR values measured during the matches were often higher than those
presented in the literature (Reilly, 1990). Only Therminarias et al. (1991) have
measured during strenuous tennis matches HR values similar to ours. The fact that the
matches were played on clay courts is the main difference from the studies quoted by
Reilly (1990). The only data available on the clay court are those of Gallozzi et al.
(1992). The $\dot{V}O_2$ and HR values in the latter case are comparable to our data. In all
the matches our subjects were requested to try as hard as possible and all of them tried
to hit the ball, if possible, as much they could.

Table 2. Mean (± standard deviation) cardiorespiratory values measured during the matches

Category of play	HR (beats.min^{-1})	%HR $_{max}$	VO$_2$ (ml.kg^{-1}.min^{-1})	VO$_2$ (l.min^{-1})	%VO$_2$max
Group A	121±15	63.6	30±7	2.28	46
Group B	165±7	82.5	39±3	2.69	59
Group C	153±6	79.6	32±4	2.38	51

As shown in Table 2 the laboratory and the field measurements were compared to illustrate the possible training effects of tennis on cardiorespiratory fitness. Considering the VO$_2$, and in accordance with the ACSM (1995), only when the match can be categorised in group B (i.e. the player in control of the play is a baseline player) is the exercise intensive enough to produce long term cardiovascular adaptations. The matches of group C (which had higher values compared with group A) can be considered as bordering on threshold values of the ACSM's limits. In fact some matches could not be considered as providing a training stimulus when the standard deviation is taken into account.

4 Conclusions

The thesis formulated in the present study (that there is an effect of the type of play on the intensity of the exercise) seems confirmed by the present data. It was found that:-

(1) The mean duration of the rally was related to the type of play in the match (short when the player in control of the rally is an attacking player, long when a baseline player, intermediate when a whole-court player).
(2) The longer the duration of the rally, the higher the intensity of the exercise.

Therefore tennis can be considered a training activity with beneficial effects on the cardiorespiratory fitness when the match is dominated by a baseline player as this prolongs the duration of the rally. In matches with other types of play, the training stimulus was not sufficient to provoke long term cardiovascular adjustments.

5 References

American College of Sports Medicine (1995) **Guidelines for Exercise Testing and Prescription.** 5th Edition, Williams & Wilkins, Philadelphia.

Bergeron, M.F., Maresh, C.M., Kraemer, W.J., Abraham, A., Conroy, B.and Gabaree,C. (1991) Tennis: A physiological profile during match play. **International Journal Sports Medicine**, 12, 474-479.

Brouns, F. (1990) Trainingsaspekte des modernen tennis. **Leistungssport**, Rijkuniversiteit Maastrricht, 4, 45-48.

Caiozzo, V.J., Davis, J.A., Ellis, J.F., Azus, J.L., Vandagriff, C.A., Prietto, C.A. and McMaster, W.C. (1982) A comparison of gas exchange indices used to detect the anaerobic threshold. **Journal of Applied Physiology,** 53, 1184-1189.

Copley, B.B. (1980) A morfological and physiological study of tennis players with special reference to the effects of training. **South African Journal of Research in Sport, Physical Education and Recreation**, 3, 33-44.

Docherty, D. (1982) A comparison of heart rate responses in racquet games. **British Journal of Sports Medicine**, 16, 96-100.

Elliott, B., Dawson, B. and Pyke, F. (1985) The energetics of singles tennis. **Journal of Human Movement Studies,** 11, 11-20.

Gallozzi, C., Amodio, F., Colli, R., De Angelis, M. and Dal Monte, A. (1992) Aspetti fisiologici del tennis maschile. **Scuola Informa-Scuola dello Sport**, 26.

Groppel, J.L., and Roetert, E.B. (1992) Applied physiology of tennis. **Sports Medicine,** 14:4,260-268.

Morgans, L.F., Jordan, D.L., Baeyens, D.A. and Franciosa, J.A. (1987) Heart rate responses during singles and doubles tennis competition. **Physician and Sportsmedicine,** 15, 67-74.

Reilly, T. (1990) The racquet sports, in **Physiology of Sports** (eds T. Reilly, N.Secher, P. Snell and C.Williams) 12, 337-369, E. & F.N. Spon, London.

Seliger, V., Ejem, M., Pauer, M., Safarik, V. (1973) Energy metabolism in tennis. **Internationale Zeitschrift fur Angew Physiologie**, 31, 333-340

Sue, D.Y., Wasserman, K., Moricca, R.B. and Casaburi, R. (1988) Use of the V-slope method for anaerobic threshold determination. **Chest,** 94, 931-938.

Therminarias, A., Danson, P.,Chirpaz-Oddou, M.F., Gharib, C. and Quirion, A. (1991) Hormonal and metabolic changes during a strenuous tennis match: effect of ageing. **International Journal of Sports Medicine,** 12,10-16.

4 Tennis versus golf: profile of demands and physical performance in senior players

A. Ferrauti[1], K. Weber[1], H.K. Strüder[1], G. Predel[2] and R. Rost[2]
[1]Institute of Sports Games and [2]Institute of Cardiology and Sports Medicine, German Sport University Cologne, Cologne, Germany

1 Introduction

Within recent years golf has become a popular sport in Germany. The number of golf clubs has increased since 1980 from 160 to 438. Where there were formerly 50,000 organised golf players there are now about 225,000 active golf players. The German Tennis Federation has also experienced an exponential growth during recent years (from 68,179 members in 1950 to 2,108,689 members in 1990). In particular the amount of middle aged and older players has constantly increased (Sklorz, 1995). Consequently, the profile of physiological demands of golf and tennis is of special interest, because of health orientated considerations.

Despite the immense increase in golf participation, representative investigations on the haemodynamic, metabolic and psychological demands are rare (Lampley et al., 1977; Murase et al., 1989). A comparison with findings in tennis (Seliger et al., 1973; Therminarias et al., 1991) is not possible due to methodological differences. Thus, the purpose of this study was to compare the profile of physiological demands in golf and tennis on senior age level players in order to evaluate the potential of both sports in the primary prevention of cardiovascular diseases.

2 Methods

2.1 Subjects
Eighteen division IV (German Tennis Federation) male senior tennis players (mean±SD: age 59.1 ±2.3 years, height 177.5 ±5.7 cm, mass 85.9 ±14.1 kg) and 21 male golfers (age 60.0 ±5.3 years, height 179.4 ±5.2 cm, mass 82.4 ±7.4 kg) with a mean handicap of 20.0 ±7.1 participated in the study. The playing experience of the tennis players was 25.4 ±8.0 years and of the golf players 10.2 ±4.4 years. The tennis players played an average of 5.2 ±3.0 hours.week^{-1} during summer and 3.1 ±1.7 hours.week^{-1} during winter. The golf players usually played 10.0±5.1 hours.week^{-1} during summer and 5.9±3.1 hours.week^{-1} during winter.

Science and Racket Sports II, edited by A. Lees, I. Maynard, M. Hughes and T. Reilly. Published in 1998 by E & FN Spon, 11 New Fetter Lane, London EC4P 4EE, UK.   ISBN: 0 419 23030 0

2.3 Procedure

The study consisted of two parts. First, all participants underwent a health and performance examination by means of cycle ergometry. Second, all subjects with negligible health problems participated in a field investigation under sports specific conditions.

No strenuous physical activity was allowed for 24 hours prior to the field investigations. On the day of investigation subjects received a standardized carbohydrate rich lunch (12:30 h). All field investigations began at 15:00 h. Only mineral water was allowed *ad libitum* during playing time. Divided into seven 3-men-groups, all 21 golfers completed 18 holes. The tennis players carried out competitive singles matches over two hours on clay courts according to the rules of the International Tennis Federation.

2.4 Measurements and analyses

Cycle ergometry was undertaken until subjective exhaustion according to the recommendations of the World Health Organisation (WHO, 1968). Absolute and relative maximal performance as well as performance at the 4 mmol.l^{-1} lactate threshold was determined. Differences in performance compared to age-related norm values were calculated according to Rost and Hollmann (1982).

During the field studies heart rate was monitored in 15 s intervals (Polar Sport-Tester, Kempele, Finland). In six golfers and six tennis players respiratory gas exchange during exercise was evaluated by means of the portable system X1$^{®}$ from CORTEX GmbH (Leipzig, Germany). Capillary blood samples were analysed for lactate in 30 min intervals (Eppendorf-Analyser 5060, Hamburg, Germany). Venous blood samples were taken from an antecubital vein at rest, during (only in golf after 9 holes) and immediately post-exercise. Serum concentrations of free fatty acids (FFA), glycerol (Cobas-Bio-System, Hoffmann-La Roche, Basel, Switzerland) and insulin (Enzym-Immunoassey ES 300, Boehringer, Mannheim, Germany) were determined. Urine concentration of adrenaline was analysed using HPLC (Chromsystems, München, Germany) and related to creatinine to eliminate differences in renal water handling. Changes in plasma volume were calculated according to Van Beaumont (1972) following the results from haematocrit measurements (Sysmex Dualdilutor DD100, Digitana AG, Germany).

2.4 Statistics

Data are presented with mean and standard deviation. Multi-factorial analysis of variance (ANOVA) with repeated measurements and unpaired t-tests were used to determine statistical differences. In the case of ANOVA significance, simple effects were verified by means of Newman-Keuls test. Significance levels were set at $P \leq 0.05$ (*) and $P \leq 0.01$ (**).

3 Results

In golf, average playing time for 18 holes was 255 ±15 min. During this time water intake was an average of 1.5 ±0.5 l. Body mass (measurement includes golf clothes) declined from 86.4 ±8.8 kg to 85.0 ±8.8 kg. Plasma volume increased by 6.2 % (Van Beaumont, 1972). The players executed 101 ±6 strokes and a walking distance of 8530 ±333 m. The net walking time was about 90 min (35 %). During the tennis matches plasma volume declined marginally (- 3%). Game analysis revealed a net playing time of 24 ±10 min (20.6 ±8.2 %).

All values related to work load showed significant differences between golf and tennis. Heart rate and lactate were at a strikingly higher level during tennis. Oxygen uptake and energy consumption in golf was only half that found in tennis (Figure 1).

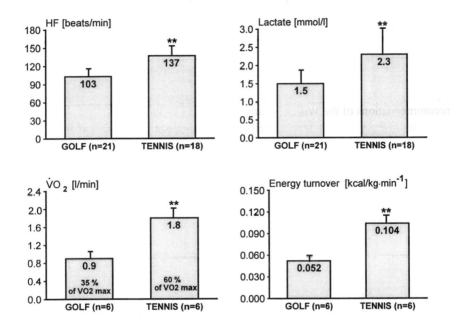

Figure 1. Heart rate, blood lactate, oxygen uptake and energy turnover during tennis and golf on senior level.

The responses of lipid metabolism and its hormonal control were more intensive in tennis than in golf. After a tennis match over two hours significantly higher serum concentrations of FFA and glycerol were found than after 9 or 18 holes of golf, respectively (Figure 2). Serum increments of products of lipolysis were found in golf only during the first half of the exercise. Alterations in serum concentration of insulin were exactly opposed to changes in FFA and declined during both forms of physical demand (Figure 2). Changes in plasma volume did not significantly affect parameters (Van Beaumont, 1972).

During cycle ergometry, tennis players reached a significantly higher power output (Table 1). Anaerobic threshold was also higher in tennis players. The age-related norm value (Rost and Hollmann, 1982) was not reached by golf players; however, it was exceeded in tennis players by 9 % (Table 1). At the point of exhaustion, the average heart rate was 144 ±19 beats.min^{-1} in golfers and 149 ±18 beats.min^{-1} in tennis players.

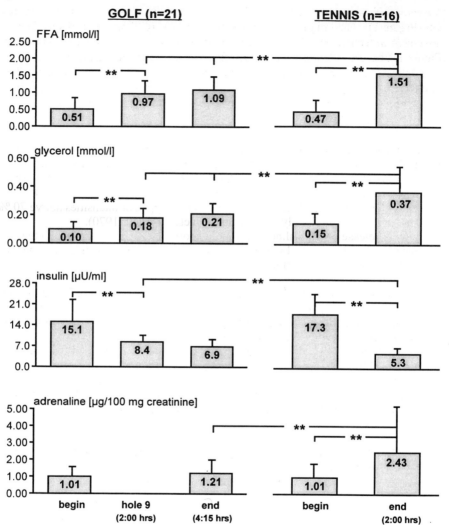

Figure 2. Serum concentrations of free fatty acids (FFA), glycerol and insulin as well as urine concentrations of adrenaline during tennis and golf on senior level.

4 Discussion

The cardiopulmonary and metabolic demands differ significantly between tennis and golf (Figure 1). This might be due to the higher intensity of strokes and speed of movement in tennis. The data on oxygen uptake obtained during the field examination (Figure 1) allow in combination with the findings during cycle ergometry (Table 1), an estimation of the percentage of the maximal performance used during exercise. Thus, for an average oxygen uptake of 0.9 ±0.2 l.min^{-1} in golf and of 1.8 ±0.2 l.min^{-1} in tennis (Figure 1) the relative demand of cadiopulmonary capacity can be estimated at about 35 % in golf and 60 % in tennis. Murase et al. (1989) found similar results in golf (38 %).

The metabolic and hormonal responses differ significantly between golf and tennis. (Figure 2). Lipolysis is activated during a tennis match earlier and higher than in golf. The main reason for this can be seen in the difference in work intensity and energy turnover between two sports (Figure 1). The rate of lipolysis usually rises with increasing physical demand and is only reduced or stopped at intensities above 70 % $\dot{V}O_2$ max due to the antilypolytic influence of lactate (Pruett, 1970).

The lower release of adrenaline in golf points toward a different exercise intensity (Lehmann et al., 1981) and a lower psychological stress or nervousness (Baron et al., 1992). A reason for this might be not only the relaxing surroundings but also the lower pressure to do well. The inter-personal evaluation of performance in all racket sports (victory or loss) is most likely associated with a higher degree of psychological pressure than the intra-personal evaluation with the respective handicap in golf.

By means of indirect calorimetry, and taking into account the respiratory exchange ratio and the mean oxygen uptake, the energy turnover in tennis and golf was calculated (Figure 1). The net turnover of a male senior sportsman with a mass of 80 kg is in golf 170 kcal (710 kJ) and in tennis 420 kcal (1760 kJ) per hour of exercise. Other authors have reached similar results (Getchell, 1968; Lampley et al., 1977). The gross turnover (including basal metabolism) during a tennis match lasting 2 hours corresponds exactly to the turnover during 18 holes of golf (about 1000 kcal or 4200 kJ, respectively).

Table 1. Results of incremental cycle ergometry. Values refer to absolute (abs) and relative performance (rel), anaerobic threshold (4 mmol.l^{-1}) as well as the age related norm (norm) and comparison of norm with actual value (rel-norm)

Performance		Golf (n=21)	Tennis (n=18)	Sig
abs	[W]	169 ± 41	196 ± 32	*
4 mmol.l^{-1}	[W]	139 ± 33	163 ± 23	**
rel	[W/kg]	2.05 ± 0.48	2.32 ± 0.53	ns
norm[1]	[W/kg]	2.11 ± 0.16	2.13 ± 0.07	ns
rel-norm	[W/kg]	-0.06 ± 0.41	0.19 ± 0.51	ns
rel-norm	[%]	-3.1 ± 19.5	9.0 ± 24.2	ns

[1]Calculated according to Rost and Hollmann (1982)

The results of incremental cycle ergometry allow conclusions if regular execution of tennis or golf over decades comes along with an improvement in general performance capacity. This is of special importance in relation to health orientated considerations because several epidemiological studies have shown that an increase in physical performance induces a decline in morbidity and mortality rate (Blair et al., 1992). The present findings suggest that corresponding adaptations can only be reached by means of tennis (Table 1). However, the data obtained do not allow a complete analysis of the causes because several factors influencing performance have not been evaluated (e.g. smoking and other physical activities). Nevertheless, the results concerning the intensity of physical demand show that the limit suggested by Blair et al. (1992) for an optimal health orientated training programme (50 % - 80 % $\dot{V}O_2$ max) is only reached in tennis (Figure 1). Consequently, a training effect is likely during tennis at senior level.

5 Conclusions

Both sports enable a significant increase in energy expenditure and an activation of lipid metabolism as well as a reduction of insulin level. This might induce positive long terms effects on body weight, lipid profile and counteract the development of the metabolic syndrome. An improvement of physical performance capacity can only be reached in tennis due to its higher hemodynamic and metabolic demands. However, golf can be suggested particularly for regeneration because of the low release of stress hormones.

6 References

Baron, R., Petschnig, R., Bachl, N., Raberger, G., Smekal, G. and Kastner, P. (1992) Catecholamine excretion and heart rate as factors of psychophysical stress in table tennis. **International Journal of Sports Medicine**, 13, 501-505.

Beaumont Van, W. (1972) Evaluation of hemoconcentration from hematocrit measurements. **Journal of Applied Physiology**, 32, 712-713.

Blair, S.N., Kohl, H.W., Gordon, N.F. and Paffenbarger, R.S. (1992) How much physical activity is good for health? **Annual Review of Public Health**, 13, 99-126.

Getchell, L.H. (1968) Energy cost of playing golf. **Archives of Physical Medicine and Rehabilitation**, 24, 31-35.

Lampley, J.H., Lampley, P.M. and Howley, E.T. (1977) Caloric cost of playing golf. **Research Quarterly**, 48, 637-639.

Lehmann, M., Keul, J., Huber, G. and Da Prada, M. (1981) Plasma catecholamines in trained and untrained volunteers during graduated exercise. **International Journal of Sports Medicine**, 2, 143-147.

Murase, Y., Kamei, S. and Hoshikawa, T. (1989) Heart rate and metabolic responses to articipation in golf. **Journal of Sports Medicine and Physical Fitness**, 29, 269-272.

Pruett, E.D.R. (1970) FFA mobilization during and after prolonged severe muscular work in men. **Journal of Applied Physiology**, 29, 809-815.

Rost, R. and Hollmann, W. (1982) **Belastungsuntersuchungen in der Praxis**. Thieme, Stuttgart/New York.

Seliger, V., Ejem, M. and Safarik, V. (1973) Energy metabolism in tennis. **Internationale Zeitschrift für Angewandte Physiologie**, 31, 333-340.

Sklorz, M. (1995) Stellung und Bedeutung der Seniorinnen und Senioren im Breitensport, in **Tennis im höheren Lebensalter aus interdisziplinärer Sicht** (eds N. Hölting, K. Weber, H. Funhoff), Czwalina, Hamburg, pp. 169-174.

Therminarias, A., Dansou, P., Chirpaz-Oddou, M.F., Gharib, C. and Quirion, A. (1991) Hormonal and metabolic changes during a strenuous tennis match. Effect of ageing. **International Journal of Sports Medicine** 12, 10-16.

WHO (1968) Exercise tests in relation to cardiovascular function. **Technicreports Series** 338, Genf.

5 Regional body composition in professional tennis players

J. Sanchis Moysi, C. Dorado Garcia and J.A.L. Calbet
Departamento de Educación Física, Universidad de Las Palmas de Gran Canaria, Campus Universitario de Tafira, Spain

1 Introduction

Tennis is an asymmetric sport that imposes a high mechanical load on the tissues of the dominant arm and as a consequence, adaptive changes take place increasing the muscle and bone mass, as well as the strength of the dominant arm (Jacobson et al., 1984; Pirnay et al., 1987; Tsuji et al., 1995). This sport offers a model for studying the adaptability of both the skeletal and the soft-tissue of the upper-limbs to physical stress, using the non-dominant arm as a control. From pioneer studies using single photon absorptiometry, it is well known that bone mineral content (BMC) and bone mineral density (BMD) increase in the dominant arm of tennis players of different ages and levels (Jones et al., 1977; Huddlestone et al., 1980; Montoye et al., 1980; Tsuji et al., 1995). Since these studies were carried out, important changes have been introduced in racket designs and grip techniques, which in turn might influence the adaptive changes (Kibler et al., 1988). Moreover, the degree of bone enhancement that professional tennis players might produce, and to what extent osteoformation acts through the growth of bone (bone hypertrophy) or through the increase of mineralization are still unkown.

The main aims of this study was to determine the effects of long term high level tennis practice on the skeletal and soft tissues of the limbs, with special reference to the dominant and non-dominant arm. Another aim was to find out the relationship between muscle hypertrophy and the enhancement of bone mass, and most importantly to determine to what degree the whole mass of the dominant arm might increase as a result of playing tennis.

2 Methods

Nine male tennis players of Gran Canaria island and 17 non-active subjects from the same Caucasian population agreed to participate in this study after being informed about the risk involved. All the tennis players had been participating in professional or first level amateur tennis competitions during, at least, the last seven years. The mean

Science and Racket Sports II, edited by A. Lees, I. Maynard, M. Hughes and T. Reilly. Published in 1998 by E & FN Spon, 11 New Fetter Lane, London EC4P 4EE, UK.   ISBN: 0 419 23030 0

time spent in tennis training or competitions was 25 ± 8 hours.week^{-1}. Subjects were ascribed to the sedentary, or control group, only if they had not been practising either any kind of sport during at least the last five years, or any physically demanding work. The nine tennis players and fourteen of the sedentary subjects were right-handed. Anthropometric measurements were first taken according to the procedures of the O-Scale system (Ward et al., 1989) as described elsewhere (López Calbet et al., 1997). Thereafter, total and regional body composition were measured by dual-energy X-ray absorptiometry (DXA) (QDR-1500, Hologic Corp., Waltham, MA). The principle of DXA, as well as its validity and reliability, have been described previously (Mazzes et al., 1990; Svendsen et al., 1993; López Calbet et al., 1996; Pietrobelli et al., 1996). Briefly, the system makes use of a dual-energy source that is pulsed between 70 and 140 kV synchronously with line frequency. The X-ray source is mounted beneath the subject and generates a thin, dual-energy X-ray beam that passes through the subject's tissues. The transmitted X-rays strike a detector mounted above the subject. A tissue-equivalent step phantom was placed alongside the subject to provide a calibration of the body composition measurements. Depending on the different attenuation experienced by the two energy beams, tissue mass and bone mass can be calculated by solving two algebraic equations. Tissue mass is further divided into fat-free non-skeletal mass and fat mass through application of an equation resulting from the calibration phantom. Body composition was analyzed assuming that the hydration of the lean body mass is 73.2 % and brain fat 17.0 %.

From the whole body scans, the lean body mass (g), body fat (g), total area (cm^2) and bone mineral content (BMC; g) were measured. Bone mineral density (BMD; g.cm^{-2}) was calculated from these measures using the formula BMD = BMC/total area. Additionally, total body scans of subregions are reported, including left and right legs and arms, and trunk (pelvis, neck, thoracic and abdominal regions). The laboratory precision error as defined by the coefficient of variation of repeated measurements for young volunteers (n=9) was for all the DXA variables less than 3 % (López Calbet et al., 1996). Fat-free lean mass was assumed to be equivalent to muscle mass in both the legs and the arms.

Data were analysed using the SPSS mainframe statistical program and statistical significance set at $P < 0.05$ level. Results are presented as means $\pm$ S.D. Group differences were evaluated using unpaired t-tests, while differences between sides were assessed using the paired Student's t-test.

3 Results and Discussion

3.1 Whole body composition
Table 1 summarises the anthropometric and whole body composition data per group. No significant differences were observed between the tennis players and sedentary subjects in age, height, body mass, BMC, total lean body mass, total body fat and in the percentage of body fat. Only limited data are available on the percentage of fat of elite

Table 1. Anthropometric and whole body composition variables

Variable	Tennis players	Control group	P
Age (years)	26.20 ± 3.8	23.90 ± 2.9	NS
Height (cm)	180.00 ± 6.0	178.00 ± 6.0	NS
Total body mass (kg)	77.30 ± 10.3	73.60 ± 9.5	NS
Total BMC (kg)	3.08 ± 0.48	2.85 ± 0.36	NS
Total lean mass (kg)	60.20 ± 5.7	56.4 ± 5.4	NS
Total body fat (kg)	13.00 ± 6.6	13.7 ± 5.4	NS
% fat	16.50 ± 6.9	18.4 ± 5.4	NS

tennis players and no study had compared the elite tennis players with a matched group of non-active subjects from the same population. This study shows that despite the tremendous amount of exercise performed by the tennis players (i.e., 25 ± 8 hours.week^{-1}) they showed only slightly lower levels of body fat than their sedentary counterparts (16.5 vs. 18.4%). These results are in accordance with those of Kibler et al. (1988) who reported a percentage of body fat between 16 and 22% in elite young tennis players, using the generalized equation of Jackson and Pollock. Nevertheless, Sinning et al. (1985) reported a mean value of 11.3% in a group of 9 tennis players (college league) assessed by hydrodensitometry.

3.2 Regional body composition: the arms
Marked differences existed between the dominant and the contralateral arm in the tennis players (mean ± S.D) for BMC (229.0 ± 43.5 vs.188.2 ± 31.9 g, P<0.001), muscle mass (3,772 ± 500 vs. 3,148 ± 380 g, P<0.001) and whole mass (4,977 ± 908 vs. 4,220 ± 632 g, P<0.001). It was noticiable that the fat mass showed a trend to be higher in the dominant arm (976 ± 567 vs. 884 ± 467 g, P=0.09), but the percentage of fat was lower in the dominant arm (18.7 ± 8.6 vs. 20.3 ± 8.8%, P<0.05). On the other hand, the control group also showed a slightly higher muscle mass in the dominant arm (3,246 ± 421 vs. 3,093 ± 388 g, P<0.01), but a lower fat mass (749 ± 274 vs. 793 ± 278 g, P<0.05), the percentage of fat also being lower in the dominant arm (17.7 ± 5.3 vs. 19.2 ± 5.7%, P<0.01). In addition the sedentary subjects showed similar BMC in both arms (194 ± 33 vs. 193 ± 32 g). When comparing the arms between groups, total and lean masses as well as BMC were higher in the dominant arm of the tennis players (P<0.05). Therefore, our study showed that in both the tennis players and the sedentary subjects the muscle mass was higher in the dominant arm. However, the inter-arm difference was much higher in the tennis players (20%) than in the control group (5%). The hypertrophy of the muscle mass of the dominant arm may be an adaptive change in response to the physical stresses imposed by daily tasks and, in the case of the tennis players, the strength necessary to grip the racket. Accordingly, Faulkner et al. (1993) have observed a 10% higher lean tissue in the dominant arm in 8 to 16 year-old children. Unfortunately, no data are available to compare with our muscle mass values of the dominant arm of professional tennis players. Nevertheless, the principal finding of our study was that tennis players had nearly 22% more mineral

content in the dominant than in the non-dominant arm. This result concords with pioneer studies in tennis players that were carried out on the radius bone with single photon absorptiometry (Jones et al., 1977; Montoye et al., 1980; Huddlestone et al., 1980; Jacobson et al. 1984; Pirnay et al., 1987). More recently, in an unpublished study, Kannus et al. (cited by Suominen, 1993), using DXA, reported a 25% higher BMC in the proximal humerus of the dominant arm in tennis players. It must be highlighted that in this study all the bones of the arm, even the hand, showed higher BMC in the dominant compared with the non-dominant arm.

With respect to the mechanism by which BMC is increased, several factors might play a role such as the type, intensity and duration of muscle contractions, as well as the degree of muscle hypertrophy elicited. For example, it has been well documented that bone tissue adapts in response to the mechanical forces acting upon it (Rawlinson et al., 1991; Fox et al., 1996). However, it appears that to increase BMC high impact or weight-bearing activity is necessary, since several studies have shown that swimmers, who perform a large number of muscle contractions, but are not involved in impact or weight-bearing tasks, have values of BMC and BMD similar to those observed in sedentary subjects. Conversely, volleyball players and weightlifters show the highest levels of BMC (Suominen, 1993).

Several studies have demonstrated that tennis players have a wider cortical bone at the distal radius (Montoye et al., 1980; Martin et al., 1987) and higher BMD in the dominant arm (Huddleston et al., 1980; Jones et al., 1977; Montoye et al., 1980; Pirnay et al., 1987). Accordingly, the area occupied by the osseous pixels was also higher in the dominant arm of the tennis players than in the contralateral arm (261 ± 42 vs. 229 ± 31 cm^2, P<0.05), while no significant differences were observed between bone areas of the arms in the control group. However, bone hypertrophy did not account for the overall increase in BMC, as BMD was also higher in the dominant arm than in the contralateral arm, in both the tennis players (0.874 ± 0.054 vs. 0.821 ± 0.083 g.cm^{-2}, P<0.05) and the control group (0.821 ± 0.087 vs. 0.808 ± 0.088 g.cm^{-2}, P<0.05). Moreover, when comparing BMD across groups, the tennis players showed a trend towards a higher BMD in the dominant arm than the control group (0.874 ± 0.5 and 0.821 ± 0.087 g.cm^{-2}, respectively, P=0.1). Nevertheless, no significant differences in BMD were observed between groups for the left arm, left leg, and right leg.

Another factor that might be associated with the high BMC in the dominant arm of the tennis players is the increased muscle and total mass of the arm. A correlation was found between BMC and both muscle mass and total mass of the dominant arm in the tennis players (r=0.76, P<0.05; and r=0.83, P<0.01, respectively) as well as the sedentary subjects (r=0.86 and r=0.86, respectively, both P<0.001). This is in accordance with other studies showing correlations between arm and leg lean mass and their respective BMD (Nichols et al., 1995; Baumgartner et al., 1996).

3.3 Regional body composition: the legs
Minor asymmetries were also observed for the legs of the tennis players, as well as in the control group. In the tennis players the right leg was slightly heavier than the left leg (13.24 ± 1.78 vs. 13.03 ± 1.83 kg, P<0.01), due to the higher fat content of the right leg (2.52 ± 1.18 vs. 2.33 ± 1.07 kg, P<0.05). Nevertheless, only the fat content was slightly increased in the right leg of the control group (3.00 ± 1.12 vs. 2.86 ± 1.05 kg,

P<0.05), while the total mass and the muscle mass, as well as the BMC were similar in both sides. In contrast, the left leg showed the highest BMD in the control group (1,426 ± 0.087 vs. 1,398 ± 0.74 g.cm^{-2}), but no differences in BMD were observed between both legs in the tennis players (1,426 ± 0.102 vs. 1,439 ± 0.101 g.cm^{-2}).

4 Conclusions

In summary, this study has shown that the marked arm asymmetry usually seen in tennis players was due to the existence of about 20% more BMC and muscle mass in the dominant than in the contralateral arm. About 2/3 of the BMC enhancement was due to bone growth, as demonstrated by the widening of the area occupied by the osseous pixels, while the rest of the BMC enhancement might be explained by a higher degree of mineralization, since BMD was about 6% higher in the dominant arm. In addition a close correlation was found between BMC and both the muscle mass and the total mass of the dominant arm. Finally, two practical implications may be derived from this study. First, the practice of tennis facilitates the maintenance of bone and muscle mass; therefore, this sport may be indicated to counteract the effects of ageing. Second, tennis players may benefit from compensatory work for the non-dominan arm. In so doing, this probably will reduce the stress on the upper dorsal spine and will decrease the risk of injuries in this region.

5 References

Baumgartner, R.N., Stauber, P.M., Koehler, K.M., Romero, L. and Garry, P.J. (1996) Association of fat and muscle masses with bone mineral in elderly men and women. **American Journal of Clinical Nutrition,** 63, 365-372.

Faulkner, R.A., Houston, C.S., Bailey, D.A., Drinkwater, D.T., McKay, H.A. and Wilkinson, A.A. (1993) Comparison of bone mineral content and bone mineral density between dominant and nondominant limbs in children 8-16 years of age. **American Journal of Human Biology**, 4, 492-501.

Fox, S.W., Chambers, T.J. and Chow, J.W.M. (1996) Nitric oxide is an early mediator of the increase in bone formation by mechanical stimulation. **American Journal of Physiology**, 270, E955-E960.

Huddlestone, A.L., Rockwell, D., Kulund, D.N. and Harrison, R.B. (1980) Bone mass in lifetime tennis players. **Journal of the American Medical Association**, 244, 1107-1109.

Jacobson, P.C., Beaver, W., Grupp, S.A., Taft, T.N. and Talmage R.V. (1984) Bone density in women: College athletes and older athletic women. **Journal of Orthopaedic Research,** 2, 328-332.

Jones, H.H., Priest, J.D., Hayes, W.C., Tichenor, C.C. and Nagel, D.A. (1977) Humeral hypertrophy in response to exercise. **Journal of Bone and Joint Surgery,** 59A, 204-208.

Kannus, P., Haapasalo, H., Sievänen, H., Oja, P., Vuori, I. (1993) The effect of long-term unilateral activity on bone mineral density and content (unpublished, cited by Suominen, 1993)

Kibler, W.B., McQueen, C. and Uhl, T. (1988) Fitness evaluations and fitness findings in competitive junior tennis players. **Clinics in Sports Medicine**, 7, 403-416.

López Calbet, J.A., Dorado García, C., Chavarren Cabrero, J. (1996) Evaluación de la composición corporal mediante absorciometría fotónica dual de rayos X: aplicaciones y limitaciones en el ámbito del deporte. **Investigaciones en Ciencias del Deporte**, 8, 53-79.

López Calbet, J.A., Armengol Ramos, O., Chavarren Cabrero, J., Dorado García, C. (1997) Anthropometric equation for assessment of percent body fat in adult males of the Canary Islands. **Medical Clinician (Barcelona)**, 108, 207-213.

Martin, A.D., Bailey, D.A., Leicester, J.B. and Gulka, I. (1987) Bone and muscle relationships in the forearm of lifetime tennis players. **Proceedings of International Symposium on Osteoporosis**, Aalborg, Denmark.

Mazess, R.B., Barden, H.S., Bisek, J.P. and Hanson J. (1990) Dual-energy x-ray absorptiometry for total body and regional bone-mineral and soft-tissue composition. **American Journal of Clinical Nutrition**, 51,1106-1112.

Montoye, H.J., Smith, E.L., Fardon, D.F. and Howley, E.T. (1980) Bone mineral in senior tennis players. **Scandinavian Journal of Sports Science**, 2,26-32.

Nichols, D.L., Sanborn, C.F., Bonnick, S.L., Gench, B. and Dimarco, N. (1995) Relationship of regional body composition to bone mineral density in college females. **Medicine and Science in Sports and Exercise**, 27,178-182.

Pietrobelli, A., Formica, C., Wang, Z. and Heymsfield, S.B. (1996) Dual-energy X-ray absorptiometry body composition model: review of physical concepts. **American Journal of Physiology**, 271, E941-E951.

Pirnay, F., Bodeux, M., Crielaard, J. and Franchimont, P. (1987) Bone mineral content and physical activity. **International Journal of Sports Medicine**, 8,331-335.

Rawlinson, S.C.F., El Haj, A.J., Minter, S.L., Tavarse, I.A., Bennett, A. and Lanyon, L.E. (1991) Loading-related increases in protaglandin production in cores of adult canine cancellous bone in vitro: a role for prostacyclin in adaptative bone remodeling? **Journal of Bone and Mineral Research**, 6:1345-1351.

Sinning, W.E., Dolny, D.G., Little, K.D., Cunningham, L.N., Racaniello, A., Siconolfi S.F. and Sholes, J.L. (1985) Validity of "generalized" equations for body composition analysis in male athletes. **Medicine and Science in Sports and Exercise**, 17, 124-130.

Suominen, H. (1993) Bone mineral density and long term exercise. An overview of cross-sectional athlete studies. **Sports Medicine**, 16, 316-330.

Svendsen, O.L., Haarbo, J., Hassager, C. and Christiansen, C. (1993) Accuracy of measurements of body composition by dual-energy x-ray absorptiometry in vivo. **American Journal of Clinical Nutrition**, 57, 605-608.

Tsuji, S., Tsunoda, N., Yata, H., Katsukawa, F. and Onishi, S. (1995) Relation between grip strength and radial bone mineral density in young athletes. **Archives of Physical Medicine and Rehabilitation**, 76, 234-238.

Ward, R., Ross, W.D., Leyland, A.J. and Selbie, S. (1989) **The Advanced O-Scale Physique Assessment System**. Kinemetrix Inc., Burnaby.

Part Two

Nutritional Aspects of Racket Sports

6 Nutrition for racket sports

D.P.M. MacLaren
*Centre for Sport and Exercise Sciences, Liverpool John Moores
University, Liverpool, UK*

1 Introduction

Nutrition and training states are two crucial aspects in determining successful
outcomes in sports performance. It is not possible to perform adequate training
regimens unless correct attention is given to nutritional support. Furthermore, good
training leading up to the day of competition can be undone by inappropriate
nutritional strategies on the day. Clearly, nutrition is a key component to success in
sport. This review considers aspects of nutrition for racket sports players such as
energy intake, the importance of carbohydrate and fluid provision, and the importance
of proteins, vitamins and minerals. Although an attempt is made to relate available
scientific information to racket sports, few good nutritional studies have been reported
in peer-reviewed journals in this specific field.

2 Energy Expenditure

In order to determine the energy needs of racket sports players, the energy expenditure
of playing tennis, squash, badminton, and table-tennis needs to be assessed. Some data
have been obtained using either heart rate measures during play and related to
laboratory determined heart rate-oxygen uptake relationships (see Reilly, 1990), or by
direct determination of oxygen uptake using portable telemetered oxygen analysers
such as the Cosmed-K2 or Metamax systems (Faccini and Dal Monte, 1996). From
such studies estimates have been made of the energy expenditure of playing the
various racket sports for a 70 kg player are:-

Badminton	- 29 to 46 kJ.min^{-1}
Squash	- 42 to 76 kJ.min^{-1}
Table-tennis	- 29 to 42 kJ.min^{-1}
Tennis	- 29 to 46 kJ.min^{-1}

Science and Racket Sports II, edited by A. Lees, I. Maynard, M. Hughes and T. Reilly. Published in
1998 by E & FN Spon, 11 New Fetter Lane, London EC4P 4EE, UK. ISBN: 0 419 23030 0

If we assume that the player is engaged in one of these activities for 2 hours in a day, the resultant is an increase in energy expenditure above an equivalent sedentary person ranging from 3480 to 9120 kJ. If body mass is to be maintained, then an equivalent energy intake is required.

3 The Need for Carbohydrate

No peer-reviewed publications have, to date, reported the influence of carbohydrates in playing racket sports. Nevertheless, there is a wealth of literature concerning the importance of carbohydrates for sports performance (Coggan and Coyle, 1991; Hargreaves, 1991; Murray, 1987; Noakes, 1991).

When played competitively, all the racket sports elicit average heart rates in excess of 150 beats.min^{-1} and involve high intensity activity of between 5 to 10 s with an equivalent recovery period. If repeated over the period of match-play lasting between 30 and 90 min, this constitutes significant portions of energy from muscle glycogen. If we assume that 50% of the energy comes from the limited carbohydrate stores in the body, then between 220 and 580 g of carbohydrate is likely to have been used up, and since the total stores in the body represent 400 - 600 g, the likely depletion is appreciable. Examination of the muscle glycogen depletion patterns in muscle fibre types following exercise of varying intensities indicates that significant depletion may occur in all fibres (Vollestad et al., 1984), but especially in type II fibres. In addition, just one 6 s sprint alone can reduce muscle glycogen by 14% (Boobis et al., 1982).

The value of carbohydrate supplementation prior to exercise has been demonstrated in the classic studies of Christensen and Hansen (1939b) and, following the introduction of muscle biopsy techniques, by Bergstrom et al. (1967). Both studies demonstrated that an increase in carbohydrate intake in the days before exercise, resulted in significant improvements in the ability to perform that exercise. In a further study, Christensen and Hansen (1939a) showed that ingestion of 200 g of carbohydrate at the point of exhaustion enabled their subjects to continue exercising for another 40 min.

More recently, research has been focused on the value of carbohydrates ingested or infused during exercise. Coyle et al. (1983, 1986) and Coggan and Coyle (1987,1991) added significantly to the understanding of how carbohydrate provision may be beneficial in prolonged activities. In the first study (Coyle et al., 1983) the subjects exercised at 70% VO_{2max} for 23 min longer after carbohydrate feedings compared with placebo; in the second study (Coyle et al., 1986) carbohydrate ingestion resulted in the subjects exercising for 60 min longer than when fed placebo; the third study (Coggan and Coyle, 1987) showed that when carbohydrate was ingested or infused to maintain euglycaemia at the point of fatigue, subjects exercised for 26 min and 43 min longer, respectively, than when placebo was ingested. In the final study (Coggan and Coyle, 1991) the subjects ingested a single large carbohydrate bolus approximately 30 min before the predicted point of fatigue, which prolonged the exercise by a further 36 min. In all these studies ingestion of carbohydrate promoted carbohydrate oxidation and elevated blood glucose concentrations.

If carbohydrate feeding during exercise enhances performance, what effect does ingestion of carbohydrate in the hour before exercise have on subsequent performance? Some early studies on glucose ingestion in the hour immediately prior to exercise have shown that this leads to an elevation of blood glucose and insulin at the onset of exercise, and has a subsequent adverse effect on metabolism during the early stages of moderate to high-intensity exercise (Costill et al., 1977; Foster et al., 1979). Under these conditions, where the percentage glucose solution ingested was high (25% solution), blood glucose declined rapidly during exercise due to the high concentrations of insulin that were induced. Fat oxidation was also depressed, and so the exercising muscle relied more heavily on muscle glycogen stores than on exogenous provision of carbohydrate.

More recently, there have been reports of the beneficial effects of ingesting carbohydrate before exercise (Gleeson et al., 1986; Neufer et al., 1987). Variations in the timing, the dose, the type of carbohydrate, and the ensuing exercise intensity make it difficult to arrive at firm conclusions. It is suggested that if carbohydrate is ingested before exercise, any possible 'rebound hypoglycaemia' may be offset by ingesting carbohydrates during exercise as well.

The effectiveness of the form of carbohydrate ingested on performance has been the subject of numerous investigations (see Maughan, 1991; Murray, 1987; Noakes, 1991). Studies in which the effects of ingesting glucose have been compared directly to maltodextrins or sucrose during exercise, either alone or in combination, have failed to demonstrate significant benefits (MacLaren et al., 1994). The only carbohydrate solution which has generally not led to improvements in performance is fructose (Murray et al., 1989). Over the last few years there has been an increase in the number of racket sports players eating bananas in between games, in conjunction with water. This is to be recommended. Table 1 illustrates some of the advantages that bananas may have when compared with other popular fruits consumed within the UK, in terms of more carbohydrate, energy, potassium, magnesium, and phosphorus. Eating 300 g (2 large) bananas per hour, together with water, will provide approximately 70 g of useful carbohydrate.

Table 1. Selected nutritional information of 4 common fruits eaten in the UK (values based upon 100 g of actual fruit, not including the skins)

	Protein (g)	CHO (g)	Energy (kJ)	K (μg)	Mg (μg)	P (μg)
Banana	1.2	23.2	380	400	34	28
Apple	0.4	11.2	180	100	3	8
Orange	1.1	8.5	148	150	10	21
Grape	0.5	16.0	240	210	7	18

The beneficial effects of carbohydrate ingestion are related to the maintenance of blood glucose levels and a high rate of carbohydrate oxidation at a time when muscle glycogen stores are low (Coggan and Coyle, 1987). At this time, blood glucose is the major source of carbohydrate for contracting skeletal muscle, which is capable of utilising glucose at a rate of 1.0 to 1.5 g.min^{-1} (Coggan and Coyle, 1987) i.e.

approximately 60 g.h^{-1}. Despite adequate blood glucose availability, exercise is eventually terminated. This illustrates the complexity of the fatigue process, and suggests that factors other than availability of carbohydrate may be involved. Nevertheless, the importance of carbohydrate for endurance exercise cannot be ignored.

In spite of the considerable weight of evidence that muscle glycogen depletion is correlated with fatigue, there is some evidence that hypoglycaemia may be a causative factor in some individuals. Hypoglycaemia may be evident in prolonged exercise, and can contribute to fatigue. This normally occurs as a result of an inadequate restoration of the liver glycogen stores, since it is unlikely that the rate of gluconeogenesis can provide sufficient glucose for the maintenance of blood glucose levels. The brain and central nervous system are dependent on glucose supplied in the blood for their metabolism, and if the levels are at or below 3.0 mmol.l^{-1}, nervousness, trembling and loss of consciousness may occur. For the skilled performer (such as racket sports players) this may result in impaired decision making and the loss of a match. Reilly & Lewis (1985) have shown that glucose feeding during prolonged activities enables mental tasks to be carried out with fewer errors than with plain water or no water.

4 Restoration of Muscle Glycogen

Since levels of muscle glycogen are likely to be significantly depleted following training and/or match-play in racket sports and the subsequent performance may be impaired if muscle glycogen levels are low prior to that activity, means to achieve rapid repletion are essential. Three reports of muscle glycogen resynthesis have focused on the effects of the timing of carbohydrate ingestion post-exercise (Ivy et al., 1988a), the dose of carbohydrate to be ingested (Ivy et al., 1988b), and the form of carbohydrate to be ingested (Reed et al., 1989). The following were concluded:-

i)   A 2 h delay in administering carbohydrate results in a slower rate of glycogen storage than if the carbohydrate is provided immediately post-exercise.

ii) Ingestion of 1.5 g.kg^{-1} body mass glucose immediately and 2 h after exercise significantly enhances muscle glycogen stores above a basal rate, and that doubling the amount of glucose ingested (3 g.kg^{-1} body mass) is of no additional benefit.

iii) The rate of muscle glycogen resynthesis is independent of the form of carbohydrate i.e. solid or liquid.

The total amount of carbohydrate necessary for consumption to restore muscle glycogen levels in 24 hours following exhaustive exercise is approximately 600-650 g. This is in line with recommendations that elite athletes need to consume 8-10 g.kg^{-1} body mass of carbohydrate per day during training or competition. For a 70 kg person this represents 560-700 g.day^{-1}.

5 Fluid Intake

At high work-rates metabolic heat production can exceed 80 kJ.min^{-1} (Maughan and Noakes, 1991). If this level of work is maintained for 1-2 h, the rate of sweat loss necessary to dissipate this heat load will result in significant losses of body water. The sweat losses incurred during activities such as tennis have been estimated as 1.5-2.0 l.h^{-1} for males and approximately 1.0 l/h for females in a hot environment (Bergeron et al., 1995). Failure to redress the loss of body fluids results in dehydration; exercise performance is impaired when an individual is dehydrated by as little as 2% of body mass, and that a loss of 5% can decrease the capacity for work by about 30% (Saltin and Costill, 1988).

The effects of imbibing different types and amounts of beverages during exercise have been well documented (see Maughan and Noakes, 1991; Murray, 1987). The majority of these studies have shown a positive effect of fluid ingestion on performance.

If muscle glycogen depletion, hypoglycaemia, and/or dehydration are potential causes of fatigue, what is the trade-off between ingestion of water or a carbohydrate solution? The American College of Sports Medicine in its Position Stand on the prevention of thermal injuries in distance running (1984) stated that cool water is the optimum fluid for ingestion during endurance exercise. This may be so for events lasting 60 min or less, and when the athlete has adequate stores of muscle glycogen. In events lasting more than 60 min, the depletion of muscle glycogen stores may present a problem. Under these circumstances consideration should be given to carbohydrate in the fluid. The problem with using carbohydrate solutions is that high concentrations delay gastric emptying, thus reducing the amount of fluid that is available for absorption (Maughan and Noakes, 1991). Sugar concentrations greater than a 10% solution may also result in gastrointestinal distress. Most sports drinks contain a carbohydrate source at a concentration of about 6%; at this concentration glucose solutions are approximately isotonic with body fluids. Depending on the duration of the match and the environmental conditions prevailing, either plain water or a dilute carbohydrate-electrolyte drink should be consumed to attempt to match the sweat losses incurred.

Most tennis matches are played outdoors and are therefore subject to the effects of the environment; hot and humid conditions result in significant sweat losses, although matches played under temperate conditions also impose thermal stress. Indeed, cramp and heat stroke whilst playing tennis have been reported in female players (Therminarias et al., 1995). Games of squash, badminton, and table tennis, although played indoors, can still be subject to alterations in heat and humidity, and thereby induce a state of dehydration in players. Sweat losses of between 1-2% of body mass have been reported for squash play (Hansen, 1995; Noakes et al., 1982). The importance of fluid replacement is paramount for racket sports players, but how should euhydration be maintained or rehydration achieved?

Matching fluid intake with changes in body mass can be achieved over periods of 24 h or longer when moving from temperate to hot climatic conditions. Frequent weighing of body mass can check for these variations. Fluid balance during match play is more difficult to achieve. Starting the match euhydrated, or even hyperhydrated, followed by frequent drinking bouts has been suggested (Maughan and Noakes, 1991). The volumes of fluid needed in hot conditions involve the ingestion of 300-500 ml before play followed by 150-200 ml every 15-20 min whilst playing; the amounts needed vary depending on the environmental factors. There are opportunities to take in fluid at the end of games/sets, and though these periods are brief, fluid ingestion must be availed of.

Rehydrating after matches and/or training is of prime importance when engaged in tournaments. Studies have highlighted the importance of drinks containing electrolytes, particularly sodium (Maughan et al, 1994). The rationale for the inclusion of sodium in the post-match drink is related to maintaining plasma osmolality and sodium concentration, thereby conserving the drive to drink. Imbibing plain water can lead to haemodilution and enhanced urine production, followed by a reduced drive to drink; the net result is maintenance of dehydration. Enough fluid should be ingested after exercise to recover any body mass decreases.

6 Protein

Recommendations have been made regarding the minimum amount of protein to be consumed per day, and these have stated a value amounting to 0.7 $g.kg^{-1}$ body mass. For a 70 kg person this would amount to 49 $g.day^{-1}$. Since the Western diet normally contains 15% energy intake in the form of protein, an individual would have to eat less than 5500 $kJ.day^{-1}$ before protein intake presents a problem. The recommendations for protein intake for athletes engaged in strength or speed events is between 1.2-1.7 $g.kg^{-1}.day^{-1}$, and 1.2-1.4 $g.kg^{-1}.day^{-1}$ for endurance athletes (Lemon, 1991). The higher values for athletes reflects the greater protein turnover as a result of increased activity and the loss of amino acids in sweat.

7 Vitamins and Minerals

Many of the vitamins play key roles in exercise metabolism although they do not possess any energy. The B-vitamins are particularly relevant to energy production in muscle. Since these vitamins are important in energy-producing reactions, a deficiency will lead to impaired performance. There is no evidence that vitamin supplementation enhances performance in athletes eating a well-balanced diet (van der Beek, 1985). Physical activity increases the need for extra amounts of vitamins, but these can be obtained by consuming a balanced diet. The Department of Health, UK (1991) has established guidelines for the nutrient needs based on age, sex and level of activity categories. These guidelines include selected vitamins and minerals. Dietary surveys of athletic populations have shown that the estimated vitamin intakes usually exceed the recommended dietary intakes (van Erp-Bart et al., 1989), and so do not appear to present a problem.

8 Conclusions

In spite of the lack of peer-reviewed publications concerning nutrition and racket sports, guidelines and recommendations can be based on the wealth of information from laboratory findings and field studies in other sports. These may be summarised as follows:-

* At least 55% of the energy intake should be in the form of carbohydrates
* Carbohydrates should form the basis of pre-competitive and post-competitive meals. The former should be consumed approximately 3 h before playing, whilst the latter (1.5 g.kg^{-1} body mass every 2 h) should be consumed within 2 h of playing.
* Carbohydrate-electrolyte drinks (6-8% solution) are beneficial and should be taken before (say up to 1 h), during (every 15-20 min), and after (within 1-2 h) competition.
* A protein intake of 1.2-1.7 g.kg^{-1} body mass per day should be consumed, although if 15% of energy intake is in the form of protein, the needs are likely to be met.
* A varied diet should ensure that the vitamin and mineral requirements are met.

9 References

American College of Sports Medicine (1984) Position stand on prevention of thermal injuries during distance running. **Medicine and Science in Sports and Exercise**, 16, IX-XIV.

Bergeron, M.F., Maresh, C.M., Armstrong, L.E., Signorile, J.F., Castellani, J.W., Kenefick, R.W., LaGasse, K.E. and Riebe, D.A. (1995) Fluid-electrolyte balance associated with tennis match play in a hot environment. **International Journal of Sports Nutrition**, 5, 180-193.

Bergstrom, J., Hermansen, L., Hultman, E. and Saltin, B (1967) Diet, muscle glycogen and physical performance. **Acta Physiologica Scandinavica**, 71, 140-150.

Boobis, L., Williams, C. and Wootton, S. (1982) Human muscle metabolism during brief maximal exercise. **Journal of Physiology**, 338, 21-22.

Christensen, E.H. and Hansen, O. (1939a) Arbeitsfahigkeit und ernahrung. **Scandinavian Archives fur Physiology**, 81, 160-171.

Christensen, E.H. and Hansen, O. (1939b) Hypoglycamie, Arbeitsfahigkeit und Ermuding. **Scandinavian Archives fur Physiology**, 81, 172-179.

Coggan, A.R. and Coyle, E.F. (1987) Reversal of fatigue during prolonged exercise by carbohydrate infusion or ingestion. **Journal of Applied Physiology**, 63, 2388-2395.

Coggan, A.R. and Coyle, E.F. (1991) Carbohydrate ingestion during prolonged exercise: effects on metabolism and performance. **Exercise and Sports Science Reviews**, 19, 1-40.

Coyle, E.F., Coggan, A.R., Hemmert, M.K. and Ivy, J.L. (1986) Muscle glycogen utilization during prolonged strenuous exercise when fed carbohydrate. **Journal of Applied Physiology,** 61, 165-172.

Coyle, E.F., Hagberg, J.M., Hurley, B.F., Martin, W.H., Ehsani, A.A. and Holloszy, J.O. (1983) Carbohydrate feedings during prolonged strenuous exercise can delay fatigue. **Journal of Applied Physiology,** 55, 230-235.

Costill, D.L., Coyle, E.F., Dalsky, G., Evans, W., Fink, W. and Hoopes, D. (1977) Effects of elevated plasma FFA and insulin on muscle glycogen usage during exercise. **Journal of Applied Physiology**, 43, 695-699.

Department of Health (1991) **Report on health and social subjects No.41: Dietary reference values for food, energy and nutrients for the United Kingdom,** HMSO, London.

Faccini, P. and Dal Monte, A. (1996) Physiologic demands of badminton match play. **American Journal of Sports Medicine**, 24, S64-S66.

Foster, C., Costill, D.L. and Fink, W.J. (1979) Effects of pre-exercise feedings on endurance performance. **Medicine and Science in Sports and Exercise**, 11, 1-5.

Gleeson, M., Maughan, R.J. and Greenhaff, P.L. (1986) Comparison of the effects of pre-exercise feedings of glucose, glycerol and placebo on endurance and fuel homeostasis in man. **European Journal of Applied Physiology**, 55, 645-653.

Hansen, R.D. (1995) Seasonal variability in physiological strain: matching performance to demand, in **Science and Racket Sports** (eds T.Reilly, M. Hughes, and A. Lees), E. & F. N. Spon, London, pp 14-20.

Hargreaves, M. (1991) Carbohydrates and exercise. **Journal of Sports Sciences**, 9 (special issue), 17-28.

Ivy, J.L., Katz, A.L., Cutler, C.L., Sherman, W.M. and Coyle, E.F. (1988a) Muscle glycogen synthesis after exercise: effect of time of carbohydrate ingestion. **Journal of Applied Physiology**, 64, 1480-1485.

Ivy, J.L., Lee, M.C., Brozinick, J.R. and Reed, M.J. (1988b) Muscle glycogen storage after different amounts of carbohydrate ingestion. **Journal of Applied Physiology**, 65, 2018-2023.

Lemon, P.W.R. (1991) Effect of exercise on protein requirements. **Journal of Sports Sciences**, 9 (special issue), 53-70.

MacLaren, D.P.M., Reilly, T, Campbell, I.T. and Frayn, K.N. (1994) Hormonal and metabolite responses to glucose and maltodextrin ingestion with or without the addition of guar gum. **International Journal of Sports Medicine**, 15, 466-471.

Maughan, R.J. (1991) Effects of CHO-electrolyte solution on prolonged exercise, in **Ergogenics: the Enhancement of Sport and Exercise Performance** (eds D.R. Lamb and M.H. Williams), Benchmark Press, Carmel.

Maughan, R.J. and Noakes, T.D. (1991) Fluid replacement and exercise stress. **Sports Medicine**, 12, 16-31.

Maughan, R.J., Owens, J.H., Shirrefs, S.M. and Leiper, J.B. (1994) Post-exercise rehydration in man: effects of electrolyte addition to ingested fluids. **European Journal of Applied Physiology**, 69, 209-215.

Murray, R. (1987) The effects of consuming carbohydrate-electrolyte beverages on gastric emptying and fluid absorption during and following exercise. **Sports Medicine**, 4, 322-351.

Murray, R., Paul, G.L., Siefart, J.G., Eddy, D.E. and Halaby, G.A. (1989) The effects of glucose, fructose, and sucrose ingestion during exercise. **Medicine and Science in Sports and Exercise**, 21, 275-282.

Neufer, P.D., Costill, D.L., Flynn, M.G., Kirwan, J.P., Mitchell, J.B. and Houmard, J. (1987) Improvements in exercsie performance: effects of carbohydrate feedings and diet. **Journal of Applied Physiology**, 62, 983-988.

Noakes, T.D. (1991) Energy utilization and repletion during endurance exercise: an historical perspective. **Journal of Human Nutrition and Dietetics**, 4, 45-55.

Noakes, T.D., Cowling, J., Gevers, W. and De V. Van Nierkerk, J. (1982) The metabolic response to squash including the influence of pre-exercise carbohydrate ingestion. **South African Medical Journal**, 62, 721-723.

Reed, M.J., Brozinick, J.T., Lee, M.C. and Ivy, J.L. (1989) Muscle glycogen storage postexercise: Effect of mode of carbohydrate administration. **Journal of Applied Physiology**, 66, 720-726.

Reilly, T. (1990) The racquet sports, in **Physiology of Sports** (eds T. Reilly, N.Secher, P.Snell and C.Williams), E. & F.N. Spon, London, pp. 337-369.

Reilly, T., and Lewis, W. (1985) Effect of carbohydrate feeding on mental functions during sustained physical work, in **Ergonomics International 85, Proceedings 9th International Ergonomics Association Congress** (eds I.D. Brown, R. Goldsmith, K. Coombes and M. Sinclair), Taylor & Francis, London, pp 700-702.

Saltin, B. and Costill, D.L. (1988) Fluid and electrolyte balance during prolonged exercise, in **Exercise, Nutrition and Metabolism** (eds E.S. Horton and R.L. Terjung), MacMillan, New York, pp150-158.

Therminarias, A., Dansou, P., Chirpaz, M.F., Eterradossi, J. and Favre-Juvin, A. (1995) Cramps, heat stroke and abnormal biological responses during a strenuous tennis match, in **Science and Racket Sports**, (eds T. Reilly, M. Hughes and A. Lees), E. & F. N. Spon, London, pp 28-31.

van der Beek, E.J. (1985) Vitamins and endurance training: food for running or faddish claims? **Sports Medicine**, 2, 175-197

van Erp-Bart, A.M.J., Saris, W.H.M. and Binkhorst, R.A. (1989) Nationwide survey on nutritional habits in elite athletes (PartII): mineral and vitamin intake. **International Journal of Sports Medicine**, 10 (Suppl 1), S11-S16.

Vollestad, N.K., Vaage, O. and Hermansen, L. (1984) Muscle glycogen depletion patterns in type I and subgroups of type II fibres during prolonged severe exercise in man. **Acta Physiologica Scandinavica**, 122, 433-441.

7 Body fluid loss during competitive tennis match-play

P.R. McCarthy, R.D. Thorpe and C. Williams
Department of Physical Education, Sports Science and Recreation Management, Loughborough University, Loughborough, UK

1 Introduction

A longitudinal study of the training of young athletes (Rowley, 1992) revealed that junior tennis players aged 12 years (group 1) and 14 years (group 2) were on court for an average of 7 and 10 hours.week^{-1}, respectively. During competition, in contrast to training, the length of time spent on court and the number of matches played, are beyond the control of the player. Even at junior level, tennis matches can extend for many hours. Furthermore, the environmental conditions throughout competition may be hot and humid. It is especially under these conditions that players must rely on their sweating mechanism to lose heat. Children have a lower sweating rate when compared with adults, even when differences in body surface area are taken into consideration (Wagner et al., 1972).

Very little research has specifically examined fluid losses in tennis (Bergeron, 1995). Furthermore, any research that has been conducted on fluid loss and replacement during tennis training and competition, has focused on the responses of adult tennis players. Progressive dehydration by as little as 3% body mass, has been shown in adult competitive tennis players to cause a 20% increase in errors during simulated tennis match-play (Burke and Ekblom, 1982).

Thus the aim of the present study was to assess the fluid losses incurred by junior tennis players, when participating in a Junior County tournament.

2 Methods

Fourteen male and six female junior county tournament standard tennis players, aged between 12 and 14 years, volunteered to be subjects whilst participating in the tournament. Prior approval of the University Ethical Advisory committee was obtained and subjects and their parents gave their signed consent for participation. All testing was conducted in August. Play was outdoors on a hard court surface (En-Tout-Cas™). Matches were the best of three sets, with a tie break played in the first two sets.

Science and Racket Sports II, edited by A. Lees, I. Maynard, M. Hughes and T. Reilly. Published in 1998 by E & FN Spon, 11 New Fetter Lane, London EC4P 4EE, UK.   ISBN: 0 419 23030 0

Subjects' dry body mass was recorded (Seca scales) before and after each match. All dry body mass measurements were taken with the subjects in their underwear. All players towelled down after the match prior to the measurement of body mass. The fluid intake of each subject was monitored throughout the match. Body mass loss was adjusted for the volume of fluid ingested. Players were permitted to drink fluids of their choice *ad libitum* throughout each match. The duration of each match was recorded to the nearest minute. It was not possible to obtain match statistics in detail as all the tournament matches were run simultaneously. Dry bulb temperature and relative humidity were recorded for each match.

A one-tailed t-test for correlated data was performed to examine the pre-match to post-match changes. A Pearson Product Moment correlation was performed between fluid intake and loss in body mass. In this study, significance was chosen as $P<0.05$. Values are presented as mean ± S.E.M.

3 Results

Match length ranged from 50 min to 140 min with a mean (± S.E.M.) of $86.3 ± 6.5$ min. Dry bulb temperature (°C) and relative humidity (%) were $27.8 ± 0.5$°C and $43 ± 3.1$ % respectively.

Dry body mass (BM) declined from a pre-match value of $54.7 ± 3.9$ kg to a post-match value of $53.4 ± 3.8$ kg ($P<0.01$). This corresponded to a body mass loss of $1.3 ± 0.1$ (0.4 to 2.3) kg or $2.3 ± 0.2$ (0.7 to 3.8) % BM. Mean *ad libitum* fluid intake was $1089 ± 95$ ml and ranged from 328 ml to 1750 ml. A negative correlation [$r=-0.54$; $P<0.05$) was observed between body mass loss and fluid intake.

4 Discussion

A main concern for the tennis specialist and/or practitioner, when working with elite junior tennis players, is to maximise playing potential and performance whilst minimising the potential health risk factors. Both hyperthermia and dehydration are potential health risk factors.

Although the rate of voluntary dehydration was reported to be independent of age, young athletes tended to store more heat (as measured by rectal temperature) in relation to body mass, than the adult athlete (Bar-Or et al., 1980). Thus for every given level of hypohydration, children's core temperature seemed to rise faster than in adults (Bar-Or et al., 1980). Furthermore, both the pre-pubescent and pubescent athlete have a lower sweating capacity compared to that of a young adult (Meyer et al., 1992). For these reasons it is important to monitor carefully the fluid losses of the junior tennis player.

Net losses in body mass were reported for the junior tennis players in the present study, reflecting fluid loss, despite the *ad libitum* ingestion of fluids. A negative correlation [$r=-0.54$] was exhibited between the amount of fluid ingested and the amount of fluid lost (as reflected in the decline in body mass). This result would support the common perception that thirst is a poor indicator of dehydration.

Nevertheless, the levels of hypohydration varied quite considerably between individuals. Thus further explanations as to why the players did not drink enough during match-play may be suggested.

Meyer et al. (1994) reported grape flavoured drinks to be more palatable than apple and orange flavours, or water in early pubertal boys and girls. Furthermore, Wilk and Bar-Or (1995) revealed that when children (aged 9 to 13 years) were allowed to drink *ad libitum* one of several grape flavoured drinks, throughout 110 min exercise in the heat, they remained in a euhydrated state throughout. Many different types of drinks were consumed by the junior tennis players in the present study. Therefore, it is possible that the junior tennis players did not voluntarily dehydrate themselves, but more that the players' willingness to rehydrate may have been influenced by the desirability or palatability of the drink.

Further, it may be that the competitive junior tennis players in this study, were not educated in, or aware of, nutritional preparation strategies and the importance of fluid intake both during competition and training.

In an environment of high ambient temperature two main demands are placed upon the junior tennis player's body; 1) the maintenance of blood flow to the exercising muscles for the supply of oxygen and substrates and 2) a high blood flow to the skin for heat dissipation. Extra-cellular volume, plasma volume and cardiac output decline with progressive dehydration, without a corresponding rise in heart rate (Nadel et al., 1980). This has the concomitant effect of reducing the rate of heat transfer to the skin and reducing cooling capacity. Eventually sweat production may decline (Nadel et al., 1980). Thus significant amounts of fluid loss may pose a health risk to the junior player, especially when competing in an environment of high ambient temperature. This has serious implications for the junior player, especially when fluid losses reach levels of 2-3% BM, such as those found in the present study.

5 Conclusions

This study has revealed that junior competitive tennis players lose up to 2.3% body mass during competitive match-play. It is important for the junior tennis player to avoid prolonged exposure to fluid losses of more than 2-3% BM, as this may pose a serious risk to health.

By encouraging the junior player to drink more than the thirst mechanism dictates, 'voluntary dehydration' may be prevented or markedly reduced. Additionally, the willingness of junior players to drink may be enhanced through the frequent administration of desirable and palatable drinks.

It is therefore important for players to understand the reasons for adopting and habituating to a frequent drinking routine during both training and match-play.

6 References

Bar-Or, O., Dotan, R., Inbar, O., Rothstein, A. and Zonder, H. (1980) Voluntary hypohydration in 10 to 12 year old boys. **Journal of Applied Physiology**, 48, 104-108.

Bergeron, M. F. (1995) Fluid and electrolyte losses in tennis, in **Tennis: Sports Medicine and Science** (eds W. Hollmann, K. Struder, A. Ferrauti, K.Weber), Rau publishers, Dusseldorf, pp.208-209.

Burke, E.R. and Ekblom, B. (1982) Influence of fluid ingestion and dehydration on precision and endurance performance in tennis. **Athlete Trainer** (Winter): 275-277.

Meyer, F., Bar-Or, O., Macdougall, D. and Heigenhauser, J. F. (1992) Sweat electrolyte loss during exercise in the heat: effects of gender and maturation. **Medicine and Science in Sports and Exercise**, 24, 776-781.

Meyer, F., Bar-Or, O., Salsberg, A. and Passe, D. (1994) Hypohydration during exercise in children: effect on thirst, drink preferences and rehydration. **International Journal of Sports Nutrition**, 4, 22-35.

Nadel, E.R., Fortney, S.M. and Wenger, C.B.(1980) Effect of hydration status on circulatory and thermal regulations. **Journal of Applied Physiology**, 49, 715.

Rowley, S. (1992) **The training of young athletes study (T.O.Y.A.): Identification of talent.** Sports Council, London.

Wagner, J. A., Robinson, S. P., Tzankoff, S. P. and Marino, R. P. (1972) Heat tolerance and acclimatisation to work in the heat in relation to age. **Journal of Applied Physiology**, 33, 616-622.

Wilk, B. and Bar-Or, O. (1995) The relationships among thirst perception, hydration status and voluntary drink intake in children during prolonged exposure to the heat (abstract) **Medicine and Science in Sports and Exercise,** 27, S18.

8 Fluid loss during international standard match-play in squash

D. Brown and E.M. Winter
De Montfort University Bedford, Bedford, UK

1 Introduction

It is well established that dehydration can reduce the endurance performance capabilities of sportspeople. For instance, Saltin and Costill (1988) reported that fluid losses in excess of 5 % of body mass can decrease exercise capabilities by about 30 %. Even at low levels (1.8 %) of dehydration exercise performance time may be reduced (Walsh et al., 1994). Armstrong et al. (1985) demonstrated that diuretic-induced water loss equivalent to approximately 2 % body mass increased the time to run simulated 1500-10,000 m races by 3-7 %. It has also been demonstrated that progressive dehydration by 2.7 % body mass can cause a 20 % increase in errors in tennis performance (Burke and Ekblom, 1982).

Squash is a sport which presents a considerable challenge to the body's thermoregulatory systems which incorporate mechanisms for fluid balance. Still air within a squash court means that the facility for convective and evaporative cooling is limited. Furthermore while a player can generate air movement on court by moving quickly, this action in itself is thermogenic.

Fluid losses in squash of 1.8 $l.h^{-1}$ (van Rensburg et al., 1982) and sweating rates in excess of 1.9 $l.h^{-1}$, corresponding to a 2 % loss in body mass (Hansen and Brotherhood, 1988), have been reported for top club players and competition level players respectively, while Noakes et al. (1982) found body fluid losses of 2 l for 90 min of match-play. Reilly (1990) stated that skill performance in sport may be affected after loss of body water equivalent to 4 % of body mass, and stressed the importance of rehydration for squash players who sweat liberally during play.

There is a dearth of information about fluid losses in elite male squash players. These players have matches which last from 40 to 90 min, although in exceptional circumstances they may be up to 2-3 hours in duration. Clearly this taxes the endurance capabilities of players and makes it harder for them to maintain skill, so it is important that they minimise dehydration. However, fluid losses in international competition are not well documented so the purpose of this study was to investigate fluid losses during international standard match-play in squash.

Science and Racket Sports II, edited by A. Lees, I. Maynard, M. Hughes and T. Reilly. Published in 1998 by E & FN Spon, 11 New Fetter Lane, London EC4P 4EE, UK. ISBN: 0 419 23030 0

2 Methods

Fluid losses were assessed in 8 matches at the squash World Cup team event in Malaysia which was held in May and June 1996. Three male members of the England national squad provided written informed consent and were recruited to the study. Fluid loss was estimated from reductions in body mass. Body mass was recorded prior to the warm up, and within 5 minutes of the match ending after the players had been towelled dry. Match time was taken as the total time between the measurements pre- and post-match. Body mass was measured to the nearest 100 g using portable electronic scales (EKS Model 6010, North Finchley, London, UK). The electronic scales were calibrated prior to and on return from the competition using laboratory based beam balance scales (Herbert and Sons, Edmonton, UK). The volume of fluid ingested by the players during the matches was measured using portable electronic food scales (EKS Model 1002, North Finchley, London, UK), where 1 g was assumed to be equivalent to 1 ml of fluid. Players were permitted to drink water *ad libitum* throughout each match.

The observed reductions in body mass (kg) combined with the fluid consumed (ml) during each match were used to calculate actual body mass loss (kg). Using match time, actual body mass loss was expressed as a rate of fluid loss ($l.h^{-1}$). It was assumed that virtually all the reductions in body mass represented fluid lost as sweat, where 1 kg of body mass loss corresponded to 1 litre of sweat. Dry bulb temperature (°C) and humidity (%) were measured on the squash court using a combined digital thermometer and hygrometer (A.T.P. Instrumentation Ltd Model HT-23, Ashby-de-la-Zouch, Leics, UK).

The relationship between match time (min) and rate of fluid loss ($l.h^{-1}$) was investigated using a Pearson's product moment correlation coefficient. The data set consisted of 8 matches: 3 matches each from two players and 2 matches from the third player. Statistical significance was set at $P < 0.05$.

3 Results and Discussion

Table 1 displays the range of data for each subject and summarises the eight matches assessed. Court temperature and humidity for the matches (n=8) were 25.1 ± 1.3 °C and 64 ± 6 % (mean ± SD) respectively.

The rates of fluid loss in this study of 2.37 ± 0.45 $l.h^{-1}$ (mean ± SD) are higher than those previously reported for squash (Noakes et al., 1982; van Rensburg et al., 1982; Hansen and Brotherhood., 1988). Although some of the reductions in body mass are attributable to substrate utilisation and respiratory fluid loss, the majority are the result of fluid lost as sweat. Approximate losses of body mass attributable to substrate utilisation would be $0.1 - 0.2$ $kg.h^{-1}$, which would account for only 4 - 8 % of the actual body mass loss.

Table 1. Range of individual and summary data (raw and adjusted) for the matches (n) played

Subject	Recorded body mass loss (kg)	Fluid consumed (ml)	Actual body mass loss (kg)	Match time (min)	Rate of fluid loss (l.h^{-1})
A (n = 3)	0.8 - 1.7	320 - 980	1.32 - 2.68	38 - 57	2.08 - 2.82
B (n = 3)	0.4 - 2.2	1000 - 2000	1.40 - 4.20	40 - 86	2.10 - 2.93
C (n = 2)	0.9 - 1.7	360 - 460	1.26 - 2.16	45 - 48	1.68 - 2.70
Mean (n = 8)	1.28	830	2.11	51	2.37
SD	0.59	556	1.02	16	0.45

The mean reduction in recorded body mass of 1.28 kg indicates that the players were incurring a mean fluid deficit of 1.28 l. Fluid deficit differed from zero ($P < 0.01$) which indicated that more fluid was lost through sweat than was ingested during the matches. Using match time, fluid deficit can be expressed as a rate of approximately 1.5 l.h^{-1} (($1.28 l \div 51$ min) $\times 60 = 1.51$ l.h^{-1}).

There was a positive relationship between match time and rate of fluid loss ($r = 0.75$, $P < 0.05$). Lower calculated rates of fluid loss in the shorter matches are probably not explained by a delay in activation of sweating mechanisms because sweating started during the warm up, not after the matches began. It is reasonable to assume that the longer matches were physically more demanding, resulting in higher rates of fluid loss. In addition there was a significant positive correlation between match time and fluid deficit ($r = 0.85$, $P < 0.05$), indicating that larger fluid deficits were incurred as the match times increased. During prolonged matches players will go for longer periods of time without drinking as they can only drink in between games. This results in a discrepancy between the rate at which a player is losing fluid through sweat and the rate at which they are able to consume fluid. Generally the longer the match time the greater this discrepancy will be, which explains the increased fluid deficit observed in the longer matches.

This is the first report of fluid losses assessed during international tournament match-play in squash. The results guide pre-, intra- and post-match hydration strategies used by elite male squash players during international competition. Pre-match hydration ensures that players do not start play already dehydrated. The short time allowed between games (90 s maximum), combined with the discomfort of large amounts of fluid in the gut, means that it is simply impractical to expect a player to consume much more than 1 litre of fluid an hour during play. Realistically players will consume at most about 200-250 ml between games. Such drinking could be considered to be a "damage limitation exercise" which minimises fluid deficits incurred during matches.

For matches lasting an hour, fluid deficits will be approximately 1.5 litres, and so considerable attention must be given to the rehydration means that players employ. The mean rate of fluid loss in this study of 2.37 l.h^{-1} provides a useful guideline to players, coaches and practitioners.

It should be noted that there is both inter- and intra-individual variability in the data. This is perhaps not surprising as the rates of fluid loss will depend on the duration and intensity of the matches, and could also be influenced by court conditions (temperature and humidity) and individual variation in sweating response.

4 Conclusions

The results demonstrate the demanding nature of international standard squash and provide guidelines which can be used to inform hydration strategies for elite male players. These strategies need to accommodate fluid losses which approximate to 2.5 $l.h^{-1}$, dependent on the intensity of play.

5 References

Armstrong, L.E., Costill, D.L. and Fink, W.J. (1985) Influence of diuretic-induced dehydration on competitive running performance. **Medicine and Science in Sports and Exercise**, 17, 456-461.

Burke, E.R. and Ekblom, B. (1982) Influence of fluid ingestion and dehydration on precision and endurance performance in tennis. **Athletics Trainer**, Winter, 275-277.

Hansen, R.D. and Brotherhood, J.R. (1988) Prevention of heat-induced illness in squash players. **Medical Journal of Australia**, 148, 100.

Noakes, T.D., Cowling, J.R., Gevers, W. and van Niekerk, J.P. (1982) The metabolic response to squash including the influence of pre-exercise carbohydrate ingestion. **South African Medical Journal**, 62, 721-723.

Reilly, T. (1990) The racquet sports, in **Physiology of Sports** (eds T.Reilly, N.Secher, P.Snell and C.Williams), E. and F.N. Spon, London, pp.337-369.

Saltin, B. and Costill, D.L. (1988) Fluid and electrolyte balance during prolonged exercise, in **Exercise, Nutrition and Metabolism** (eds E.Horton and R.Terjung), Macmillan, New York, pp. 150-158.

van Rensburg, J.P., van der Linde, A., Ackermann, P.C., Keilblock, A.J. and Strydom, N.B. (1982) Physiological profile of squash players. **South African Journal for Research in Sport, Physical Education and Recreation**, 5, 25-56.

Walsh, R.M., Noakes, T.D., Hawley, J.A. and Dennis, S.C. (1994) Impaired high intensity cycling performance time at low levels of dehydration. **International Journal of Sports Medicine**, 15, 392-398.

9 Metabolic responses and performance in tennis after caffeine ingestion

A. Ferrauti and K. Weber
Institute of Sports Games, German Sport University Cologne, Cologne, Germany

1 Introduction

Controversy still exists concerning the potential ergogenic benefit of caffeine. A decreased glycogen depletion due to an increased lipolysis and lipid oxidation, an enhancement of neuromuscular function and an optimisation of central nervous system function has been discussed (Powers and Dodd, 1985; Jacobson and Kulling, 1989). In some cases increases in aerobic (Ivy et al., 1979) and anaerobic endurance (Anselme et al., 1992) were found after caffeine ingestion. Nevertheless, several studies have failed to exhibit a beneficial effect (Butts and Crowell, 1985; Powers et al., 1983).

The ergogenic value of caffeine has not yet been investigated in ball games. In addition to metabolic effects, positive responses can be expected to occur, due to the high mental and neuromuscular demands in this type of sports. From a practical viewpoint, commercially available beverages are of special interest due to the current flood of caffeine-containing "designer-energy drinks" on the European market. Thus, the purpose of this investigation was to determine the effects of caffeine in amounts typically used in soft drinks, on metabolic responses, playing success, hitting accuracy, running speed and perception during a long-lasting and interrupted tennis competition.

2 Methods

2.1 Subjects

Sixteen tournament tennis players (division II in German Tennis Federation), eight male (mean±SD: age 25.4 ±1.9 years, height 184 ±5 cm, mass 81.1 ±7.3 kg) and eight female (age 20.4 ±2.8 years, height 170 ±4 cm, mass 65.0 ±4.6 kg) participated in the study. Subjects were not regular consumers of caffeine (< 150 mg.day^{-1}), were non-smokers and were not taking any medication during the experimental period. The players were familiar with all test procedures.

Science and Racket Sports II, edited by A. Lees, I. Maynard, M. Hughes and T. Reilly. Published in 1998 by E & FN Spon, 11 New Fetter Lane, London EC4P 4EE, UK.   ISBN: 0 419 23030 0

2.2 Procedure

Each player was tested on two occasions separated by at least three days. Subjects were asked to refrain from exercise during the last three days before trials and to abstain from caffeine consumption and also to maintain the same prescribed diet 24 hours prior to each trial. During the test days subjects received a standardized breakfast (08:00 h) and a carbohydrate-rich lunch (12:30 h) in order to simulate typical pre-match conditions. Between 15:00 h and 19:30 h players participated in a singles competition of 240 min on clay courts, according to the rules of the International Tennis Federation. The competition was interrupted after 150 min by a 30 min break. Immediately after the end, players were asked to perform a ball-machine test (BMT) to assess hitting accuracy and a tennis-sprint test (TST). Perception ratings were recorded continuously during match-play.

Players ingested an orange flavoured placebo (PLA) with no caloric value (provided by Sandoz Nutrition Ltd, Bern, Switzerland) or PLA supplemented with 130 mg.l^{-1} caffeine (CAF). In CAF, the drink treatment matched the average caffeine content of coke drinks. Fifteen minutes after starting to play, and every following 15 min (at court changeover) the players consumed 150 ml (men) or 100 ml (women) of the assigned fluid. During the break 400 ml were ingested containing 52 mg caffeine in CAF. Additionally, the subjects were allowed to drink water *ad libitum*. The total amount of standard ingestion in men (women) was 2.8 l (2.0 l) of fluid, supplemented with 364 mg (260 mg) caffeine in CAF. The treatment drinks were assigned double-blind in a counter-balanced pattern.

2.3 Measurements and analyses

Metabolic parameters: Capillary blood samples were analysed for glucose (0, 15, 30, 90, 150, 180, 195, 210, 270 min; Cobas-Bio-System, Hoffmann-La Roche, Basel, Switzerland) and lactate (0, 75, 150, 270 min; Eppendorf-Analyser 5060, Hamburg, Germany). Venous blood samples were taken from an antecubital vein at rest and immediately post-exercise. Serum concentrations of free fatty acids (FFA) and glycerol (Cobas-Bio-System) as well as haemoglobin and haematocrit (Sysmex Dualdilutor DD100, Digitana AG, Germany) were determined. Urine concentrations of adrenaline and noradrenaline were analysed using HPLC (Chromsystems, München, Germany) and related to creatinine (Creat) to eliminate differences in renal water handling. Caffeine determination was carried out with HPLC by direct urine injection. Heart rate was monitored in 15 s intervals (Polar Sport-Tester, Kempele, Finland).

Hitting accuracy: A standardized ball-machine test (BMT) was applied (Weber, 1987). Two players were instructed to return a randomized sequence of four successive forehand (FH) or backhand (BH) ground-strokes (20 balls.min^{-1}) alternating cross and long-line into a target area at the opponents´ base-line. Percentage of valid strokes during a 10 min test-period was recorded. Before each skill session, a 60 s warm-up period was permitted.

Running speed: Specific sprint performance was determined by a tennis-sprint test (TST) with electronic time measurement (Ferrauti, 1993). Subjects performed six base-line sprints (from central position to FH(BH)-corner and back to BH(FH)-corner), each a total of 15 m length and interrupted by a 30 s break. A newly developed stroke simulator transferred stop signals and guaranteed a tennis-specific movement pattern.

Perception: A newly developed perception scale was applied to assess "energetic drive" (ED-scale). This scale consists of numbers ranging from 1 to 10 with description words printed beside them (range from "very low" to "very high energetic drive"). The intention was not to investigate acute central or local exertion (Borg, 1982), but rather to evaluate superior items. In the present study the rating of energetic drive appeared to be advantageous, since other perception scales described in the literature are primarily reflecting the cardiopulmonary aspects of exertion (Borg 1982). Perception was estimated simultaneous to measurements of glucose. Sufficient time for recovery from the preceeding rallies was ensured.

2.4 Statistics
Data are presented as means and standard deviations. A multifactorial analysis of variance (ANOVA) with repeated measurements was used to determine statistical differences. In case of significance, simple effects were verified by means of Newman-Keuls test. Significance level was set at $P \leq 0.05$.

3 Results

Glucose in capillary blood decreased in both treatments from beginning to end by 15 % (Figure 1). During the first 15 min a distinct decrease in glucose immediately followed by an increase, was noted. This recurred after the break only in PLA. At this time point, glucose was maintained in CAF at a significant higher level (Figure 1). No considerable differences in glucose were found between men and women. Serum FFA and glycerol changes during competition were nearly identical in PLA and CAF but tended to a higher increase in women in case of caffeine ingestion (Figure 2). Plasma volume increased in both treatments equally by 5-6 % (Van Beaumont, 1972).

   Urine concentrations of adrenaline and noradrenaline were significantly elevated after the competition. No differences as to gender and treatment were found for noradrenaline (Figure 2). In contrast, increases of adrenaline were significantly higher in men than in women and in women higher in CAF than in PLA. Urine post-exercise caffeine concentration increased only in CAF (6.6 ±1.1 $\mu g.ml^{-1}$), ranged from 5.5 to 9.3 $\mu g.ml^{-1}$ and did not differ between men and women. In all subjects caffeine concentration remained below the doping limit (12 $\mu g.ml^{-1}$) of the International Olympic Committee.

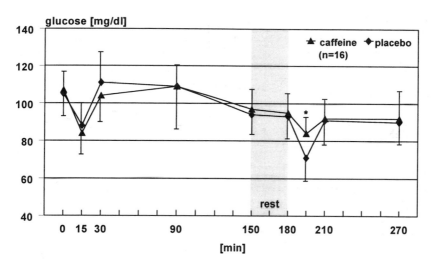

Figure 1. Capillary blood glucose during a tennis competition under caffeine feeding.

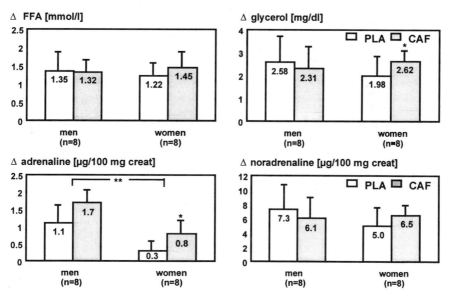

Figure 2. Absolute changes (Δ) of serum free fatty acids (FFA) and glycerol as well as urinary adrenaline and noradrenaline concentrations during a tennis competition under placebo (PLA) and caffeine feeding (CAF) in men and women.

Table 1. Heart rate (HF), blood lactate and playing success (won games) during a tennis competition and post-exercise hitting accuracy (BMT) and sprint performance (TST) under placebo (PLA) and caffeine (CAF) feeding in men and women (n=8)

test			drink	men (n=8)	women (n=8)
match		HF [beats/min]	PLA	143 ± 7	139 ± 17
			CAF	143 ± 6	137 ± 17
		lactate [mmol/l]	PLA	2.1 ± 0.5	1.2 ± 0.4 *
			CAF	1.8 ± 0.5	1.5 ± 0.4 *
		won games [n]	PLA	22.6 ± 7.5	20.9 ± 0.4 ⌐ **
			CAF	21.1 ± 5.3	27.8 ± 6.8 ⌐
BMT		valid strokes [%]	PLA	47.4 ± 7.6	43.9 ± 9.4
			CAF	45.6 ± 8.3	46.1 ± 9.9
TST		running time [s]	PLA	3.21 ± 0.13	3.36 ± 0.08 *
			CAF	3.17 ± 0.13	3.37 ± 0.12 *

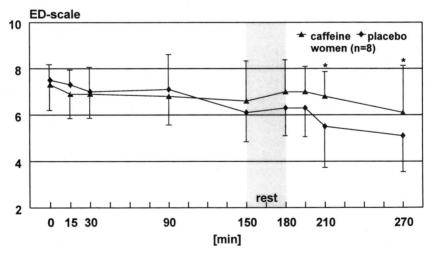

Figure 3. Perceived energetic drive (ED-scale) during tennis competition under caffeine feeding in women.

Blood lactate and heart rate did not differ between CAF and PLA but were higher in men than in women (Table 1). These findings were significant only for lactate (P≤0.05). Significant differences in TST and BMT depending on the fluid supplementation did not occur. The only statistically significant effect on performance was gender-specific and occurred in respect to the measured game success. Women in CAF played more successfully (won games) than in PLA (P≤0.01) and achieved a better hitting accuracy in BMT (Table 1). These data correspond to the results of our perception ratings. In women, there was a significantly higher "energetic drive" during the last hour of the CAF trial, while no such effects were found in men (Figure 3).

4 Discussion

Blood glucose levels in CAF and PLA tended to be almost identical (Figure 1). Obviously, there was no evidence that the caffeine beverage provided had any glucose sparing effect during continuous match-play in tennis. Blood glucose data corresponded with the fact that there was no influence on lipolysis in CAF. Although both FFA and glycerol concentrations tended to be higher under caffeine treatment, these values did not differ significantly from those in PLA (Figure 2). This would contradict the observation of increased FFA levels and fat oxidation following caffeine ingestion (Ivy et al., 1979). The carbohydrate-rich pre-exercise meal was provided in the present study to simulate a typical match condition. According to other researchers, caffeine does not have significant metabolic effects after a high carbohydrate diet (Weir et al., 1987). Moreover, metabolic benefits of caffeine were usually measured after providing a higher caffeine dosage during the pre-exercise phase (Costill et al., 1978). In the present study a lower amount and a continuous form of administration was applied. It is concluded, that under these conditions no clear beneficial effects of caffeine on energy metabolism can be expected.

Caffeine ingestion resulted in a higher rise of urine adrenaline concentrations (Figure 2). Thus, we assume an augmented overall sympathetic activity in CAF. As expected, the effects of caffeine on adrenaline were independent of noradrenaline changes due to an immediate central nervous system stimulation of the adrenal medulla (Graham and Spriet, 1991). In contrast to the PLA trial there was no significant decline of blood glucose following the break of competition in CAF, but rather a more harmonious curve (Figure 1). It cannot be ruled out that the increased sympathetic activity, especially after previous rest, guarantees a quicker glycogenolytic response to the sudden occurrence of glucose oxidation under beginning physical demands. This observation hints at an ergogenic effect of caffeine as a pre- or inter-exercise drink. Thus, beverages containing caffeine may improve the metabolic transition from rest to physical activity in tennis.

In men, the players´ success (games won) and hitting accuracy (BMT) did not benefit from caffeine. Nevertheless, a higher performance was shown by the women, who won significantly more games in CAF (Table 1). Furthermore, only women registered an elevated "energetic drive" during the last hour of competition (Figure 3). The underlying causes for these results are unknown. Gender-specific reactions to caffeine have not yet been proved (Butts and Crowell, 1985). A doseage effect can be ruled out, since in relation to body mass the women were given less caffeine (40 vs 4.5

mg.kg^{-1}). Thus, the lower intensity in the women's matches (Table 1) and their smaller usual caffeine consumption (70 vs 110 mg.day^{-1}) offer the only grounds for explanation. It has been shown that caffeine effects are increased in caffeine-naive subjects (Dodd et al., 1991). In fact, the women tended to reveal a more sensitive reaction in catecholamines after caffeine ingestion (Figure 3). In view of the lower physical demands, this might have stimulating mental effects. Caffeine had been shown to have a positive influence on alertness, wakefulness and mental activity at rest (Goldstein et al., 1965). As the exercise intensity was higher in men, these effects may be masked by the elevated exercise induced sympathetic responses (Perkins and Williams, 1975).

5 Conclusions

Results of the present study indicate that caffeine had no definite ergogenic effects on energy metabolism during long-lasting tennis competitions. Nevertheless, there were some indications that caffeine accelerates the regulation of blood glucose at the beginning of match-play and has specific ergogenic effects on performance and perception in women's tennis. The intake of caffeine containing beverages can be suggested only for those players who 1) frequently complain about hypoglycaemic symptoms at the beginning of match-play and/or 2) usually achieve an insufficient level of physical and mental activity during the match.

The study was supported by the German Federal Institute for Sport Science, Cologne (BISP: VF 0407/01/52/95).

6 References

Anselme, F., Collomp, K., Mercier, B., Ahmaidi, S. and Prefaut, C.H. (1992) Caffeine increases maximal anaerobic power and blood lactate concentration. **European Journal of Applied Physiology**, 65, 188-191.

Beaumont Van, W. (1972) Evaluation of hemoconcentration from hematocrit measurements. **Journal of Applied Physiology**, 32, 712-713.

Borg, G.A.V. (1982) Psychophysical bases of percieved exertion. **Medicine and Science in Sports and Exercise**, 14, 377-381.

Butts, N.K. and Crowell, D. (1985) Effect of caffeine ingestion on cardiorespiratory endurance in men and women. **Research Quarterly**, 56, 301-305.

Costill, D.L., Dalsky, G.P. and Fink, W.J. (1978) Effects of caffeine ingestion on metabolism and exercise performance. **Medicine and Science in Sports and Exercise**, 10, 155-158.

Dodd, S.L., Brooks, E., Powers, S.K. and Tulley, R. (1991) The effects of caffeine on graded exercise performance in caffeine naive versus habituated subjects. **European Journal of Applied Physiology**, 62, 424-429.

Ferrauti, A. (1993) Relevance, diagnosis and training of running speed in high performance tennis, in **Proceedings of 2ⁿᵈ Maccabiah-Wingate International Congress in Sport Science and Coaching** (eds G. Tenenbaum, T. Raz-Liebermann), Wingate Institute for Physical Education and Sport, Netanya, pp. 214-229.

Goldstein, A., Kaizer, S. and Warren, R. (1965) Psychotropic effects of caffeine in man. II. Alertness, psychomotor coordination and mood. **Journal of Pharmacological Experimental Therapeutics**, 150, 146-151.

Graham, T.E. and Spriet, L.L. (1991) Performance and metabolic response to a high caffeine dose during prolonged exercise. **Journal of Applied Physiology**, 71, 2292-2298.

Ivy, J.L., Costill, D.L., Fink, W.J. and Lower R.W. (1979) Influence of caffeine and carbohydrate feedings on endurance performance. **Medicine and Science in Sports and Exercise**, 11, 6-11.

Jacobson, B.H. and Kulling F.A. (1989) Health and ergogenic effects of caffeine. **British Journal of Sports Medicine**, 23, 34-40.

Perkins, R. and Williams, M.H. (1975) Effect of caffeine upon maximal muscular endurance of females. **Medicine and Science in Sports and Exercise**, 7, 221-224.

Powers, S.K., Byrd, R.J., Tulley, R. and Callender, T. (1983) Effects of caffeine ingestion on metabolism and performance during graded exercise. **European Journal of Applied Physiology**, 50, 301-307.

Powers, S.K. and Dodd S. (1985) Caffeine and endurance performance. **Sports Medicine**, 2, 165-174.

Weber, K. (1987) **Der Tennissport aus internistisch-sportmedizinischer Sicht**. Richarz, St. Augustin.

Weir, J., Noakes, T.D., Myburgh, K. and Adams, B. (1987) A high carbohydrate diet negates the metabolic effects of caffeine during exercise. **Medicine and Science in Sports and Exercise**, 19, 100-105.

10 The effect of carbohydrate ingestion on shot accuracy during a conditioned squash match

J. Graydon, S. Taylor and M. Smith
School of Sports Studies, Chichester Institute of Higher Education, Chichester, UK

1 Introduction

Squash is a game of continuous movement for both players. Each player is aiming to make the opponent cover as much ground around the court as possible, forcing him/her from one corner to the other at maximum stretch. The rules of the game state that 'play shall be continuous' (The Squash Rackets Association, 1993), and apart from the stipulated 90 s rest between games, the only respite players have is the short interval of approximately 7 s between points (Sharp, N.C.C., 1990, Personal Communication). For the elite male player this activity may last for up to, and even beyond 2 hours. For the good club player sessions of 45 minutes to an hour are more usual.

Sustaining this level of activity makes severe demands upon the body's systems of both aerobic and anaerobic energy supply (Sharp , 1979). The game is characterised by a player needing to maintain submaximal exercise continuously, yet repeatedly undertake short dashes at maximal speed. This type of exercise is maintained by both aerobic and anaerobic metabolism (Wilmore and Costill, 1994). Lamb (1978) has suggested that exercise which results in exhaustion in less than 150 min draws mainly on the aerobic breakdown of muscle glycogen and blood glucose. This contention has been supported in a number of studies of another, somewhat different, high intensity intermittent activity, that of soccer (Bangsbo, 1994). Furthermore it has been shown by Saltin (1973) that muscle glycogen levels are depleted at half time in a soccer match, and even more so at full time.

It is logical to assume then that depletion of glycogen levels is likely to occur in a squash match where both players are continuously active. It may also be the case therefore that replenishment of muscle glycogen and blood glucose supplies may function to maintain performance. The ingestion of carbohydrate (CHO) solutions have been shown to enhance endurance performance (Coggan and Coyle, 1987) and to improve sprint performance following exercise (Neufer et al., 1987). Furthermore Kirkendall et al. (1988) have shown that exercise performance in soccer was enhanced when a glucose polymer solution was consumed pre-game and at half time. It is logical to assume that a similar mechanism may occur in the game of squash, but to the authors' knowledge this has not yet been documented.

Science and Racket Sports II, edited by A. Lees, I. Maynard, M. Hughes and T. Reilly. Published in 1998 by E & FN Spon, 11 New Fetter Lane, London EC4P 4EE, UK.   ISBN: 0 419 23030 0

The mechanism by which glycogen depletion may affect performance may be by reducing the number of muscle fibres capable of producing the force needed for exercise (Wilmore and Costill, 1994). Squash is a whole-body activity requiring continuous running and hitting of the ball. It has been estimated that a good male player is making up to 22 strokes per minute (Sharp, 1990). Accuracy is extremely important. If a player is incapable of reaching the ball and making accurate shots performance will inevitably deteriorate. It may be the case therefore that reduced levels of muscle glycogen could limit performance as detailed above, and that CHO ingestion may serve to maintain performance by its action on muscle glycogen and thus fibre recruitment.

It was the aim of the study therefore to examine the effect of CHO ingestion on squash performance as assessed by an accuracy test, and also on subjective feelings of exertion.

2 Methods

2.1 Design
The design was a repeated measures (RM) design with all subjects completing all levels of both factors. The independent variables were the carbohydrate supplementation condition (CHO-trial and Placebo(PL-trial), and the game condition (3 simulated squash games with a 90 s rest period between each). The dependent variables were measures of shot accuracy, heart rate (beats.min^{-1}) and Perceived Rate of Exertion (Borg, 1973).

2.1 Participants
Eight good club standard male players participated in the study. All were regular players and accustomed to high levels of exertion. The mean age was 20.13 (±1.55) years, and the mean mass was 70.75 (±13.55) kg. During the period of testing all subjects were matched with an opponent deemed to be of approximately equal ability. This was agreed by an SRA Intermediate level coach and confirmed by the players.

2.2 Materials
The carbohydrate solution used was a commercially available glucose polymer energy fuel (Maxim AMS Ltd.). The amount given to each subject was calibrated according to body mass (8.0g 100 ml^{-1}.kg^{-1}, CHO-trial), and was flavoured with a sugar free orange drink (1:16 parts concentrate to water). The PL-trial solution was also based upon the above fraction of drink to body mass, but contained only the sugar free orange drink.

Participants played 3 simulated games of squash, consuming 50% of the solution before game 1, and 25% after each of games 1 and 2.

The conditioned game was devised as a result of analysing 12 high standard men's club matches, recording the type of shots played, rally, game and match length. A detailed description of these data are not possible here, but resulted in the following simulated match being devised:

game 1:	29 rallies (16 short, 11 medium, 2 long)
game 2:	26 rallies (14 short, 11 medium, 1 long)
game 3:	24 rallies (13 short, 10 medium, 1 long)

The analysis resulted in the length of a short rally being determined as 13 s, a medium length rally being 33 s, a long rally being 112 s. The order of the rallies was randomly chosen, but constant throughout the testing period.

The accuracy test was conducted with a feeder and consisted of the participant moving from the 'T' area of a standard international size squash court to hit a straight forehand drive into the back corner of the court. The ball was fed onto the front wall by the feeder such that the participant had to move forward to hit it. Scoring was by a predetermined marking scheme, such that the closer the ball landed to the back corner of the court the higher the points scored. After each shot the participant returned to the 'T' before moving towards the next ball. Each testing session consisted of 20 trials preceded by 10 practice trials.

Heart rate monitoring was conducted using a heart rate monitor (Polar Sports Tester, Kempele, Finland) and perceived exertion was rated using the Rate of Perceived Exertion Scale (Borg, 1973).

All participants were allowed to use their regular squash rackets together with a Dunlop X2 yellow dot squash ball. A new ball was used for each set of trials.

2.3 Procedure

Participants were asked not to consume any food substrates up to 2 hours before testing. They were given their first drink, either CHO or PL-trial condition 30 minutes prior to testing, and fitted with the heart rate monitor.

As on-court testing began they were allowed a 5 min warm up (to simulate match conditions) followed by the first accuracy test. All scores were recorded by the experimenter. The first simulated game then began. The rallies progressed as outlined in 2.2 above. At the end of the time allotted to a given rally, the experimenter called 'STOP', whereupon a participant would pick up the ball and serve to start the next rally. The order of servers was alternated, as was the side of the court from which they served. All games were separated by a 90 s rest interval (The Rules of Squash SRA, 1993), during which time the participants consumed the designated drink.

Heart rate values were recorded at the end of rallies 6, 12, 18, 24 and at the end of the game for game 1, and at the end of rallies 5, 10, 15, 20 and at the end of the game for games 2 and 3. A rating on the Perceived Exertion Scale was recorded at the completion of each game.

Participants completed the CHO and P-trials in a counterbalanced order to minimise order effects. A check was performed to ascertain if they could determine the nature of the drink consumed, but they were unable to do so. Trials were separated by a period of 7 days.

3 Results

3.1 Accuracy test
The scores on the accuracy test were collected at two points; after the 5 min warm up but before game 1, and immediately after the end of game 3. The results are shown in Table 1.

Table 1. Mean scores (±SD) for accuracy (max.100) for subjects in CHO and PL-trials

	CHO trial	PL trial
Pre-game 1	62.6 (±9.8)	59.1 (±8.7)
Post-game 3	60.6 (±11.6)	47.6 (±8.4)

The data were analysed using a two-way RM ANOVA (condition x game). There was a significant condition by game interaction effect ($F_{1,7}$=12.4, P<0.01), and a significant main effect of condition ($F_{1,7}$=63.0, P<0.001). The main effect of game failed to reach significance. Follow up Tukey analysis showed a significant effect on accuracy performance in the (PL-trial) (P<.01). This would indicate that participants maintained accuracy of performance in the CHO-trial but not in the PL-trial. The effect of the manipulation is depicted graphically in Figure 1.

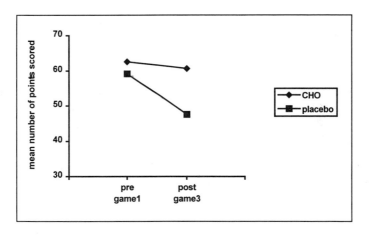

Figure 1. Mean accuracy scores in CHO and placebo conditions.

3.2 Heart rate changes
Heart rate data were taken at 4 points during each game, and at the end of each game. The mean of the values for each game were used for data analysis, and are shown in Table 2.

Analysis was by two-way RM ANOVA (condition by game). There were no significant main effects or interactions. Inspection of Table 2 would indicate slightly higher heart rates for the PL-trial, particularly as the series of games progressed. Although not significant, some trends are worthy of note as the main effect of game achieved a significance level of $P=0.059$, with the interaction effect reaching $P=0.073$.

Table 2. Mean heart rates (beats.min^{-1}) ($\pm$SD) for the three game conditions for CHO and PL-trials

Game	CHO-trial	Pl-trial
Game 1	142 ($\pm$14)	147 ($\pm$10)
Game 2	145 ($\pm$11)	150 ($\pm$8)
Game 3	146 ($\pm$13)	153 ($\pm$10)

3.3 Rating of perceived exertion

At the conclusion of each game subjects were asked to rate their perceptions of exertion on the Borg RPE-Scale (Borg, 1973). The results are shown in Table 3.

Statistical analysis was by a 2-way RM ANOVA (condition x game). A significant interaction effect, game by condition, was found ($F_{2,14}=10.4$, $P<0.01$). There was also a significant main effect of game ($F_{2,14}=150.8$, $P<0.001$), and a significant main effect of condition ($F_{1,7}=6.3$, $P<0.05$). Follow up Tukey analysis indicated a significant difference between games 1 and 3 of the (CHO-trial), and between all games of the (PL-trial) ($P<0.05$). It would appear that CHO ingestion may have mitigated participants' perceptions of exertion as the simulated match progressed.

Table 3. Mean RPE scores ($\pm$SD) for the three games in the CHO and PL-trials

Game	CHO-trial	PL-trial
Game 1	12.2 ($\pm$.9)	12.7 ($\pm$.8)
Game 2	13.2 ($\pm$.9)	14.5 ($\pm$1.2)
Game 3	14.7 ($\pm$.9)	16.1 ($\pm$1.1)

4 Discussion and Conclusions

The results of the accuracy performance analysis confirm the suggestion that the ingestion of the glucose polymer solution was effective in influencing the maintenance of performance. This confirms previous findings concerning the effectiveness of CHO ingestion on endurance performance (Coggan and Coyle, 1987; Neufer et al., 1987) and extends the research into the area of motor skill and motor control.

The change in performance for the PL-trial was of the order of a 19% drop in performance accuracy. In a game between evenly matched opponents this decrease could prove to be crucial. It is still unclear why such a decrease should occur. It is possible, as suggested by Wilmore and Costill (1994) that the problem concerning motor control is in the reduced recruitment of muscle fibres due to the unavailability of substrate. In the absence of muscle glycogen or blood glucose monitoring suggestions concerning the locus of the effect must remain tentative, but clearly a future research direction is signalled.

Another avenue it may be useful to explore is the nature of accuracy problem. As the current test involved the participant moving from the 'T' to make the shot, it could be that the ability to move quickly from the 'T' to the ball has been affected, thus not enabling the player to arrive at the correct position to hit an accurate shot, or it may be the ability to control the ball. It is of course possible that both factors are affected.

Analysis of the heart rate data showed non-significant results, but a clear trend towards increasing mean heart rates as the number of games played increased. Previous research (Reilly, 1990) has indicated that mean heart rates during squash match play have varied from 147 to 161 beats.min^{-1}. It could be considered therefore that the values obtained in this study are somewhat low, thus questioning the ecological validity of the simulated game. This may be due to the fact that the game was not intended to be competitive and therefore participants may not have extended themselves to their normal competitive values. Clearly the game could be modified to introduce a stronger element of competition which may produce elevated heart rates. Additionally extending the test period to the possible 5 games may have provided data similar to that of Reilly (1990).

The ratings of perceived exertion increased as the 'match' progressed for both the CHO and the PL-trial. This finding was more pronounced in the PL-trial as ratings increased significantly game by game, whereas in the CHO-trial the only significant increase was from game 1 to game 3. It is possible that CHO ingestion may have delayed the onset of feelings of exertion, but the mechanism by which this could occur is unclear. It may concern levels of glycogen in the active muscles or may be related to levels of blood glucose, either centrally and/or peripherally. Again, without analysis of these variables, these proposals must remain tentative and are suggestions for future work.

There is clearly much work still to be done to understand the demands of squash match-play. Nevertheless this study has extended previous work concerning the benefit of CHO ingestion on endurance performance into a sport making high demands both for endurance and fine motor control. This suggests that it may be of benefit for players at this level of competition to maintain CHO levels as a match progresses.

5 References

Bangsbo, J. (1994) Energy demands in competitive soccer. **Journal of Sports Sciences**, 12, S5-S12.

Borg, G. (1973) Perccieved exertion: A note on history and methods. **Medicine and Science in Sports**, 5, 90-93.

Coggan, A.R., and Coyle, E.F. (1987) Reversal of fatigue during prolonged exercise by carbohydrate infusion or ingestion. **Journal of Applied Physiology**, 63, 2388-2395.

Kirkendall, D.T., Foster, C., Dean, J.A., Grogan, J. and Thompson, N.N. (1988) Effect of glucose polymer supplementation on performance of soccer players, in **Science and Football** (eds T. Reilly, A. Lees, K. Davids and W.J. Murphy) E. and F.N. Spon, London, pp.33-41.

Lamb, D.R. (1978) **Physiology of Exercise: Response and Adaptations**. Collier Macmillan Publishers, London:

Neufer, P.D., Costill, D.L., Flynn, M.G., Kirwan, J.P., Mitchell, J.B., and Houmard, J.A. (1987) Improvement in exercise performance: effects of carbohydrate feeding and diet. **Journal of Applied Physiology**, 62, 983-988.

Reilly, T. (1990) The racket sports, in **Physiology of Sports** (eds T. Reilly, N. Secher, P. Snell and C. Williams) E. and F.N. Spon, London, pp.337-379.

Saltin, B. (1973) Metabolic fundamentals in exercise. **Medicine and Science in Sports and Exercise**, 5 137-146.

Sharp, N.C.C.(1979) Fitness for squash; how to build your aerobic power. **Squash Player International**, 8, 15-17.

The Squash Rackets Association (1993) **The Rules of Squash**. p.10.

Wilmore, J.H. and Costill, D.L. (1994) **Physiology of Sport and Exercise**. Human Kinetics Publishers, Champaign, Illinois.

Part Three

Preparation for Play in Racket Sports

11 Conditioning for tennis: preventing injury and enhancing performance

T.J. Chandler
Lexington Clinic Sports Medicine Center, Lexington, Kentucky, USA

1 Introduction

A sport-specific tennis conditioning programme for competitive tennis players is necessary to maximise performance and reduce the risk of injury. As a framework for developing this programme, both the physiological demands of the sport and the musculoskeletal base of the individual player should be evaluated. The physiological demands of tennis include such aspects as work/rest intervals, primary energy systems, forces related to injuries common in the sport, and sport-specific movements. The musculoskeletal base of the athlete includes physical fitness items such as cardiorespiratory fitness, muscular strength and endurance, joint range of motion, muscle inflexibilities, muscle weakness, and muscle strength imbalances, as well as athletic fitness items including speed, quickness, agility, power, and balance. Fitness testing can provide a baseline level for the individual athlete to begin a conditioning programme, and can provide useful normative data to compare between athletes at various levels of performance. This approach for evaluating the demands of the sport of tennis, as well as musculoskeletal performance characteristics, can be applied to other racket sports.

2 The Musculoskeletal Base of the Athlete

Competitive tennis has evolved into a game requiring high levels of physical and athletic fitness. Conditioning for tennis should involve building a general athletic fitness base (strength, muscular endurance, cardiorespiratory endurance), then progressing to sport-specific fitness (speed, power, agility, balance). General athletic fitness is important both in recreational and competitive players. For a competitive player to reach maximal levels of performance, sport-specific athletic fitness should be developed. Many resistance training regimens have been shown to improve strength (Atha, 1981). Plyometric exercises have also proved to be effective in improving performance-related parameters (Hewett et al., 1996). Power, as well as speed, agility,

Science and Racket Sports II, edited by A. Lees, I. Maynard, M. Hughes and T. Reilly. Published in 1998 by E & FN Spon, 11 New Fetter Lane, London EC4P 4EE, UK. ISBN: 0 419 23030 0

and coordination are components of tennis performance, and should be addressed in the conditioning programme.

Planning conditioning programmes for tennis players is challenging for several reasons, including (a) frequent travel at some competitive levels of play, and (b) a very long in-season. A conditioning programme for tennis based on defined specific "periods", and by using each "period" to train specific aspects of tennis performance, progressing from general athletic fitness in the off-season to sport specific fitness as the competitive season approaches, will most likely maximise performance.

3 The Demands of the Sport

The metabolic and mechanical demands of tennis have been reported in recent literature (Bergeron et al., 1991; Kibler et al., 1989; Kibler and Chandler, 1994a; Kraemer et al., 1995). Tennis requires repeated bouts of moderate to high-intensity exercise. Evaluation of the individual player in terms of muscle strength, muscle balance, and joint range of motion provides important information about his/her strengths and weaknesses. Work-rest intervals during high levels of tennis play are comprised of an approximate 1:2 work-rest interval, with the duration of the points averaging 8-10 s on a hard surface (Chandler, 1990). Flexibility decrements in tennis players have been demonstrated in the dominant shoulder in internal rotation, believed to be related to the demands on the posterior shoulder musculature in decelerating the tennis racket (Chandler et al., 1992; Kibler et al., 1996). These decreases in internal rotation increase as a function of both age and years of tournament play. Isokinetic muscle strength imbalances have been identified in college tennis players in the dominant shoulder compared to the non-dominant shoulder (Chandler et al., 1990). Ongoing tennis research in such areas as metabolism, fluid replacement, work-rest intervals, muscle firing patterns and musculo-skeletal adaptations, will continue to provide useful information that can be incorporated into the tennis conditioning programme.

4 Testing Tennis Players

Evaluation of the individual player in terms of muscle strength, muscle balance, and joint range of motion provides important information about his/her strengths and weaknesses. A player may enter the sport with a fitness level anywhere along a continuum from very poor to excellent. Testing is crucial to the conditioning programme because it allows determination of the entry level of fitness, comparisons to other athletes, and provides information regarding the current fitness level. The evaluation should match the demands of the sport, and may include a variety of tests for (a) physical fitness, such as muscular strength, muscular endurance, cardiorespiratory endurance, and joint range of motion, as well as (b) sport-specific athletic fitness tests for speed, power, quickness, and agility.

5 General Principles of Exercise Programme Design

The principles of exercise programme design refer to adaptation, specificity, recovery, variety, individuality and progression, and are important both to maximise performance and to modify injury risk (Chandler, 1995). Repetitive strain injuries are common in the tennis player. The goal of "preventing" injuries is commonly discussed, but is unlikely to be reached in high-intensity ballistic sports such as tennis. Injuries, both traumatic and overuse, will continue to occur.

5.1 Adaptation
This is a process which the body goes through in order to be able to meet better the demands placed upon it. Running distances causes adaptations to occur to the aerobic systems of the body, resulting in an increased ability to transport and utilise oxygen for the production of energy. Resistive training causes adaptations to occur to the specific muscles involved, increasing the strength and muscular endurance of the player. With the improper application of training stresses, adaptation may be abnormal, in the form of injury, inflexibility, or muscle strength imbalances.

5.2 Specificity
Specificity of exercise means that training should be specific both metabolically and mechanically to the activity for which the player is training. Metabolic specificity deals with the energy systems used during the performance of a sport or activity. A simple way to achieve metabolic specificity is to study the work-rest intervals of a particular sport, in combination with the relative intensity of exercise. By working over longer intervals in the off-season progressing to sport-specific intervals in the pre- and in-seasons, conditioning is more likely to enhance performance in a particular sport. Metabolically, the conditioning programmes should be specific to the energy systems used in the sporting activity, progressing from general to more specific as the season   approaches. Mechanical specificity involves conditioning the muscles in a way similar to that in which they are used in a sport. Mechanical specificity, as well as metabolic specificity, should progress from general to specific as the season approaches.

5.3 Recovery
It is necessary for the player to allow time for adaptation to take place. Without proper time for recovery fatigue, overtraining, and injury could result. The body needs time for rest and repair, both within an exercise session, and between sessions. The amount of recovery time depends on the type and intensity of exercise, as well as the tissue that is stressed.

5.4 Variety
By choosing a variety of exercises within the limits of specificity, certain muscles are allowed more time for recovery from a particular exercise. Progressing from general to specific from the off-season to the in-season allows variety to be incorporated into the programme. A variety of exercises may also help to prevent "staleness" and "boredom" from doing the same drills repeatedly.

5.5 Individuality

It is important to recognise individual differences in players when designing conditioning programmes. Each player is an individual with unique skills and abilities, and each may bring a different level of physical fitness to the conditioning programme. Similarly, each player has a different rate of adaptation to the conditioning process. Individual players may enter a sport with a history of previous injury, that calls for individualisation of the exercise programme. Exercise prescriptions should be formulated for each player to take into account these variations in fitness and adaptation.

6 Periodisation

Periodisation is a plan for conditioning based on scientific principles of programme design (Stone and O'Bryant, 1987), which involves manipulation of the volume (frequency x duration) and intensity of the work an athlete performs during various periods of competitive season. The goal of the periodised conditioning programme is to manipulate these variables planning for peak performance during certain competitions. To accomplish this, the athletic season is broken down into cycles, which contain various phases. The simplest format is to fit the cycles into a calendar year, which works very well for seasonal sports such as basketball or football. A cycle is divided into shorter phases, generally including pre-season, in-season, and off-season phases. In each phase, different amounts of general fitness, sport-specific fitness, and skill work are included. The general concept is to concentrate on specific fitness items at specific times in the developmental process, and to use the sets, repetitions, and durations that are most effective at producing the specific benefits for which the athlete is training. Tennis, as mentioned earlier, presents unique challenges to the conditioning specialist. Tennis is an almost year-round sport, with little time for an "off-season".

6.1 Active rest

Active rest is the phase immediately after the competitive season. In this stage the athlete will have some period of complete rest followed by a period of remaining physically active by participating in a variety of recreational activities. Cross-training may be a major component of this phase. This phase gives the athlete a mental and physical break from the sport. The pre-conditioning evaluation should be performed in between the active rest and general preparation phases, and should be the basis for designing the individualised conditioning programmes.

6.2 Preparation phase

This phase marks the start of the conditioning process and prepares the body for more intense training. General athletic fitness is emphasised, including exercises for basic strength, general flexibility, cardiorespiratory endurance, and muscular endurance. There should be some skill work, along with some occasional sport-specific play, but ideally, no competition. This phase may need to be longer in young players who need to build their general fitness base. Recovery periods should be built in to the schedule, particularly with the utilisation of heavy weight training, plyometrics, and intense running. It is important that athletes reach and maintain a general athletic fitness base of muscular strength and flexibility. This base prepares the musculoskeletal system to reach the sport-specific level of conditioning

6.3 Pre-competitive phase

Skill work begins to predominate in the pre-season phase. Conditioning becomes more sport specific, with a transition from general to sport-specific work in flexibility, strength, and endurance. The general fitness activities such as weight training for general strength may be continued as a maintenance activity, generally with a decreased frequency and intensity. In sports with high risk of overload injuries, prehabilitation exercises, exercises designed to modify strength imbalances and range of motion deficiencies that may be related to the athletes risk of overload injuries, should be prescribed to minimise these musculoskeletal adaptations. Sport specific sprint and plyometric drills may be used during this phase to bring sport specific fitness to a peak. Due to the high intensity of work, recovery periods should be emphasised and scheduled. Plyometrics should be done no more than two times per week to allow time for recovery.

6.4 Competitive phase

This phase applies to sports with a long regular season for the purpose of maintaining athletic fitness during the competitive year. Competition is frequent in this phase. Prehabilitation exercises are emphasised in this phase, and strength and endurance work is continued on a regular basis, but with less intensity as competition increases. Adequate recovery periods must be planned after competitions. In sports that have weekly or bi-weekly competitions, hard practices and conditioning should come early in the week, with tapering one to two days before competition.

6.5 Peaking or maintenance phase

In the peaking phase, conditioning is minimal. The skill work that is performed is sport specific and of high intensity. Rest is a major component of this phase. Estimates of how long athletes can remain in a peaking phase range from one to three weeks without some decrease in fitness. Sport-specific sample conditioning programmes for a variety of sports and levels of participation can be found in the current literature (Kibler et al., 1994b).

7 Planning the Conditioning Programme

7.1 Prehabilitation

"Prehabilitation" is that part of a conditioning programme designed to modify injury risk. It should be based, as discussed previously, on a thorough evaluation of the strengths and weaknesses of the individual athlete, as well as the measurable physiological demands of tennis. Sport-specific research is an important factor in the exercise prescription for prehabilitation. Areas of common injury risk can be identified and focused on. The exercise prescription for prehabilitation exercises depends on the nature of the problem (muscle weakness, inflexibility, muscle imbalance, and so on) and the type of conditioning activity (strength training, flexibility training, and so on). Prehabilitation exercises are generally low in intensity, and can be performed once or more a day.

7.2 General physical fitness

The general physical fitness component of conditioning for tennis is comprised of a general strength programme, a general aerobic fitness programme, and a general flexibility programme. While these programmes are planned in the "off-season" for many sports, the lack of a lengthy off-season in tennis may complicate the plan in some players. In tennis, it may be that general physical fitness is built in the off-season and during the early months of the in-season, then maintained during the remainder of the season.

An exercise prescription for strength training of tennis players should generally be planned for 3 days per week, and perhaps 4-5 days per week in advanced competitive players. Core body exercises should make up the bulk of the programme, using 3-5 sets of 8-12 repetitions. Flexibility exercises can be performed daily or almost daily for 15-20 min.

The aerobic exercise prescription is somewhat more controversial, since tennis is primarily an anaerobic sport. Recent evidence indicates that interval training at high intensities improves aerobic fitness to the same extent as traditional aerobic training (Tabata et al., 1996). Low intensity aerobic training may be used in the initial phases of training to reduce the chance of injury. The general aerobic fitness programme should gradually progress to high-intensity interval training, since it is more specific to the sport, and since it has the same positive effect on aerobic fitness. In general, the programme should begin with running 2-5 km 3-5 days per week for 1-2 months. As the season progresses, intervals should become gradually shorter and higher in intensity.

7.3 Sport specific athletic fitness

Once the player has attained a base level of general athletic fitness, he/she can progress to sport-specific functional activities. Athletic fitness, speed, power, quickness, balance, agility, are important in most sports. By exposing players to a variety of conditioning activities that require "athletic" movements, the individuals will improve their athletic abilities.

Exercises that improve lower body power include the squat, the power clean, vertical jumping drills, bounding, and box jumping. As many of these drills are plyometric in nature, they must be introduced slowly and cautiously as a part of the functional rehabilitation programme. Power in the trunk can be improved by using medicine balls and performing simulated tennis strokes using the forehand, backhand, and service motions.

Quickness can be improved in the upper body by using hand slap drills, boxing drills, and an irregularly shaped ball that bounces in unpredictable directions. Quickness for the lower body can be improved using a number of quick foot drills including ladder drill, hexagon drill, five dot drill, and others. In these drills, the

Table 1. Exercises for building a physical fitness base

(a) Activities for general strength
- Medicine ball: squats, lunges, curls, presses, triceps extensions, arm curls, etc.
- Body weight: squats, lunges
- Barbell free weight: squats, lunges, curls, presses, triceps extensions, arm curls, etc.
- Dumbbell free weight: squats, lunges, curls, presses, triceps extensions, arm curls, etc.
- Machines: leg press, leg extension, leg curl, pullovers, triceps extensions, arm curls, etc.

(b) Activities for flexibility
- Total body flexibility: hamstring stretch, quadriceps stretch, shoulder internal rotation stretch, iliotibial band stretch, cross-body stretch, calf stretch.
- Individual needs

(c) Activities for building the aerobic base
- low intensity running
- cycling
- jumping rope
- sprint/interval training

Table 2. Exercises for improving athletic fitness

(a) Exercises for power
- Vertical jumps
- Bounding
- Barrier jumps
- Heel to butt, knee to chest, single and double
- Bounding ladder drills
- Tennis stroke medicine ball drills

(b) Exercises for hand and foot quickness
- Hand slap drills
- Crazy ball
- Punching bag
- Hexagon
- Five dot drill
- Line jumps
- Quick foot ladder drills
- Cone drills

(c) Exercises for balance and agility
- Ladder drills
- Shuffle drills
- Cone drills
- Single leg drills

(d) Exercises for speed
- Ladder drills
- Form sprints
- Resisted/assisted sprints
- Changing footwork pattern sprints

player is pushed to move the feet as fast as possible while minimising contact time with the ground. The footwork ladder (Speed City, Portland, Oregon) is an excellent tool for all areas of athletic fitness, including quickness of foot.

Balance and agility are important and can be improved using drills such as the footwork ladder and cone drills (Wojtys et al., 1996). Single leg drills, including strengthening exercises such as single leg squats and lunges as well as single leg movement drills, such as the hexagon and five dot drill can also improve balance. These drills are particularly important in the case of a lower extremity injury.

Speed is dependent on stride frequency and stride length. Stride frequency is a function of neural drive, causing the muscles to contract and relax as rapidly as possible. Speed is also a function of stride length, which can be improved with a number of exercises, including ladder drills, form sprints, and changing foot pattern sprints. Speed can be improved using both resistance training and high-velocity movement training (Delecluse et al., 1995). By evaluating the footwork patterns in tennis, the need for changing from one footwork pattern to another can be determined. Most often, the tennis player hits a shot, shuffles to the middle of the court, then reacts by moving in the direction of the next shot. Players can practice changing footwork patterns, concentrating on changing from one pattern to another rapidly and efficiently.

The exercise prescription for speed, power, quickness, balance, and agility is individualised according to the needs of the individual players. Although these skills are used in tennis practice, it is best to devote time specifically to their improvement. Athletic fitness can easily be incorporated into the tennis practice as an "on court" activity. Athletic fitness drills are generally performed 10-20 min each day, decreasing in length and frequency as a tournament approaches. It is important to choose a variety of exercises from each group, and not to repeat the same exercises on consecutive days. The duration of each drill should match the approximate work/rest intervals of the sport.

8 Summary

Conditioning for improved performance is widely practised among tennis players at all levels of competition. With the variety of techniques and equipment available, the simple process of conditioning can become quite involved. A proper conditioning plan includes several components, such as prehabilitation, the general athletic fitness base, and sport specific athletic fitness. By integrating these components into a periodised conditioning plan, and by combining this plan with the appropriate volume and intensity of tennis skill practice, performance in the sport will be enhanced. This same process, evaluating the demands of the sport and the musculoskeletal base of the individual athlete, can be applied to other racket sports also.

9 References

Atha, J. (1981) Strengthening muscle. **Exercise and Sport Science Review**, 9, 1-73.

Bergeron, M.F., Maresh, C.M., Kraemer, W.J., Abram, B., Conroy, B., and Gabaree, C. (1991) Tennis: A physiological profile during match play. **International Journal of Sports Medicine**, 12, 474-479.

Chandler, T.J. (1990b) Work/rest intervals in world class tennis. **Tennis Pro, 3** (1), 4.

Chandler, T.J., Kibler, W.B., Uhl, T.L.,Wooten, B.P., Kiser, A.K. and Stone, E. (1990a) Flexibility comparisons of junior elite tennis players to other athletes. **American Journal of Sports Medicine**, 18, 134-136.

Chandler, T.J., Kibler, W.B., Stracener, E.C., Ziegler, A.K. and Pace, B. (1992) Shoulder strength, power, and endurance in college tennis players. **American Journal of Sports Medicine**, 20, 455-558.

Chandler, T.J. (1995) Exercise training for tennis. **Clinics in Sports Medicine**, 14(1), 33-46.

Delecluse, C., Van Coppenolle, H., Willems, E., Van Leemputte, M., Diels, R. and Goris, M. (1995) Influence of high-resistance and high velocity training on sprint performance. **Medicine and Science in Sports and Exercise**, 27, 1203-1209.

Hewett, T.E., Stroupe, A.L., Nance, T.A., and Noyes, F.R. (1996) Plyometric training in female athletes; decreased impact forces and increased hamstring torques. **American Journal of Sports Medicine**, 24, 765-773.

Kibler, W.B., Chandler, T.J. (1994a) Racquet Sports, in **Sports Injuries, Mechanisms, Prevention, and Treatments**, (ed. F. Fu), Baltimore, Williams and Wilkins.

Kibler, W.B. and Chandler, T.J. (1994b). Sport-specific conditioning. **American Journal of Sports Medicine**, 22, 424-432.

Kibler, W.B., Chandler, T.J., Livingston, B.P., and Roetert, E.P. (1996) Shoulder range of motion in elite tennis players; effects of age and years of tournament play. **American Journal of Sports Medicine**, 24, 1-7.

Kibler, W.B., Chandler, T.J., Uhl, T.L. and Maddux, R.E. (1989) A musculoskeletal approach to the preparticipation physical examination; preventing injury and improving performance. **American Journal of Sports Medicine**, 17, 525-531.

Kraemer, W.J., Triplett, N.T., Fry, A.C., Kosiris, L.P., Bauer, J.E., Lynch, J.M., McConnell, K.T., Newton, R.U., Gordon, S.E., Nelson, R.C., and Knuttgen, H.G. (1995) An in-depth sports medicine profile of women college tennis players. **Journal of Sport Rehabilitation**, 4, 79-98.

Stone, M.H. and O'Bryant, H.S. (1987) **Weight Training, A Scientific Approach**. Bellwether Press, Minneapolis, MN.

Tabata, I., Nishimura, Kouji, Kouzaki, M., Hirai, Y., Ogita, F., Miyachi, M. and Yamamoto, K. (1996) Effects of moderate-intensity endurance and high-intensity intermittent training on anaerobic capacity and VO$_2$max. **Medicine and Science in Sports and Exercise**, 28, 1327-1330.

Wojtys, E.M., Huston, L.J., Taylor, P.D. and Bastian, S.D. (1996) Neuromuscular adaptations in isokinetic, isotonic, and agility training programs. **American Journal of Sports Medicine**, 24, 187-192.

12 A preliminary investigation into a sport specific fitness test for table tennis players

M.A.K. Bawden and I.W. Maynard
Chichester Institute of Higher Education, Chichester, UK

1 Introduction

When developing any sport-specific test, it is essential that the test protocol should accurately reflect the physiological and technical demands of the sport (Hughes and Fullerton, 1994). The physiological demands of table tennis require players to have speed, agility, strength, power, flexibility and endurance. All of these physical demands interact and complement each other when in the playing environment. To test endurance, it is important that all the physical demands are considered alongside the technical aspects of performance. Despite the sport itself being primarily interval based and thus anaerobic in nature, players still need to have a high level of aerobic fitness in order to meet the demands of the sport when played at the highest level.

Lundin (1973, cited in Astrand and Rodahl, 1986) reported that elite table tennis players have a very good base of exercise fitness. Laboratory based $VO_{2\ max}$ tests were conducted on seven elite Swedish players which gave a mean value of 65 $ml.kg^{-1}.min^{-1}$. Laboratory based tests on elite senior England players have also demonstrated the high level of endurance fitness that table tennis players possess with $VO_{2\ max}$ results comparing favourably with elite performers from other sports that require high levels of endurance fitness (Houghton, 1987). Laboratory based measures are effective in assessing a player's general aerobic fitness level, although such measures are not specific to the sport of table tennis and thus do not reflect the demands of the game (Ellwood, 1992). Therefore there is a need to develop tests that are specific to the demands of the sport being tested. Such tests should reflect both the physiological and the technical demands of the sport in order to give a more accurate measure of a player's fitness for the sport. Sport-specific fitness tests in racket based sports have been developed in both squash (Chin, Steininger, So, Clark & Wong, 1995) and badminton (Chin, Wong, So, Siu, Steininger & Los, 1995; Hughes & Fullerton, 1995). To date, no endurance sport-specific field based fitness test exists for table tennis.

The purpose of this study was to develop a practical field-based sport-specific aerobic fitness test for table tennis players and to compare the results of players

Science and Racket Sports II, edited by A. Lees, I. Maynard, M. Hughes and T. Reilly. Published in 1998 by E & FN Spon, 11 New Fetter Lane, London EC4P 4EE, UK. ISBN: 0 419 23030 0

completing the table tennis specific field-based test with a previously validated non sport-specific field-based test, the multi-stage shuttle run test (Leger & Lambert, 1982). The criteria for the test design were that it should be performed in the match-play situation and not involve complex equipment so that the test would be practical to use in the training environment. It was also required that the movements made by the players in the test, were highly specific to table tennis, involving both the upper and lower body, and thus accurately reflect both the physical and technical demands of the game.

2 Methods

2.1 Participants
The participants in this study were 14 elite (National Junior Squad) table tennis players age (mean ± S.D.) 14.9 ± 1.6 years of mixed gender (9 males, 5 females).

2.2 Procedure
The experiment took place at a national training camp. The 14 players were split into two groups and performed the test in a randomised counter balanced order. The variables that were collected were pre-test and post-test heart rates (beats.min^{-1}), perceived exertion (RPE) and the level reached in each test.

2.3 The sport-specific test
The sport-specific test was performed in a table tennis playing area and required a table tennis table and a ball projection machine (see Figure 1). The test began with the subject playing a rally using alternate backhand and forehand strokes for a 6 s period. The player was given the instruction to hit the balls as hard and as accurately as possible. The balls were projected from a ball projection machine straight down the centre of the table. In order to play backhand and forehand strokes correctly the players had to move as they would in a game to get into the correct position to play each stroke. When the 6 s rally was completed the player had a set period of time in which to complete a side-stepping circuit as indicated by markers on the floor. The player was required to side-step out to each marker and then back to the ready position in turn within a set time period. At the end of this time period (25 s for level one) a ball was released from the ball projection machine to begin the next 6 s rally. If the subject was not back in the ready position, having completed the side-stepping circuit then he/she was eliminated from the test. If the player was successful in getting back to the starting position, then he/she had completed level one of the test. The players then repeated the same protocol; however, the time that the player has to complete the side-stepping circuit decreased progressively (1 s decrease) as each level was completed. The player continued until they could not keep up with the progressive demands of the test. The timing of the test was controlled by an audio tape which indicated when the 6 s playing period started and finished and also when the time for the side-stepping movements was started and completed. A count down from ten to one for the last 10 s of each level acted as an indication to the players as to how quickly they should be moving so to avoid players being unable to get back to the start

position through lack of judgement rather than fitness limitations. The time taken to complete each side-stepping circuit was progressively decreased to 14 s. At that point the time period was fixed with subjects continuing at this level until they were unable to meet the demands of the test. Pre-test and post-test heart rates recorded on short range telemetry (PE3000 Polar Sports Tester) perceived exertion (RPE) and the level that the player reached were recorded.

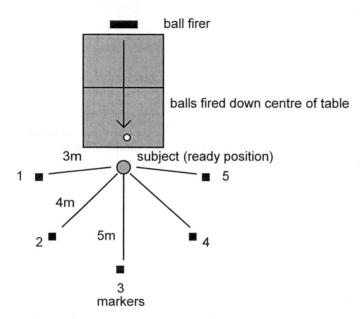

Figure 1. Table tennis specific test.

2.4 Multi-stage shuttle run

The multi stage shuttle run (Leger and Lambert, 1982) required players to run between two markers placed 20 m from each other. Players had to run between these markers in time with the sound of an audio tape. The time to complete each shuttle decreased progressively as the test continued. Subjects were eliminated from the test when they could no longer run to the markers in time with the signal on the audio tape. As each player was eliminated from the test, the level reached was recorded. Other variables measured were pre-test and post-test heart rates and perceived exertion (RPE).

3 Results

The sport-specific fitness indices were compared to results from the multi-stage shuttle run test. The levels reached by the players were compared using a Pearson product moment correlation coefficient (r = 0.30, P = 0.29). The low correlation between the two tests suggest that the tests were not measuring the same parameters. Other variables measured from both tests were post-test heart rates (table : 200 ± 8 beats.min^{-1}, multi stage : 200 ± 8 beats.min^{-1}) perceived exertion (table :16.9 ± 2.07, multi stage : 16.7 ± 2.1) and elimination level. The results showed no significant difference using a paired t-test for post-test heart rates or perceived exertion (P>0.05). This indicated that both the sport-specific test and the multi-stage fitness test achieved similar levels of maximum heart rate and perceived exertion.

4 Discussion and Conclusion

The low correlation established when comparing the results of the two tests suggests that the tests were not measuring the same parameters. The movements that the players are required to perform in the sport-specific test are similar to those used when they are actually playing in the table tennis match/practice situation. The movements used in the multi-stage fitness test (running and turning) are not similar to those required for table tennis performance and thus those players that perform well in a general fitness test are not necessarily those that do well in a sport-specific test. The sport-specific test required a combination of many other physical demands such as speed, agility, flexibility, quick reactions and power, all of which comprise endurance fitness for table tennis performance. Therefore those players that have a good level of endurance fitness specific to the demands of table tennis should be able to perform well on such a test.

When comparing the intensity of the two tests, it was found that the heart rate data indicated that the players were working close to their maximum at the end of both tests. This suggests that both tests were highly intensive; however, the RPE values did not reflect this level of exertion for either test. These slightly low (RPE) values may be explained by the situation in which the tests were conducted, in that subjects may not prefer to indicate openly in front of their peers, that a maximal effort had been given.

Current weaknesses of the table tennis test are that, unlike the multi-stage shuttle run, only one player can perform the test at a time. Hence, testing larger groups/squads may be time consuming and therefore sometimes not be practical in a training environment. The lack of sensitivity of the test also needs to be addressed. In order to detect changes in fitness, more stages need to be added to each level of the test as with the multi-stage shuttle run. This could be implemented by making the players perform three complete circuits at each level of the test, before progressing to the next level. A weakness that cannot be controlled by the experimenter is the level of effort that the player puts into the forehand and backhand strokes. A future development could have target zones both 'on' and 'behind' the table. The 'on table' targets could be used to assess accuracy compared to fatigue rates throughout the test and the standing targets could be used as a measure of the power of the strokes. Such measures will enhance consistency and provide quality assurance (in terms of 'all out' effort from the players).

The table tennis test accurately reflects the demands of the sport in the use of upper body technique and lower body footwork. Players have indicated that they find such a test more applicable and relevant to the requirements of their fitness. This was reflected in the fact that there was a definite trend of higher standard players performing significantly better in the specific test regardless of their fitness as indicated by other aerobic tests. A similar trend was also found on specific testing with elite squash players (Chin et al., 1995).

A strength of the table tennis test was that very little equipment was required in order to conduct the test. A ball projection machine is not a necessity as a coach can feed balls to the players for the 6 s period. The limited need for essential equipment (audio tape player and a tape measure) will have positive implications for the practical application of the sport specific test at all levels of table tennis and should ensure its widespread adoption.

Further research may compare the correlation between validated laboratory based endurance measures and the sport-specific field based test to establish aspects of concurrent validity. Other physiological measurements, possibly including oxygen consumption and pre-test and post-test blood lactate concentration, would be beneficial in comparing the physiological demands of the sport-specific test to more traditional tests of aerobic fitness. Furthermore, predictive validity of the sport-specific measure could be evaluated by assessing the discriminatory ability of the test across table tennis players of different ability groups. The initial findings of this study suggest that there is a need for sport-specific testing in table tennis and that such measures could help to gain a greater understanding of an individuals fitness specific to the demands of the game.

5 References

Chin, M.K., Wong, S.K.A., So, R.C.H., Siu, T.O., Steininger, K. & Los, D.T.L. (1995) Sport Specific fitness testing of elite badminton players. **British Journal of Sports Medicine**, 29, 153-157.

Chin, M.K, Steininger, K, So, R.C.H, Clark, C.R & Wong, A.S.K.(1995) Physiological profiles and sport specific fitness of Asian elite squash players. **British Journal of Sports Medicine**, 29,158-164.

Ellwood, J.D. (1992) Is the Sub-maximal treadmill test an accurate predictor of oxygen uptake in table tennis? **International Journal of TableTennis Sciences**, 1, 33-38.

Houghton, N. (1987) Psychology and Science: England Squad's annual test. English Table Tennis Association.**Table Tennis News**, 170, 34-35.

Hughes, M.G. and Fullerton, F.M. (1995) Development of an on-court aerobic test for elite badminton players, in **Science and Racket Sports** (eds T.Reilly, M.Hughes and A.Lees) E. & F.N. Spon, London, pp.51-54.

Leger, L.A and Lambert, J. (1982) A maximal multi-stage 20m shuttle test to predict VO$_2$ max. **European Journal of Applied Physiology**, 49,1-12.

Lundin, A. (1973) "Bordtennis", Idrottsfsiologi, rapport no.12, Trygg-Hansa, Stockholm, cited in **Textbook of Work Physiology** (eds P.O. Astrand and K.Rodahl, 1986, McGraw-Hill, NewYork.

13 The efficacy of training routines as a preparation for competitive squash

M.K. Todd[1], C.A. Mahoney[2] and W.F.M. Wallace[3]

[1]Department of Physical Education and Sports Studies, Worcester College of Higher Education, Worcester, UK; [2]Department of Sports Studies, Roehampton Institute London, UK and [3]School of Biomedical Sciences, The Queen's University, Belfast, UK

1 Introduction

Squash requires a high level of physical fitness and good gross and fine motor control. Top players are expected to have a good aerobic capacity, and to be agile, powerful, and flexible (Todd and Mahoney, 1995), and previous work from this study has found the average energy cost of county level squash to be 60.7 kJ.min^{-1} (Todd et al., 1996). Part of an effective training regimen for the competitive squash player will take place on the court involving activities which resemble or mimic the game situation.

1.1 Oxygen uptake

The estimation of oxygen consumption on court has been rather ineffective in the past. The most suitable method of expired air sampling on court has been done by Montpetit et al. (1977; 1987) where expired air was collected in a Douglas bag for one minute at three points during a 25 min game. The authors reported values of 57% $\dot{V}O_2$ max for recreational players, and 62.5% $\dot{V}O_2$ max for elite players. On court measurements of $\dot{V}O_2$ have been estimated from heart rate recordings during a competitive match against a player of similar standard. Values have been reported of 83% $\dot{V}O_2$ max for nationally ranked players and 75.7% $\dot{V}O_2$ max for University league players during a game (Loots and Thiart, 1983; Van Rensburg et al., 1982).

1.2 Heart rate

Heart rate is a relatively easy variable to measure and gives a good indication of exercise intensity, though in squash, this is subject to variation due to the ambient temperature, humidity, use of the arms (Mercier et al., 1987; Loots & Thiart, 1983; Northcote et al., 1982; Van Rensburg et al., 1982) and adoption of the crouched position. A game of squash, when played for 20 min or more, against an opponent of similar standard, is sufficient to raise the heart rate to between 150 and 185 beats.min^{-1} (Mercier et al., 1987; Montpetit et al., 1987; Northcote et al., 1983; Loots and Thiart, 1983; Van Rensburg et al., 1982) and the mean heart rate for the game increases as the players become closer matched by ability.

Science and Racket Sports II, edited by A. Lees, I. Maynard, M. Hughes and T. Reilly. Published in 1998 by E & FN Spon, 11 New Fetter Lane, London EC4P 4EE, UK.   ISBN: 0 419 23030 0

1.3 Blood lactate
Generally, during a squash game lasting from 30 to 90 minutes, average lactate values in the blood range from 2.5 to 3.5 mmol.l^{-1} with peak lactate values of 5.3 and 8.0 mmol.l^{-1} (Mercier et al., 1987; Garden et al., 1986; Van Rensburg et al., 1982).

1.4 Aim of the study
The aim of the study was to investigate the efficacy of three commonly used court routines as a preparation for competitive squash. The intensity of the routines was determined by measurement of three physiological responses: $\dot{V}O_2$, heart rate and blood lactate concentration. The warm-up, boast and drive, and boast, drop and drive routines were investigated and compared to a competitive game situation.

2 Methods

2.1 Subjects
Twelve county players (mean age ($\pm$ SD) 33.1 $\pm$ 6.3 years) gave their informed consent and baseline data were collected in the Laboratory. For the determination of the intensity of county level squash, each player was monitored for $\dot{V}O_2$ on a treadmill using a portable telemetric gas analyser (Cosmed K2) with readings taken every 15 seconds; for heart rate using a telemetric heart rate analyser (Polar Electro PE3000); and for blood lactate via capillary sampling (Analox, England).

2.2 Court test
The Court test was performed on a county squad during the mid-season, and is outlined more clearly in Todd et al., (1996). The subjects were fitted with the Cosmed K2 device on arrival at the laboratory and a pre-test lactate sample was obtained from the ear lobe prior to the start of the test. An opponent of similar standard and the subject both performed a 'normal' self-determined squash warm-up on court for 3 min after which a blood sample was obtained. Then followed 3 min of a 'boast and drive' routine, during which the opponent boasted and the subject hit the ball straight down the side wall returning to the 'T' after each drive. Immediately following this a further blood sample was obtained. A 'boast, drop and drive' routine followed for 3 min with the subjects boasting on their forehand and 3 min on their backhand side; after each, blood samples were obtained. Finally the opponent and the subject played two games 'as normal' (including pauses for service and retrieving the ball after a point), which were stopped after 3 min and blood samples were obtained after each 3 min game. The blood samples were all collected within 30 s and were analysed within 30 min of collection.

The statistical significance of the different court routine measurements on heart rate, oxygen uptake and blood lactate concentration taken at four points during the court routine was determined using an analysis of variance with repeated measures to determine F values. A post hoc Scheffé test was used to determine the significance of the difference between any two groups.

3 Results

Table 1 shows the mean $\dot{V}O_2$, heart rate and blood lactate concentration to be lowest during the self determined warm-up phase, and highest during the boast, drop and drive routine. The mean ($\pm$SD) game blood lactate concentration of 2.9 ± 0.9 mmol.l^{-1} would indicate that squash is predominantly an aerobic sport, supported by the taxation of the aerobic capacity of 74.3 ± 9.3 % $\dot{V}O_2$ max when measured on court using the K2 analyser. The anaerobic demands of squash can be seen in the boast, drop and drive routine where lactate responses of 4.1 ± 0.9 mmol.l^{-1} and an oxygen demand of 84.4 ± 9.1% $\dot{V}O_2$ max are reported.

Table 1. Absolute and relative intensity of the squash routines

Routine	$\dot{V}O_2$ (ml.kg.$^{-1}$min^{-1})	% $\dot{V}O_2$ max	Heart rate (beats.min^{-1})	% HRmax	Blood lactate (mmol.l^{-1})
Warm-up	29.4 ± 3.9	51.8 ± 5.9	120 ± 19	64.5 ± 9.0	1.8 ± 0.6
Boast & drive	41.2 ± 4.4	73.5 ± 13.8	153 ± 15	81.1 ± 6.5	2.7 ± 0.7
Boast, drop, drive	48.1 ± 5.7	84.4 ± 9.1	168 ± 12	90.3 ± 4.4	4.1 ± 0.9
Game	42.2 ± 4.6	74.3 ± 9.3	160 ± 15	85.9 ± 6.0	2.9 ± 0.9

Modified with permission from Todd et al., Portable telemetry as a method of measuring energy cost in high level squash. in Robertson S.A.(ed) *Contemporary Ergonomics* 1996 p439-444. London. Taylor & Francis Ltd

Table 2. Statistical significance of the difference in intensity between the squash routines as measured by $\dot{V}O_2$, heart rate, and blood lactate concentration

	$\dot{V}O_2$ $F_{3,40} = 30.67$	Heart rate $F_{3,40} = 21.09$	Blood lactate $F_{3,42} = 15.89$
Game V warm-up	*	*	*
Game V boast & drive	NS	NS	NS
Game V boast, drop & drive	*	NS	*
Boast, drop & drive V boast & drive	*	NS	*
Boast, drop & drive V warm up	*	*	*
Boast & drive V warm-up	*	*	NS

* = P<0.001

The results of the statistical analysis are given in Table 2, and show that $\dot{V}O_2$ during the warm-up differed significantly from the other routines. The $\dot{V}O_2$ was also significantly higher during the most intense boast, drop and drive routine, compared with warm-up, boast and drive routine and the game. The mean $\dot{V}O_2$ for the game was not significantly different from the boast and drive routine, though both were significantly different from warm-up and boast, drop and drive. Heart rate during the warm-up was significantly lower than for the boast and drive routine, boast, drop and drive routine, and the game. Heart rate did not differ significantly between either the game, or the two routines. The Scheffé test revealed a significant difference between the game and both the warm-up and the boast, drop and drive routine, but not the boast and drive routine. The blood lactate concentration during the intense boast, drop and drive routine was significantly higher than all other routines. The Scheffé test showed no significant differences for the blood lactate concentration between the boast and drive routine and the game.

4 Discussion

4.1 The warm-up

There were significant differences in intensity as measured by $\dot{V}O_2$, heart rate and blood lactate concentration between the game and the warm-up routine, indicating that the warm-up can be considered a useful training routine for preparation for a game, for court movement and motor skill rehearsal, though not for overload of the cardio-respiratory system. The intensity of the self-selected warm-up of the county players in this study was more intense than the warm-up routine of recreational players as reported by Garden et al. (1986).

4.2 The game

There were no significant differences observed between the intensities of the game and the boast and drive routine as measured by $\dot{V}O_2$, heart rate or blood lactate concentration. This would indicate that the boast and drive routine places similar physiological demands upon the player as the game and would therefore be a scientifically appropriate routine to include in a training regimen. There can be no true comparison of this study with other literature since this study has employed a novel method for measurement of on-court oxygen uptake to a new dimension. In the present study, $\dot{V}O_2$ was measured every 15 s using the Cosmed K2 device during a game, and during three other intensities all of which would be expected to form a component of the game. The mean $\dot{V}O_2$ for the county players during the game was similar to university league players, $75.7 \pm 2.9\%$ $\dot{V}O_2$ max (Loots and Thiart, 1983) although the $\dot{V}O_2$ was estimated from heart rate recordings, while national players recorded an estimated $83.0 \pm 12.6\%$ $\dot{V}O_2$ max (Van Rensburg et al., 1982). Montpetit et al. (1987; 1977) took expired air collections for one minute with a Douglas bag harnessed to the player's back, on three occasions during the game and calculated an intensity of 57% $\dot{V}O_2$ max for recreational players and $62.5 \pm 6.8\%$ $\dot{V}O_2$ max for elite players respectively.

   Squash entails intermittent activity and players do not reach steady state as they might do during a dynamic court routine where the emphasis is placed upon continuity. Heart rate during a game of squash can be so high as to induce ventricular arrhythmias, which are not invoked during treadmill running (Northcote et al., 1983). Since heart rate is the easiest of the three variables to measure, some authors have simply measured heart rate on court and estimated the corresponding $\dot{V}O_2$ intensity. This practice could lead to inaccurate results since the heart rate on court may be elevated due to factors already mentioned. During the game phase of the present study, the mean heart rate was $85.9 \pm 6\%$ HRmax. This follows the general consensus that squash raises the heart rate to between 80 - 85% HRmax, which seems to be independent of skill level, while higher values occur when playing against an opponent of a greater standard (Mercier et al., 1987). South African national players worked at an intensity of 88.3 ± 7.4% HRmax, (Van Rensburg et al., 1982) which is similar to the heart rate of the county players during the high intensity boast, drop and drive routine, 90.3 ± 4.4% HRmax.

The mean blood lactate concentration during the game routine for these county players was 2.9 ± 0.8 mmol.l^{-1}, which is similar to that of nationally ranked players (Mercier et al., 1987; Van Rensburg et al., 1982), and is slightly higher than the top level league players, 2.5 mmol.l^{-1} of Noakes et al. (1982). Squash seems to be an endurance event, which invades the anaerobic energy system periodically, with mean game blood lactate concentrations ranging from 2.5 - 3.5 mmol.l^{-1} (Mercier et al., 1987; Garden et al., 1986; Van Rensburg et al., 1982).

4.3 The routines

The warm-up may be considered a preparatory routine, and the intensity of the boast and drive routine was found to be similar to that of a game. The intensity of the boast, drop and drive routine as measured by $\dot{V}O_2$ and blood lactate concentration, was found to be significantly greater than the boast and drive routine and the game. However, there was no significant difference in the intensities of the boast, drop and drive routine, the boast and drive routine or the game when measured by heart rate. This indicates that heart rate during squash may be affected by factors other than intensity of play, and this variation is adequately encompassed by the heart rate response required by the other two routines.

Average peak lactate values for national players have been reported at 5.3 ± 2.5 mmol.l^{-1} when playing against opponents of similar standard, which are considerably higher than the average values for the county squad during the boast, drop and drive routine (4.1 ± 0.9 mmol.l^{-1}). The individual blood lactate levels of the same national players did not rise above 2 mmol.l^{-1} (mean values 1.5 ± 0.7 mmol.l^{-1}) when playing against lesser opponents (Mercier et al., 1987). This would indicate the need to train at intensities above those mean values reported for a game, if the player intends to play against opponents of similar or better standard. With a $\dot{V}O_2$ of 84.4 ± 9.1% $\dot{V}O_2$ max, a heart rate of 90.3 ± 4.4% HRmax, and a blood lactate concentration of 4.1 ± 0.9 mmol.l^{-1}, the boast, drop and drive routine of this study would be considered to overload the cardiovascular system sufficiently to elicit training effects, since the intensity of this routine is statistically greater than the average intensity of a game when measured by $\dot{V}O_2$ and blood lactate concentration.

5 Conclusion

Squash is an aerobic event with frequent invasions upon the anaerobic energy system. For sport specific training adaptations to occur, it is important to overload the muscular and cardiovascular systems involved in the sport. For training purposes, intensity of routines, as measured by heart rate, is less sensitive than measurements of $\dot{V}O_2$ or blood lactate due to other factors affecting the heart rate such as ambient temperature and humidity, use of the arms, and adoption of the crouched position. A self-selected warm-up may be a useful preparatory tool for grooving motor skills prior to a game, but is less intense than a competitive game, and therefore ineffective as an overload training tool. The boast and drive routine most closely resembles the average intensity of a competitive game when measured by $\dot{V}O_2$, heart rate and blood lactate concentration, while the boast, drop and drive routine is more intense than both the game and the boast and drive routine, overloads the cardio-respiratory system, and prepares the player for the more intense periods of the game experienced by competitive squash players.

6 References

Garden, G., Hale, P.J., Horrocks, P.M., Crase, J., Hammond, V. and Nattrass, M. (1986) Metabolic and hormonal responses during squash. **European Journal of Applied Physiology**, 55, 445-449

Loots, S.L. and Thiart, B.F. (1983) Energy demands of league and social squash players. **South African Journal of Research Sport**, 6(1), 13-19.

Mercier, M., Beillot, J., Gratas, A., Rochcongar, P., Lessard, Y., Andre, A.M. and Dassonville, J. (1987) Adaption to work load in squash players: laboratory tests and recordings. **Journal of Sports Medicine and Physical Fitness**, 27, 98-104.

Montpetit, R.R., Beauchamp, L. and Leger, L. (1987) Energy requirements of squash and racquetball. **Physician and Sportsmedicine**, 15, 106-112.

Montpetit, R., Leger, L. and Girardin, Y. (1977) Racquetball, le squash et la condition physique. **Racquetball-Canada**, 3(2): 6-11.

Noakes, T.D., Cowling, J.R., Gevers, W. and Van Niekerk J-P de V. (1982) The metabolic response to squash including the influence of pre-exercise carbohydrate ingestion. **South African Medical Journal,** 62, 721-723.

Northcote, R.J., MacFarlane, P. and Ballantyne, D. (1983) Ambulatory electrocardiography in squash players. **British Heart Journal**, 50, 372-377.

Todd, M.K. and Mahoney, C.A. (1995) Determination of pre-season physiological characteristics of elite male squash players, in **Science and Racket Sports** (eds T. Reilly, M. Hughes and A. Lees), E. & F.N. Spon, London, pp. 81-86.

Todd, M.K., Mahoney, C.A. and Wallace, W.F.M. (1996) Portable telemetry as a method of measuring energy cost in high level squash, in **Contemporary Ergonomics** (ed. S.A. Robertson), Taylor & Francis Ltd, London, pp. 439-444.

Van Rensburg, J.P., Van der Linde, A., Ackermann, P.C., Kielblock, A.J. and Strydom, N.B. (1982) Physiological profile of squash players. **South African Journal of Research in Sport**, 5(2), 25-26.

14 The travelling racket sports player

T. Reilly, G. Atkinson and J. Waterhouse
*Centre for Sport and Exercise Sciences, School of Human Sciences,
Liverpool John Moores University, Liverpool, UK*

1 Introduction

Sports tournaments, particularly events in the racket sports, tend to be distributed throughout the world and over the complete year. This has been encouraged by the growth in televised competitions for professional players and flourishing indoor as well as outdoor tournaments. It is facilitated by the ease of contemporary air-flight which makes it possible to travel quickly from one side of the globe to the other, for example by means of long-haul flights between Europe and Asia or Australia. The potential financial rewards on offer in sports competitions tend to predominate over the biological stress that such itineraries entail.

A typical regimen is illustrated by the competitive programme of British lawn tennis player Tim Henman at the beginning of the present year. In three successive weeks he was engaged in competitions in Germany, Dubai and Australia. Coping with such a schedule is aggravated by the necessity or desire to return to one's home country between tournament engagements. Where players have commitments close together in time but in countries far apart, they are unlikely to perform at their best. The experience of one of the British table-tennis participants at the Atlanta Olympics - delayed in China prior to travelling to USA via Europe - is not an uncommon experience in the racket sports.

2 Travel Fatigue

Travel is nowadays an accepted part of the habitual activity of athletes. It may entail travel across one's own country for domestic contests as well as travel overseas to training camps or competitive venues. Besides, many athletes may not reside close to good quality training facilities and may regularly have to travel by car or public transport for the purpose of training. The stresses associated with habitual travelling have been studied in 'commuters' to work but little is known about the phenomenon of 'travel fatigue' in athletes. It is likely that any detrimental effects are compounded by subjective feelings of tiredness associated with training and by boredom. Fatigue

Science and Racket Sports II, edited by A. Lees, I. Maynard, M. Hughes and T. Reilly. Published in 1998 by E & FN Spon, 11 New Fetter Lane, London EC4P 4EE, UK.   ISBN: 0 419 23030 0

may also be precipitated by a failure to allow for brief stops in the journey to alleviate postural discomfort, permit drinking and eating if necessary.

Travel fatigue linked with long distance air-flights poses a different range of problems for athletes and team management. In general these travel stresses apply to all visitors to overseas countries. They include the procedures associated with obtaining and presenting the necessary travel documents, enough money, checking in and getting through security, passport and customs screening and so on. These stresses are common irrespective of direction or distance of travel and can be accentuated by delay in boarding at take-off. They call for a positive psychological approach to facing these routines and overriding any negative feelings.

Travel fatigue in long-haul flights may be due to a gradual dehydration as a result of ambient conditions on board. This is due to the water vapour content of the cabin air which is low in comparison with fresh air. Headaches may also be linked to a combination of low air pressure and the loss of body water to the dry air within the aeroplane (de Looy et al., 1988). Caffeine and alcohol may compound the effect as they are diuretics and so are unsuitable for rehydration purposes. Stiffness due to spending a long time in a cramped posture can be relieved by simple stretching or by isometric contractions of the muscles affected. These exercises should help to eliminate residual stiffness at the end of the journey.

Flights within the same time-zone, such as to South Africa from the United Kingdom or between the east coast of USA and South America, may have residual effects due to the duration of the journey. These are not as disturbing as are flights across multiple time-zones. After-effects attributable to the flight itself wear off quickly once the destination is reached. Flights eastward or westward that entail travel across time-zones additionally lead to a disturbance of the circadian body-clock. This desynchronisation of biological rhythms is the cause of 'jet-lag' and one of the problems that arises may be a difficulty in sleeping, thereby accentuating travel fatigue.

3 Jet-lag

The group of symptoms affecting travellers following rapid journeys to distant places across multiple time-zones is referred to as jet-lag. There is a general malaise and a sense of feeling and acting 'below par' associated with the collective symptoms (see Table 1). Physical exercise will be more difficult and fine skills (including difficult serves or volleys) are likely to be executed less well until the symptoms abate.

Jet-lag affects individuals differently, but in general:
◊ It is more pronounced (that is, it is more severe and lasts longer) after a flight to the east than one to the west through the same number of time-zones.
◊ It is more pronounced the more time-zones that are crossed.
◊ Younger and fitter people tend to suffer less than do older persons.
◊ Women may be affected more than men.

Table 1. Symptoms associated with the phenomenon of jet-lag

- ◆ Fatigue during the new daytime, and yet inability to sleep at night.
- ◆ Decreased mental performance, particularly if vigilance is required.
- ◆ Decreased physical performance, particularly with regard to events that require stamina or precise movement.
- ◆ A loss of appetite, coupled with indigestion and even nausea.
- ◆ Increased irritability, headaches, mental confusion and disorientation

---

The disruption of the body's 'circadian rhythm' is the root cause of jet-lag. This rhythm is a function of the body-clock which controls a whole host of physiological functions. It determines the cyclical rise in body temperature during the day to an evening peak and a subsequent drop in the trough in the middle of the night's sleep. It also determines the sleep-wakefulness cycle, sleep being easier to initiate and maintain when body temperature is low. Research evidence shows that the body-clock also affects physiological measures that themselves influence sports performance (Reilly, 1994b). They include leg strength and back strength (Coldwells et al., 1994), metabolism (Reilly and Brooks, 1982), power output (Reilly and Marshall, 1994) and self-paced exercise (Atkinson et al., 1994).

The racket sports incorporate a range of complex skills as well as fast actions. The data in Table 2 illustrate that diurnal rhythms and force variability principles interact to effect a diurnal increase in the velocity of the tennis serve, accompanied by a decrease in accuracy. In this study of six tennis players the high points of alertness, muscle strength and ball velocity coincided with the peak value of tympanic temperature which was observed at 18:00 hours (Speers and Atkinson, unpublished observations 1996, Liverpool). The results for the second serve did not reach significance ($P > 0.05$).

Table 2. Diurnal variations in alertness, strength and performance of a tennis serve. Mean values of 15 trials of 1st and 2nd serves were calculated prior to establishing mean ± S.D. for the group

	09:00	14:00	18:00
Alertness (Scale 0-10)	5.7 ± 1.7	6.4 ± 1.8	7.2 ± 1.0
Grip strength (N)	391.6 ± 11.0	410.2 ± 105.9	417.4 ± 9.8[b]
V - 1st serve (m.s^{-1})	23.3 ± 3.4	23.8 ± 3.2[a]	24.2 ± 3.3[b]
V- 2nd serve (m.s^{-1})	20.8 ± 2.5	21.1 ± 2.6	21.1 ± 2.5
Accuracy - 1st serve	29.0 ± 9.8	27.0 ± 5.2	24.0 ± 8.9[b]
Accuracy - 2nd serve	30.0 ± 11.8	32.0 ± 11.8	33.0 ± 5.9

[a] denotes difference between 09:00 and 14:00 ($P < 0.01$)
[b] denotes difference between 14:00 and 18:00 ($P < 0.01$)

The body-clock is normally in harmony with the 24-hour changes between daylight and darkness. Since the earth spins on its axis, the sun is at its maximum height above the horizon at any point on the earth's surface once in every 24-hour period. This time is called *local noon*. The world has been divided into 24 time-zones in order to standardise all these times. The time-zone that all others are related to passes through England i.e. *Greenwich Mean Time* (GMT). Countries to the east of the UK have clocks that are ahead of this, because the sun rises earlier, whereas time to the west appears delayed with respect to this reference. Having a local time that reflects the position of the sun in the sky is a simple idea - but adjusting to a new local time on flying to a new time-zone presents difficulties for the internal body clock (de Looy et al., 1988).

The body-clock is slow to adjust to the change in schedule that is required on travelling to a new country with its own local time. Before adjustment takes place, the player might train or compete at a time when the body's signal denotes a preference to be asleep, and attempt to sleep when the body-clock is directing wakefulness. It is during this period - before adjustment has taken place - that jet-lag is experienced. Once the body-clock has adjusted, jet-lag disappears - until the next journey across time-zones (usually on the return trip home).

Females may be more affected by jet-lag than male racket sports players because the severity of symptoms can be related to menstrual cycle phase. Disruptions of the menstrual cycle in female travellers have been linked to disturbances in melatonin secretion. In Scandinavia, it has been found that higher melatonin levels in the winter compared with summer values have an inhibiting effect on lutenizing hormone. As a consequence, ovulation might not occur during that cycle (Harma et al., 1994). The extent to which the menstrual disturbances accompanying travelling across multiple time-zones in themselves alter athletic performance is uncertain.

It will take on average about 1 day for every time-zone crossed to recover fully from the effects of jet-lag (Reilly and Mellor, 1988). Experience at the 1994 British Olympic Association's training camps in Tallahassee was that it took 5 days for the majority of athletes to be completely clear of jet-lag symptoms, although a few had recovered by the third day in the USA (Reilly 1994a). The journey entailed a 5-hour time-zone transition. It should be noted that the effects are periodic and can be more intense at particular times of the day. The athlete may be totally unaware of any adverse effects, unless he/she has to do something quickly, take decisions or perform sports skills.

Local environmental factors may also influence the effects of jet-lag symptoms. Dehydration associated with heat stress, for example, may accentuate difficulties in concentration and mental fatigue. A programme of heat acclimatisation prior to departure across multiple time-zones can benefit the players and was implemented as a formal strategy by British competitors at the 1996 Atlanta Olympic Games (Reilly et al., 1997c).

4 Adjusting the Body-clock

The body clock is a poor time-keeper. Left to itself, it would run slow, with a period of 24 to 25 hours rather than the 24-hour day which is required in order to stay in time with the alternation of light and dark (Minors and Waterhouse, 1981). Under normal circumstances, the body-clock is adjusted in the same way as a watch that keeps poor time - by external signals. Several signals adjust the circadian rhythms, and making use of them helps the body to adjust to time-zone transitions.

The main signals are:
◊ Exposure to light, particularly receiving direct sunlight out of doors.
◊ The pattern of sleep and activity (including exercise).
◊ The timing and type of meals.
◊ Exposure to social influences and the alternation of natural daylight and darkness in the environment.

5 Promoting Adjustment

5.1 The process of adjustment
Complete adjustment of the body-clock takes several days. The aim is to speed up this process of adjustment as much and as safely as possible. Only when fully adjusted to the new time-zone can performance be at its peak. This applies to training as well as to competition. Until that time, it will be more difficult for an individual to produce maximal effort. While adjustment is taking place, the shape of the normal rhythm is changed. It displays a lower amplitude, a lower peak value and a lower average value (Reilly et al., 1997b).

A manoeuvre frequently adopted by athletes prior to flying overseas in a westward direction is to go to bed 1-2 hours later than normal each night and get up 1-2 hours later each morning. It might not always be possible to do this, but its main benefit is to promote thinking ahead about times in the country of destination. It is not useful to try to adjust fully to the time-zone transition before the journey, since this will interrupt training schedules and lifestyle too much and will not adjust the body-clock very much (Reilly and Maskell, 1989). This advice applies to both a phase delay (getting to sleep later) and a phase advance (getting to bed earlier). Where there is a choice of flight times and airports, the player or team manager should select a schedule that makes planning to adjust all the easier. A flight that gets the European traveller to the USA destination in the evening, for example, would be helpful. The ideal travel schedule is seldom available but at least alternatives that are on offer can be consulted.

5.2 Possibilities for speeding adjustment
The perturbation of the body's circadian rhythms following rapid travel across time-zones has been outlined. Players and coaches must acknowledge this phenomenon if they are to take steps to promoting adjustment to the new time-zone. Several methods have been suggested (see Waterhouse et al., 1997), differing in their practicality and in

their potential side-effects. They encompass manipulations by means of nutritional, pharmacological, environmental and behavioural factors.

5.3 Timing and composition of meals

It has been suggested that high protein breakfasts promote alertness and that high-carbohydrate evening meals (vegetables, potatoes, rice, bread, pasta, desserts, etc.) promote sleep (Graeber et al., 1981). The theoretical grounds for this include the effects that such meals would have upon plasma amino acids and, thence, the uptake of the amino acids into the brain, their incorporation into neurotransmitters, and the release of the neurotransmitters. High protein meals (meat, cheese, eggs, etc.) raise plasma tyrosine, but whether this promotes the release of catecholamines by the activating systems of the brain and so promote alertness, is less clear. Similarly, high-carbohydrate meals promote the concentration of plasma tryptophan, but whether this stimulates the raphé nucleus and sleep is also uncertain (Leathwood, 1989). Electroencephalographic waves have shown some changes in athletes on a carbohydrate rich diet, but effects on the quality of sleep have not been demonstrated. The two-phase dietary method was promoted in the USA under the title 'President Reagan's Anti-jet-lag-Diet'.

Scientific tests of the efficacy of the diet are few and poorly designed. Even so, a variant of this proposal has been marketed. It consists of two types of pills, one to be taken in the morning and the other in the evening. Each pill is a mixture of substances, the morning pill containing tyrosine and the evening one, tryptophan. The accompanying literature does not enable a judgement to be made on the scientific evaluation of these preparations. Besides, tryptophan achieved adverse publicity in the early 1990s owing to the finding of impurities in commercially available products and its use is no longer recommended.

5.4 Sleeping pills

Disturbance of sleep is one of the unwanted corollaries of jet-lag syndrome. Resynchronising the normal sleep-wakefulness cycle seems to occur first, prior to restoration of physiological and performance measures to their normal circadian rhythm (Reilly et al., 1997a).

British sports teams travelling to Australia have used sleeping pills to induce sleep while on board. Military aircraft pilots flying from Britain to the Falkland Islands have also used minor tranquillizers (temazepam) to get to sleep so as to be refreshed for immediate activities on arrival, or in preparation for the return journey. Although drugs, such as benzodiazepines, are effective in getting people to sleep, they do not guarantee a prolonged period asleep. Besides, they have not been satisfactorily tested for subsequent residual effects on motor performance, such as sports skills. They may be counter-productive if given at the incorrect time. A prolonged sleep at the time an individual feels drowsy (presumably when he or she would have been asleep in the time-zone departed from) simply anchors the rhythms at their former phases and so operates against adjustment to the new time-zone (Reilly et al., 1997b).

The administration of one benzodiazepine (temazepam) was found to have no influence on subjective, physiological and performance measures following a westward flight across five time-zones (Reilly et al., 1997a). The circadian rhythms of athletes differed from those of sedentary subjects, although neither group benefitted from the sleeping pill. Jet-lag and sleep disturbances may be more severe in members of the team management than in players, the former being generally older and less fit than the latter.

5.5 Melatonin capsules

In normal circumstances, melatonin from the pineal gland is secreted into the blood stream between about 21:00 and 07:00 hours. It can be regarded as a 'dark pulse' or 'internal time cue'. Several studies have shown that melatonin capsules taken in the evening by local time in the new time-zone reduce the symptoms of 'jet-lag' (Arendt et al., 1987). This is an important finding, but there are some caveats:-

1. Jet-lag, as defined in these studies, has concentrated on subjective symptoms. It is not known if there would also be improvements in mental and physical performance, and in motivation to train hard - or even if there would be further decrements.
2. It is not clear if melatonin produces its effect by promoting adjustment of the body clock or by some other means (increasing a sense of well-being or the ability to sleep, for example). Recent work suggests that melatonin should adjust the body clock, but this requires careful timing of ingestion according to whether the need is to advance or delay the clock.
3. Melatonin is only just becoming commercially available (largely in the USA) and the results from many clinical trials are still awaited.

In summary, more information is required before melatonin can be recommended. Systematic monitoring of racket sports players voluntarily taking melatonin (freely available in USA but not licenced for Europe) during long haul flights and days afterwards would help in this respect.

5.6 Bright light exposure and physical activity

Bright light (that is, of an intensity found naturally but not normally indoors) can adjust the body-clock. The timing of exposure is crucially important (Minors et al., 1991) and is the opposite of that for melatonin ingestion; thus, bright light in the morning (05:00-11:00 hours) on body time advances the clock and bright light in the evening (21:00-03:00 hours) on body time delays it. As part of this treatment, there are also times when light should be avoided (those times which produce a shift of the body-clock in a direction opposite to that desired). Table 3 gives times when light should be sought or avoided after different time-zone transitions; the timing will vary as the body-clock adjusts.

Table 3. The use of bright light to adjust the body-clock after time-zone transitions

	Bad local times for exposure to bright light	Good local times for exposure to bright light
Time zones to the west		
4 h	01:00-07:00*	17:00-23:00†
8 h	21:00-03:00*	13:00-19:00†
12 h	17:00-23:00*	09:00-15:00†
Time zones to the east		
4 h	01:00-07:00†	09:00-15:00*
8 h	05:00-11:00†	13:00-19:00*
10-12 h	#Treat this as 12-14 hours to the west	

* Will advance the body-clock; † will delay the body-clock; # note that this is because the body-clock adjusts to delays more easily than advances.

Even though 'bright light' is of an intensity normally not achieved in domestic or interior lighting, light boxes and visors are now available commercially that produce a light source of sufficient intensity. Light visors, in particular, might prove useful.

Since outdoor lighting is the obvious choice, it would be natural, therefore, to consider training outdoors - such as jogging, a brisk walk, a swim or a light training session - when light is required, and to relax indoors when it should be avoided. This raises the question whether physical exercise and inactivity can, in some way, add to the effects of light and dark respectively. Current evidence is not conclusive.

For the first few days in the new time-zone, training sessions should not be all-out efforts. Skills requiring fine coordination are likely to be impaired and this might lead to accidents or injuries if, for example, racket sports players conducted training matches too strenuously. Where a series of tournament engagements is scheduled, it is useful to have at least one friendly match during the initial period, that is before the end of the first week in the overseas country. Subject to these caveats, exercise for racket sports players is recommended also since it helps them psychologically in their preparations for competition.

In practice, therefore, to combine exposure to bright light and exercise, and to combine dim light and relaxation, would seem practicable. However, there is very little evidence to suggest that exercise by itself will alter the speed of adjustment of the body-clock.

To a large extent it might be considered that to adjust as fully as possible to the *lifestyle and habits* in the new zone would be the best advice. This is not always the case on the first day or so after the flight. Consider a westward flight through eight time-zones. To delay the clock requires bright light at 21:00-03:00 hours body time and its avoidance at 05:00-11:00 hours. By new local time, this becomes equal to 13:00-19:00 hours for bright light and 21:00-03:00 hours for dim light (see Table 2). It can be seen that natural daylight and night would provide this. Consider, by contrast, a flight to the east through eight time-zones. Now light is required 05:00-11:00 hours body time (13:00-19:00 hours local time) and should be avoided 21:00-03:00 hours body time (05:00-11:00 hours local time). That is, morning light for the first day or so *would be unhelpful and tend to make the clock adjust in the wrong direction* (though afternoon and evening light are fine). The timing of exposure to bright light is critical on the first days after the flight. After a couple of days, when partial adjustment has occurred, it is then advised to adjust the timing of the light exposure towards that of the local inhabitants, so that the visitors' habits become synchronized with those of locals.

Sleep loss itself is unlikely to have a major adverse effect on exercise performance. In normal conditions the effects of substantial sleep disturbances are more pronounced on complex tasks than on gross measures such as muscle strength (Reilly and Piercy, 1994). Indeed the circadian variation in sports performances was greater than that induced by partial sleep deprivation over three consecutive nights (Sinnerton and Reilly, 1991). Difficulties in sleeping after crossing multiple time-zones are eventually self-correcting but disturbances may last longer following eastward compared to westward flights.

6 Overview

Circadian rhythms should be taken into account when travelling across multiple time-zones to compete in racket sports. Deleterious effects of jet-lag will be exacerbated if there are additional environmental stresses, such as heat or altitude, to be encountered. Performance can be adversely affected even when flights are within one country, coast to coast in USA and Australia, for example (Jehue et al., 1993). Whilst jet-lag symptoms persist, even if only periodically during the day, it is recommended that training is light in intensity to reduce possibilities of accidents and injuries occurring. Individuals may be more vulnerable to defeat in the early rounds of tournaments at the hands of home-based players, unless the need for adjustment to the new time-zone is considered in the timetable of the 'tour'.

7 References

Arendt, J., Aldhous, M., English, J., Marks, J., Arendt, J.H., Marks, M. and Folkard S. (1987) Some effects of jet-lag and their amelioration by melatonin. **Ergonomics**, 30, 1379-1393.

Atkinson, G., Coldwells, A., Reilly, T. and Waterhouse, J. (1994) The influence of age on diurnal variations in competitive cycling performance. **Journal of Sports Sciences**, 12, 127-128.

Coldwells, A., Atkinson, G. and Reilly, T. (1994) Sources of variation in back and leg dynamometry. **Ergonomics**, 37, 79-86.

de Looy, A., Minors, D.S., Waterhouse, J., Reilly, T. and Tunstall-Pedoe, D. (1988) **A Coach's Guide to Competing Abroad.** National Coaching Foundation, Leeds.

Graeber, R., Sing, H. and Cuthbert, B. (1981) The impact of transmeridian flight on deploying soldiers, in **Biological Rhythms, Sleep and Shift-work** (eds L. Johnson, D. Tepas, P. Colquhoun), MTP Press, Lancaster, pp. 513-537.

Harma, M., Laitinen, J., Partinen, M., Savanto, S. (1994) The effect of four-day round trip flights over 10 time zones on the circadian variation of salivatory melatonin and cortisol in air-time flight attendants. **Ergonomics**, 37, 1479-1489.

Jehue, R., Street, D. and Huizenga, R. (1993) Effects of time-zone and game time changes on team performance; National Football League. **Medicine and Science in Sports and Exercise**, 25, 127-131.

Leathwood, P. (1989) Circadian rhythms of plasma amino acids brain neurotransmitters and behaviour, in **Biological Rhythms in Clinical Practice** (eds J. Arendt, D. Minors, J. Waterhouse), John Wright, Bristol, pp. 146-159.

Minors, D.S. and Waterhouse, J. (1981) **Circadian Rhythms and the Human**. John Wright, Bristol.

Minors, D., Waterhouse, J., Wirz-Justice, A. (1991) A human phase-response curve to light. **Neuroscience Letters**, 133, 36-40.

Reilly, T. (1994a) Body clock and lifestyle disturbances, in **Proceedings, British Olympic Association International Conference "The Travelling Athlete's Environment"**, British Olympic Association, London, pp. 40-48.

Reilly, T. (1994b) Circadian rhythms, in **Oxford Textbook of Sports Medicine** (eds M. Harries, C. Williams, W.D. Stanish and L.J. Micheli), Oxford University Press, Oxford, pp. 238-254.

Reilly, T. and Brooks, G.A. (1982) Investigation of circadian rhythms in metabolic responses to exercise. **Ergonomics**, 25, 1093-1107.

Reilly, T. and Maskell, P. (1989) Effects of altering the sleep-wake cycle on human circadian rhythms and motor performance, in **Proceedings First IOC Congress on Sports Sciences** (Colorado Springs), pp. 106-107.

Reilly, T. and Mellor, S. (1988) Jet lag studies on Rugby League players following a near-maximal time-zone shift, in **Science and Football** (eds T. Reilly, A. Lees, K. Davids, W. Murphy). E. and F.N. Spon, London, pp. 249-256.

Reilly, T. and Piercy, M. (1994) The effect of partial sleep deprivation on weight lifting performance. **Ergonomics**, 37, 107-115.

Reilly, T., Atkinson, G. and Budgett, R. (1997a) Effect of temazepam on physiological and performance variables following a westerly flight across five time zones. **Journal of Sports Sciences**, 15, 62.

Reilly, T., Atkinson, G. and Waterhouse, J. (1997b) **Biological Rhythms and Exercise**. Oxford University Press, Oxford.

Reilly, T., Maughan, R.J., Budgett, R. and Davies, B. (1997) The acclimatisation of international athletes, in **Contemporary Ergonomics 1997** (ed. S.A. Robertson). Taylor and Francis, London, pp. 136-140.

Sinnerton, S. and Reilly, T. (1992) Effects of sleep loss and time of day in swimmers, in **Biomechanics and Medicine in Swimming: Swimming Science VI** (eds D. MacLaren, T. Reilly and A. Lees), E. and F.N. Spon, London, pp.399-405.

Waterhouse, J., Reilly, T. and Atkinson, G. (1997) Travel and body clock disturbances. **Sports Exercise and Injury**, 3, 9-14.

Part Four

Psychology of Racket Sports

15 From the laboratory to the courts: understanding and training anticipation and decision-making

R.N. Singer

Department of Exercise and Sport Sciences, University of Florida, Gainesville, Florida, USA

1 Overview

Great advancements have been made in recent years as to conditioning racket sport athletes, establishing guidelines for nutritional requirements, and facilitating the mastery of technical skills and tactics. However, in spite of the realisation of the importance of possessing exceptional anticipatory strategies and decision-making skills in situations with tight time constraints and uncertainty of opponent's intentions, little practical information has been generated from science as to how to improve the ways one might prepare to function most effectively in these situations.

In many respects, reactive behaviours on the court may be referred to as mental quickness (Singer, 1995). Typically, quickness on the court is perceived by many competitors, coaches, and spectators as reflected by fast hand and foot movements as well as changing directions immediately and appropriately depending on the demands of the activity. The emphasis is on the physical or motoric elements of quickness. Not realised is the role of cognitive processes and strategies that enable one to be in the right place at the appropriate moment. The result is more time to return an opponent's shot effectively.

A conceptualisation of mental quickness has been proposed recently by Singer (1995) and Singer et al. (1994). The outcome of overall quickness is movement reactions and completion of the act. This is the basis of the typical interpretation of an athlete's quickness. However, much information processing has to occur prior to the act itself. Attention to the most salient opponent cues, an awareness of his or her shot selection tendencies in particular situations, anticipating intentions, and making good decisions in response to the opponent's actions constitute those mental quickness processes that enable one to appear quick on the court. Obviously, physically and mechanically trained foot and hand movements per se complement the overall notion of quickness.

The premise here is that it is possible and indeed necessary to identify the most significant components of quickness which appear to interact in the production of skilled movement in reactive fast-paced racket sports. Perceptive assessments of players can determine specific deficiencies. Special training programmes can be

Science and Racket Sports II, edited by A. Lees, I. Maynard, M. Hughes and T. Reilly. Published in 1998 by E & FN Spon, 11 New Fetter Lane, London EC4P 4EE, UK. ISBN: 0 419 23030 0

designed to remedy shortcomings and to improve upon limitations. Assuming that all players have room to improve (within genetic constraints) upon the way they activate and implement personal resources, competitive play should be enhanced as well.

Therefore, the intention in this paper is to elaborate upon scientific perspectives related to attention, cue selection, anticipation, decision-making, and reactions. Three scientific paradigms can generate meaningful and practical insights about this motion: (1) the case study approach, in which high level athletes are asked about how they prepare for competition, cues they try to use to anticipate better in order to be in better court position, and how they activate good decisions; (2) the experimental approach, in which a group of athletes are trained with specific techniques to improve upon their strategies, and are compared in performance measures with a control group; and (3) the descriptive approach, in which experts are compared to novices in such measures as visual search and cue utilisation, anticipatory accuracy and speed related to the intentions of an opponent, and the quality of decision-making in response to an opponent's actions. The objective will be first to review briefly literature regarding these approaches, followed by what little is known about the viability of training programmes, and then to offer possible techniques that players can use to be at an advantage during competition.

2 What Does the Research Suggest with Regard to Understanding Attention, Anticipation and Decision-making?

Little is known about the complex interaction of the various cognitive components that contribute to reacting effectively under tight time constraints, as there is a scarcity of data related directly to quickness. Yet, there are many concepts from signal detection theory (Swets, 1964) and various models of attention (e.g., Broadbent, 1958; Theeuves, 1993; Treisman, 1988) that can offer insight. Likewise, research paradigms associated with understanding the nature of selective attention and the processing of information (Abernethy, 1993), decision-making (Tenenbaum & Bar-Eli, 1993), reaction time/movement time (Singer, 1980), as well as the dynamic aspects of human movement from cognitive-neuroscience perspectives (e.g., Stelmach & Requin, 1992) provide helpful perspectives. Indeed, a major contribution toward understanding visual perception and its relation to action in dynamic sport settings has been advanced by Williams et al. (in press).

In other words, there are rich bodies of literature that describe insights into information processing processes as well as the nature of the interplay of perception and action. They provide conceptual and research perspectives about the nature of the interests in this paper. However, the focus here on in will be oriented to sport-specific approaches that might reveal compelling evidence for the existence of a profile of the expert as to the productive use of internal processes under dynamic reactive circumstances.

2.1 Case studies
Typically in the case study approach, an athlete might be asked to reflect on what he or she thought about during a contest. Was it the opponent's tendencies to go for certain

shots in particular situations? Was it the attempt to pick up specific opponent cues that might help in anticipating shots? Was it the ability to make good decisions as to court position and shot selection?

Unfortunately, reflections on these situations are difficult to make accurately. High-level competitive racket sport contests are filled with continuous action. Indeed, skilled athletes performing at their very best often describe general personal states that have been termed "flow," "peak," or "the zone." Comments are made about the ease in execution, that there seemed to be plenty of time to hit good shots, and, in general, that the feeling was exhilarating. However, the details related to information pick-up, anticipation, and decision-making are rather vague. It is little wonder that case study research in this area has not been undertaken satisfactorily.

Another form of the case study approach was reported by Singer et al. (1996). Thirty highly-skilled collegiate tennis players were compared with 30 beginners in a laboratory using a variety of measures presumably related to tennis success. A subjective analysis was made of two of the best expert subjects (one female who had just turned professional and was doing exceptionally well, and one male who turned professional) and two randomly chosen subjects from the beginner subject pool. The qualitative analysis involved examining the eye scanning patterns of the four subjects. Specifically, the visual searching pathways were superimposed on filmed serves and ground strokes of an opponent. The overlaying technique involved the vertical and horizontal positions of the eyes dynamically superimposed on the two strokes (the model strokes that the players saw during testing). These two signals (eye position data and the models) were recorded on a separate videotape for later visual inspection. This technique allowed us to make qualitative assessments of what the players were focusing on and for how long.

In viewing the visual scanning information this way, a few obvious dramatic patterns emerged. During the serve, the highly-skilled players first focused on the racket arm and racket region, tracked the ball as it was tossed to the point of racket-ball contact, and then tracked the ball after it was hit. During the ground strokes, they first focused on the waist area, then the racket and racket-ball contact, and then tracked the ball. The experts were quite consistent in their visual search patterns, from trial to trial and between each other. Beginners were very scattered in their focus. They seemed to scan in many areas, were highly variable in their search process, and finally attempted to track the ball after it was contacted. Implications are that beginners badly need to be educated about relevant anticipatory cues!

2.2 Experimental evidence

A few studies have demonstrated improvement in predicting events; however, the training method was simply repeatedly exposing subjects to relevant task stimuli. Burroughs (1984) demonstrated enhanced prediction accuracy of pitch location in intercollegiate baseball players. In this study, players were asked to predict the location of a simulated pitch within the contexts of a rating grid. However, instruction in this programme only involved persistent exposure to the training film and feedback concerning the correctness of a subject's responses. In addition, Haskins (1965) found a decrease in response time to determine the direction of a tennis serve due to continual familiarity with a training film. Similarly, Day (1980) observed an increase in prediction accuracy of the landing position of a tennis ball over a 10-week training programme that only involved task repetition.

In these studies, training experiences primarily consisted of nothing more than repeated experiences with task-specific stimuli. However, better anticipation reflects a combination of directing attention early to appropriate cues, as well as extracting meaning from them to make appropriate conclusions about the intentions of the opponent. Therefore, the purpose of a study undertaken by Singer et al. (1994) was to determine if a training programme that included these two considerations was better than mere task exposure in contributing to one's ability to predict an opponent's intentions effectively in various tennis situations. More specifically, through simulated tennis situations in a laboratory setting, one group of beginning/intermediate tennis players was taught to attend to appropriate cues, as well as to derive meaning from them. The other group only received continued exposure to the same simulated tennis situations. Subjects in both groups were trained concurrently on the tennis court and in the laboratory. Generally speaking, the laboratory tests were encouraging in showing that players can learn to make faster and more accurate decisions in filmed tennis situations as a result of experiencing an appropriate anticipating training programme.

2.3 The expert-novice design

A very popular approach in the last 20 years to understand the attentional, perceptual, and decision-making processes of skilled performers is the use of the expert-novice design. Typically, beginners are compared to proficient performers in the way they function while attempting to accomplish the same sport tasks. On other occasions, experts only are studied to determine commonalities among them. Such was the case with the table tennis players to determine their visual search patterns, such as tracking a ball (Ripoll, 1988, 1989).

One primary component of mental quickness is the ability of an athlete to search visually for early cues with high predictive value as to the opponent's intentions. Researchers have used tracking systems that monitor eye positions to measure visual search strategies. The basic assumption of this assessment is that the characteristics of eye fixation patterns (e.g., location and duration) reflect the underlying perceptual strategies activated by the performer in order to selectively attend to and make meaning of relevant cues (Abernethy, 1988, 1993). (It should be pointed out that Viviani (1990) and Theeuwes (1993), among others in recent years, suggest that the role of cognition may not be inferred from eye movement data.)

Nonetheless, in a number of studies in a variety of sport situations, for example table tennis (Ripoll & Fleurance, 1988), scanning patterns of experts have been demonstrated to be more efficient than those of the novices. In monitoring the search patterns of tennis players while viewing a videotaped serve, Goulet, Bard, and Fleury (1989) observed a preponderance of fixations by the expert on the arm and racket to determine the outcome of the shot, whereas the novice focused primarily on the ball. Singer et al. (1996) compared high-level tennis players and novices under a variety of simulated tennis playing situations in a laboratory setting to test for visual search patterns, anticipation/decision-making, reactions, and movements. Visual search patterns were fairly similar between the groups (although the novices fixated on more irrelevant information, such as the opponent's head). Decision-making accuracy and speed, reflecting anticipation, was shown to be associated with the skilled players. The assumption is that they could make more and earlier meaning of the available cues (pattern recognition).

Findings of the research generally indicate the importance of mental quickness (from cue pick-up to anticipation to decision-making) leading to initiating and completing actions in a timely manner. The implications are that these behaviours can be improved upon through appropriate training, for all skill-level racket sport players. Instructors and coaches have predominately tried to improve speed on the court with physical drills such as quick sprints, line drills, and split steps. However, the mental aspect of quickness training is not typically emphasised in practice sessions.

2.4 A conceptualisation of quickness

For the purpose of scholarly and practical perspectives, it is believed that an information processing framework is appropriate. The most important objective is to determine the primary components of mental quickness in order to identify more precise strengths and limitations in players. This would lead to the formulation of appropriate training techniques to improve deficits.

If an athlete is said to be lacking quickness, it is necessary to know in what ways such shortcomings are exhibited. What is contributing to the problem? The first step in attempting to fix something is to understand what it is. Proposed here is that quickness can be analysed within an information processing model, and is composed of at least five components. It appears to be influenced by:

[1] Visual searching for the minimal number of cues but the most relevant opponent and situational ones at the right time[1].
[2] Anticipating early what the opponent will do on a probability basis, depending on the availability and recognition of these cues, knowing the opponent's tendencies, and considering the situation.
[3] Decision-making about what to do, with sufficient time to be effective
[4] Initiating the appropriate movements in a timely manner.
[5] Moving to complete the execution, considering the parts of the body (hands and/or feet) and perhaps the entire body placement, timed perfectly to accommodate the response.

As can be seen in Figure 1, the sequence can be depicted rather simply. Figure 2 presents the same ideas in the terms just described. Quickness in general involves well-trained attentional processes as well as visual and perceptual operations. It also requires rapid and accurate information processing, effective decision-making, and timely reacting. Physical capabilities then take over to implement the results of all of this processing. A break-down in any of these processes can contribute to a deficit in quickness.

It is difficult for expert players and coaches to appreciate the sequence of events which includes early cue identification, perceptions of the situation and anticipation,

---

[1] It is difficult to determine to what degree a player searches for certain cues and then anticipates what will happen, or if anticipation occurs first, leading to a visual search. They may indeed occur somewhat simultaneously. For convenience here, however, searching is suggested as preceding anticipation.

decision-making, and the initiation and completion of action, all of which must operate under extremely high time constraints. In fact, sport situations are even more complex than this. Once an action is being activated, the process continues so as to out-manoeuvre the opponent. Deceiving and anticipating go back and forth, and decisions and movements must occur with great rapidity. The challenge is also great for scientists and scholars to attain a significant level of understanding of what goes on internally, and how these operations can be improved upon. Nonetheless, it is fairly well-agreed that trying to infer the reasons for successful or unsuccessful actions by only observing the end result of performance is inadequate. In the last section, suggestions will be made for improving the mental side of performance.

3 Bridging Research and Practical Implications

So, how can research findings be of value to racket sport athletes? How can they improve upon attentional, anticipatory, and decision-making processes while in the midst of competition? First of all, an assumption must be made that these behaviours can be modified and improved upon.

3.1 Heredity vs. trainability

Many coaches and athletes seem to believe that concentration and attentional flexibility, court awareness, and strategic playing ability are genetically determined. Another view is that athletes can acquire relevant skills to sharpen the way ideal cognitive behaviours are exhibited. There is little doubt that genetics shape our anatomical structure, tendencies toward particular diseases, functional capabilities, and even personality. Indeed, an impressive amount of research has been generated in recent years about the genetic base of health and disorders. An issue of Science (1994) was dedicated to presenting the latest developments and issues regarding different topics associated with behavioural genetics. Continually discussed were intriguing possibilities about the impact of genes on behaviours. However, at the same time, frequently pointed out was the complex interaction between genetic determinants and environmental opportunities/experiences, resulting in such individual differences that generalisations in this area are somewhat hazardous.

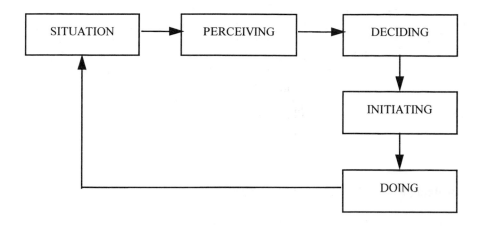

Figure 1. Simplified components of quickness.

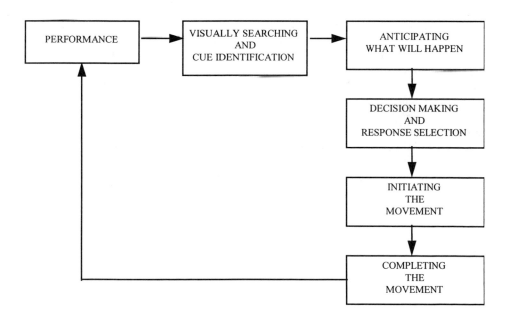

Figure 2.   Quickness as a function of information processing
            processes. Ultimate quickness in any situation depends upon
            the optimal function of these processes as well as body and
            limb movement applications.

Therefore, it is reasonable to expect that anyone can improve strategically in sport performance, within genetic limitations (or advantages). Improving on-court anticipation and decision-making, and overall quickness on the court, is dependent on learning relevant mental skills and physical/motoric conditioning. "Mental conditioning" can occur off-court, during practice, and immediately prior to and during competitive matches.

3.2 Off-court preparation

The serious racket sport competitor can allocate some off-court time periodically to "homework." This would take the form of mental rehearsal sessions as well as video sessions. The purpose of these would be to prepare oneself to think intelligently on the court.

Mental rehearsal (imagery, visualisation) has been demonstrated to enhance performance in a wide range of sport skills (e.g., Suinn, 1993). However, typically of focus is the act, such as serving the shuttlecock in badminton or hitting forehand and backhand strokes in squash. If the intention is to improve cue-pick-up, anticipation, decision-making, and reacting, then why not visualise a variety of game situations which require these behaviours? See that these processes are done well, as mental practice sessions remind one what to do and build confidence in being able to follow through successfully when in action.

Visualisation for return of serve in tennis, for example, might include: initial focus on chest/shoulder area of the opponent, with gaze shifting to ball toss and then to serving shoulder, to racket, to ball contact, to finally tracking the ball until the return is made. Ball toss (more forward or behind the head) will probably indicate the intent to hit a flat serve or a spin serve. Shoulder rotation can reveal an attempt to direct the serve to a certain location on the receiver's court. Such cues, along with an understanding of the capabilities and tendencies of the server, provide advance information that can be useful in estimating the intentions of the server. Such anticipation knowledge can help the receiver to get to the correct location more quickly, and to beplanning the return shot with sufficient time to execute ideally.

The serious minded competitor might consider the use of video - of self in previous competitions and of future opponents. Currently, videos are used frequently by athletes in basketball, American football, soccer, and other sports, but rarely in racket sports. Self-film of previous competitions is good for critiquing; determining whether good position is being realised, the appropriateness of court playing strategies, and the effectiveness of decisions made with regard to shot selection. Film of future opponents leads to knowing what playing style and tendencies to expect. Also, mannerisms and techniques preliminary to executing certain shots may lead to tipping off intentions. Essentially, this is homework - mental preparation for the next opponent with advance information.

3.3 On-court preparation

Key concepts here are simulation and designing special drills. Practice sessions, on occasion should be approached as if they were "the real thing." This means attempting to generate the context, the mood, the expectations, and the planning for them. Concentration, attentional distribution, anticipation, decision-making, and reacting should be worked on with the same dedication exhibited for improving the skills and tactics of the sport as well as conditioning for it.

Special drills with partners can be designed for each sport. With a little creativity, "games" can be made out of drills, making them more fun. (We have just created one for tennis; Singer & Steinberg, 1996). Drills work toward perfecting how one activates appropriate behaviours. Take the serve as an example. Two players can take turns as server and receiver. The server attempts to be consistent in preparatory and execution techniques while varying serve placement, velocity, and spin. Deception is important. The receiver works on attentional focus, cue scanning techniques, anticipation, decision-making, and stroke execution.

A "game" can be made of this drill. For example, the object of the game could be to determine who makes the most points - the server or the receiver. Each player hits 20 serves. The process will be similar as in a contest situation.

The server receives 2 points for each ace and 1 point for causing the receiver to make an in effective return. The receiver receives 2 points for a return "winner" and 1 point for a satisfactory return. Play stops following 20 serves for each player, with the winner" being the player with the most points.

If the coach or instructor is present, cuing the receiver at the right time would help. The coach or instructor could provide constructive feedback following the return of service as to what was done right and what could have been done more quickly and better. The emphasis would be on the way mental operations seem to be, or should be, functioning.

Similar drills could be established for aspects of game play. Objectives have to be defined clearly to improve upon the activation of appropriate mental operations. Boredom can be reduced if drills are made into games (as in the server example described previously). Coach/instructor prompting and feedback can help to facilitate the learning process.

Another type of one-on-one drill could be with the intention of working on approaching the net. Both players start at their respective baselines. The first player puts the ball in play with a firm stroke placing the opponent somewhat on the defensive. At the same time, he or she comes to the net. The object for the first player is to estimate where to be in position in anticipation of the opponent's return. The opponent will attempt to conceal the intended return and to vary the type of return. The first player not only should be in the ideal position, but then be able to put the ball away.

Each player would have 20 consecutive opportunities as "the aggressor." For the offensive player, 2 points would be awarded for being in the right place at the right time; 1 point for almost being there. Two points would be awarded for a put-away. For the defensive player, 2 points would be awarded for stroking the ball which is not returned; 1 point for a weak return by the offensive player that in turn would allow him/her to go the offensive. The player with the most points after each has played 20 approaches each would be the winner.

Drills need to be meaningful. In many practice situations, players respond too mechanically and indifferently without attempting to train their mental processes. It is one thing to strengthen stroke production over and over. It is another matter to train mental effectiveness leading to the stroke production. Mental operations can become more automatised, in the same way strokes can. Repeated practice in various situations with the intention of attaining goals will lead to their realisation.

3.4 Pre-competition and during competition

As in simulation practice, the key is mental preparation before competition and refining cognitive processes during competition so that a mental edge leads to more productive performance.

Mental preparation for a match should begin before even stepping on the court. If there is a familiar opponent, it is important to be aware of his/her strengths and weaknesses as well as preferred tendencies toward certain strokes and strategies. Visualising early cue-pick situations, good anticipation and decision-making, favourable court position, and making good decisions and strokes is helpful as a preparatory technique and a confidence-builder.

While warming up with the opponent, an attempt should be made to ascertain performance style and any cues as to what type of game he or she will play. Once in a match, continued concentration is necessary for everything to go right. During the early points, much can be learned about the opponent's strengths, weaknesses, tendencies, and "gift" cues about intentions. Court awareness is crucial. A point should never be played until and unless the player is mentally and emotionally ready to play that point. An initial optimal ready state leads to better focus, decisions, and execution. Prior to and during competition, self-verbal cues may be helpful or reminders to play opponents and points strategically.

Training mental processes is like training strokes. Both take time and deliberate intent to improve upon as was mentioned earlier. Both require a degree of conscious awareness and purpose. With consistency and excellence, both are produced as if automatically. Automatic behaviours are effortless. They involve fast information processing, and result in efficient and productive skills. However, there are times when the unexpected requires adaptive behaviours, more conscious control over what to do. The best players learn how to operate as if in a state of automaticity. They also seem to know intuitively when to accommodate the unexpected, to issue adaptive responses. Both automatic and adaptive behaviours can be acquired with appropriate practice.

Great players train with the intent of improving upon their conditioning, their sustained competitive intensity, their emotional control, their skilled production of accuracy of strokes, their tactics and their confidence. They also train their minds to read situations quickly and accurately, and to meet the challenge of preparing responses. But they are not satisfied only with making any kind of return. With efficient and effective mental functioning in crucial situations, they want to, and many times are able to, make offensive returns that will put their opponents on the defensive.

4 Conclusions

A "mental" player is one who effectively anticipates an opponent's intentions, is usually in the right location at the right time, and has sufficient time to make good decisions and movement reactions. With the objective of playing each match intelligently, and with more experience, less effort and deliberate consciousness will be expended toward cue awareness, anticipating and reacting. Research and intuition are strongly suggestive of the importance to the racket player of developing appropriate strategies to channel attention, direct focus toward valid anticipatory cues, and to "read" situational probabilities and specific opponent tendencies and intentions quickly in any competitive situation. A particular response repertoire needs to be adequately developed and associated with intentions and actions of any opponent. These behaviours can be improved in players of virtually any level of skill player who possesses the right intentions and appropriate experiences.

5 References

Abernethy, B. (1988) Visual search in sport and ergonomics: Its relationship to selective attention and performer expertise. **Human Performance**, 1, 205-235.

Abernethy B. (1993) Attention, in **Handbook of Research on Sport Psychology** (eds R.N. Singer, M. Murphey and L.K. Tennant) Macmillan, New York, pp. 127-170.

Broadbent, D.E. (1958) **Perception and Communication**, Pergamon, London.

Burroughs, W. (1984) Visual simulation training of baseball batters. **International Journal of Sport Psychology**, 15, 117-126.

Day, L. (1980) Anticipation in junior tennis players, in **Proceedings of the International Symposium on the Effective Teachings of Racket Sports** (eds J.L. Groppel and R. Sears) Champaign, IL, University of Illinois Press, pp.108-116.

Goulet, D., Bard, D. and Fleury, M. (1989) Expertise difference in preparing to return a tennis serve: A visual information processing approach. **Journal of Sport Psychology**, 11, 382-398.

Haskins, M. (1965) Development of response recognition training films in tennis. **Perceptual and Motor Skills**, 21, 201-211.

Ripoll H. (1989) Uncertainty and visual strategies in table tennis. **Perceptual and Motor Skills**, 68-507-512.

Ripoll, H., and Fleurance, P. (1988) What does keeping one's eye on the ball mean? **Ergonomics**, 31, 1647-1654.

Science (June 1994) Genes and behavior, 264, 1635-1816.

Singer, R.N. (1995) Mental quickness in dynamic sport situations, in **Sport Psychology: Perspectives and Practices Toward the 21st Century** (eds F.H. Fu and M.L. Ng), Baptist University Press, Hong Kong, pp. 63-82.

Singer, R.N. and Steinberg G. (1996) The Mental Side of Quickness (video). (Available from Gregg Steinberg, Dept. Of Health and Human Performance, Austin Peay University, Clarksville, Tennessee, USA).

Singer, R.N., Cauraugh, J.H., Chen, D., Steinberg, G.M., Frehlich, S.G., and Wang, L. (1994) Training mental quickness in beginning/intermediate players. **The Sport Psychologist**, 8, 305-318.

Singer, R.H., Cauraugh, J.H., Chen, D., Steinberg, G.M., and Frehlich, S.G. (1996) Visual search anticipation, and reactive comparisons between highly-skilled and beginning tennis players. **Journal of Applied Sport Psychology**, 8, 9-26.

Stelmach, G.E. and Requin, J. (eds) (1992) **Tutorials in Motor Behavior: II**. Elsevier Science, Amsterdam, Netherlands.

Suinn, R. (1993) Imagery, in **Handbook of Research on Sport Psychology** (eds R.N. Singer, M. Murphey, L.K. Tennant) Macmillan, New York, pp. 492-510.

Swets, J.A. (1964) Signal Detection and Recognition by Human Observers, Wiley, New York.

Tenenbaum, G. and Bar-Eli, M. (1993) Decision-making in sport: A cognitive perspective, in **Handbook of Research on Sport Psychology** (eds R.N. Singer, M. Murphey and L.K. Tennant) Macmillan, New York, pp. 171-192.

Theeuwes, J. (1993) Visual selective attention: A theoretical analysis. **Acta Psychologica**, 83, 93-154.

Treisman, A. (1988) Features and objects: The Fourteenth Bartlett Memorial Lecture. **The Quarterly Journal of Experimental Psychology**, 40A, 201-237.

Viviani, P. (1990) Eye movements in visual search: Cognitive, perceptual, and motor control aspects, in **Eye Movements and Their Role in Visual and Cognitive Processes** (ed. E. Kowler) Elsevier, Amsterdam, pp. 353-393.

Williams, A.M., Davids, K. and Williams, J.G. (in press). **Visual Perception and Sport Performance**, E. & F. N. Spon, London.

16 Visual search strategy in 'live' on-court situations in tennis: an exploratory study

A.M. William[1], R.N. Singer[2] and C. Weigelt[1]

[1]Centre for Sport and Exercise Sciences, Liverpool John Moores University, Liverpool, UK and [2]Department of Exercise and Sport Sciences, University of Florida, Gainesville, Florida, USA

1 Introduction

It is now widely accepted that skilled perception is an important characteristic of high level sports performance (Williams et al., 1993). This is particularly the case in fast ball sports such as tennis where ball velocity during the serve can reach values above 200 km.hr^{-1}. In such circumstances, the speed of play dictates that the receiver has to make a decision based on information arising prior to, or at least very soon after, ball-racket contact by the server. This suggests that the ability to use early advance cues from the opponent's service action as well as the effective co-ordination of head, eye and postural movements during ball flight would appear to be pre-requisites for successful performance.

During the past decade, researchers have attempted to identify important distinguishing characteristics between experts and novices with regard to perceptual skill in tennis (e.g., Goulet et al., 1989; Singer et al., 1996). Typically, these studies have highlighted the skilled tennis players' superior anticipatory performance, with this ability being due, at least in part, to their more appropriate visual search patterns. It appears that skilled performers fixate on more informative areas of the display, employ more efficient search rates and exhibit search patterns which are more systematic and consistent.

Although such studies have been successful in identifying some of the differences between experts and novices, they have not been without criticism. First, research has typically been conducted under laboratory situations with participants required to make simple responses to slide or film presentations. Not surprisingly, questions about the ecological validity of these contrived situations have increased in recent years (see Williams et al., 1993). Simplistic or artificial laboratory tasks may: a) negate the expert's advantage; b) cause them to function differently by denying them access to information they would normally use; or c) cause them to use different information to solve a particular problem.

Second, previous studies have only focused on the search behaviours employed prior to ball-racket contact by the server. The use of filmed displays has prevented scientists from investigating differences in search strategy while the ball is in flight as well as

Science and Racket Sports II, edited by A. Lees, I. Maynard, M. Hughes and T. Reilly. Published in 1998 by E & FN Spon, 11 New Fetter Lane, London EC4P 4EE, UK.   ISBN: 0 419 23030 0

during the execution of the service return. Bahill and LaRitz (1984) suggested that during the ball flight phase skilled tennis players may demonstrate faster smooth-pursuit eye movements, a good ability to suppress the vestibular-ocular reflex, and the occasional use of an anticipatory saccade. As yet, this suggestion has not been addressed empirically. Moreover, previous research has not examined the coupling between visual search behaviours (as inferred from point-of-gaze) and physical actions (as determined by the participant's movements) during the return of serve in tennis. Such an approach would enable researchers to address interesting questions regarding visual search strategy during different sub-phases of the return stroke.

Finally, the typical protocol in the past has been to compare experts with novices, rather than undertaking a within-group comparison of high-level performers on the variables of interest. Although previous research has highlighted large intra-group variability in visual search behaviours (see Williams et al., 1993), this has not been systematically investigated within a dynamic sports context. Clearly, such variability in search patterns suggests that factors other than visual search strategy may contribute to proficiency in sport.

The purpose of this study was therefore twofold. First, the study represents an initial attempt to assess visual search patterns in a dynamic 'on-court' situation in tennis. More specifically, we examined whether accurate visual search data could be collected whilst players prepared for and executed the return of serve. An attempt was also made to relate participants' physical actions to their visual search behaviours during the return of serve. Second, we examined the extent to which performance among expert tennis players could be differentiated on the basis of their visual search patterns.

2 Methods

2.1 Participants
Three male and two female highly-ranked players from the University of Florida tennis team were selected to participate in the study (mean age = 20.5 years). The women's team was ranked the number one collegiate team in the country, whilst the men's team was ranked in the top twenty.

2.2 Apparatus
An ASL 4000SU (Applied Science Laboratories, Waltham, Massachusetts, USA) eye movement registration system was used to collect visual search data. This is a video-based monocular system which measures eye-line-of-gaze with respect to a head-mounted scene camera. The system works by detecting two features, the pupil and the corneal reflex (reflection of a light source from the surface of the cornea), in a video image of the eye. The relative position of these features is used to compute visual gaze with respect to the optics. Displacement data from the left pupil and cornea were recorded by a small camera, processed by computer, and superimposed as a cursor on the scene camera image to highlight the point of gaze. The system was accurate (i.e., the difference between true eye position and measured eye position) to within ± 1 degree visual angle. System precision (i.e. the amount of instrument noise in the eye position

measure when the eye is perfectly stationary) was better than 0.5 degree in both horizontal and vertical directions.

In addition to the visual search data recorded, participants' physical responses were videotaped from behind at an angle of 45^0. This video image was temporally synchronised with the head-mounted scene camera image on the eye movement system, enabling a precise comparison of the players' physical actions relative to their visual search behaviours. These video images were interfaced using a digital effects mixer to obtain a split-screen effect such that the two images were located side-by-side on the same video image for subsequent analysis. Figure 1 shows the typical scene observed using the split-frame video technique.

2.3 Procedures

Since the eye movement registration system is particularly sensitive to direct sunlight, data were collected at night under floodlights. Upon arrival at the tennis courts, the test procedure was explained and the head-mounted optics were fitted on the participant's head. The system was then calibrated using a 9-point reference grid so that the recorded indication of fixation position corresponded to the participant's visual gaze. Thereafter, the calibration was checked every 3 to 4 serves. All participants reported that the helmet was comfortable and did not interfere with performance. After initial calibration, participants positioned themselves near the baseline and prepared to return serves as well as possible, as if they were playing in a competitive match. Participants' visual search behaviours as well as their physical actions were then recorded as they prepared for and executed returns of service. Service return data were collected for a total of 10 good serves (placement). Participants were tested in pairs with one acting as server and the other as receiver. The servers were informed to serve in a manner similar to a match situation.

Qualitative measures as to the effectiveness of each service return were also obtained by asking two experienced tennis coaches to rate each return on a 1 (poor) to 10 (excellent) Likert scale based on shot placement and velocity. The test session lasted approximately 20 minutes.

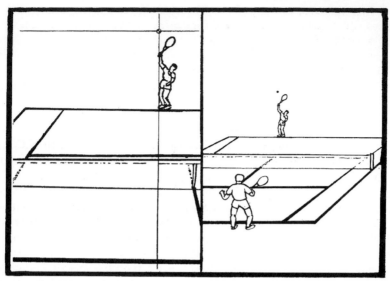

Figure 1. The scene observed using the split-screen approach. The right side of the screen shows the image from the external scene camera highlighting the participant's movements during the return of serve, whilst the left side of the screen illustrates the typical image obtained from the head-mounted scene camera with visual point-of-gaze highlighted by the cross-hairs.

2.4 Analysis of data

The Observer (Noldus, Wayeningen, The Netherlands) software system for the collection and analysis of observational data was used to analyse the video-taped image on a frame-by-frame basis. This enabled the participants' visual search behaviours (pursuit tracking, saccades, visual fixation) and their physical actions (ritual, backswing, foreswing, follow through phases of the service return) to be analysed relative to each other and to the different temporal phases of the serve (ritual phase, ball toss, ball-racket contact by server to ball bounce, ball bounce to ball-racket contact by receiver).

3 Results

3.1 Ball velocity and quality of service return

The mean values for ball velocity (as determined by video analysis) during the initial 'pre-bounce' portion of the serve and the qualitative assessment of the return of serve are highlighted in Table 1.

Table 1. Mean ball (±SD) velocity during the serve for male (M) and female (F) players

	M1	M2	M3	F1	F2
Mean Ball Velocity m.s^{-1}	53.5 (8.6)	34.8 (2.8)	37.0 (8.0)	29.0 (2.2)	31.4 (2.5)
Quality of Service Return (1-10 Likert Scale)	5.0 (1.8)	7.6 (1.8)	6.8 (0.8)	7.4 (1.1)	5.3 (1.9)

3.2 Visual behaviours during the temporal phases of the serve

Ritual phase - The higher ranked players (M3, F1), as determined by their N.C.A.A. (US National Collegiate Athletic Association) rankings and qualitative assessment of the service return, fixated on the arm-racket-shoulder region during this phase (see Table 2). However, two participants tended to focus specifically on the racket rather than the more general arm-racket-shoulder region. Surprisingly, these two players also tended to move their fixation towards the expected ball toss area even during this early stage. Finally, most players occasionally fixated on the server's head.

Table 2. Mean percentage of total number of fixations on each of the locations during the ritual phase

	M1	M2	M3	F1	F2
Arm-racket-shoulder			80%	60%	100%
Racket	40%	60%			
Head	20%	20%	20%	40%	
Expected Ball Area	40%	20%			

Ball toss phase - Three types of visual behaviours were observed (see Table 3). Participants M3 and F1 always tracked the ball using smooth-pursuit eye movements to the highest point of the ball toss. In contrast, M2 used a visual saccade to follow the ball to the apex of the toss. Participant M1 didn't maintain fixation on the ball via pursuit or tracking eye movements, but rather tended to fixate a-priori the expected ball toss area. Finally, F5 tended to maintain fixation on the racket during the ball toss phase.

Table 3. Mean percentage of visual behaviours during the ball toss phase

	M1	M2	M3	F1	F2
Pursuit tracking of the ball	40%		100%	100%	
Saccades to follow the ball		100%			
Fixations on areas other than the ball	60% (expected ball toss area)				100% (racket)

Ball-racket contact by server to ball bounce - Perhaps the most significant variation in visual search behaviour between players was observed after ball contact by the server. Table 4 highlights the different search strategies employed during the initial portion of ball flight.

Participants M1 and M2 made no attempt to visual track the ball during flight, rather they employed an anticipatory or predictive saccade to fixate the expected ball bounce area. In contrast, the higher ranked players (M3, F1) nearly always maintained fixation on the ball via pursuit tracking eye movements, whilst M2 used a combination of these two visual behaviours.

Table 4. Mean percentage of visual behaviours during the initial portion of ball flight

	M1	M2	M3	F1	F2
Pursuit tracking only			90%	100%	
Saccade only	100%				100%
Combination of pursuit tracking and saccades		100%	10%		

Ball bounce to ball contact by receiver - Table 5 highlights the search behaviours observed. Participants M3 and F1 tracked the ball via smooth-pursuit eye movements until the ball was 184 (SD$\pm$60) ms and 160 (SD$\pm$28) ms away from racket contact respectively. Initially, participant M2 tended to pursuit track the ball before it bounced. Thereafter, he employed a visual saccade to bring the eye onto the ball and then pursuit tracked the ball until it was 120 (SD$\pm$56) ms away from racket contact. Participants M1 and F2 did not fixate the ball, but employed a predictive saccade to bring the eye into the general vicinity of ball-racket contact.

Table 5. Mean percentage of visual behaviours during the final portion of ball flight

	M1	M2	M3	F1	F2
Pursuit tracking only			100%	100%	
Saccade only	100%				100%
Combination of pursuit tracking and saccades		100%			

3.3 Temporal characteristics of the return of serve

Subtraction of a visual reaction time latency value of 200 ms (based on the work of McLeod, 1987) suggests that participants made a decision regarding whether to return the serve via forehand or backhand stroke some 16-152 ms after the ball left their opponent's racket, whilst a decision regarding the return stroke (i.e., initiation of foreswing) was made 296-416 ms before ball arrival.

Table 6. Mean (±SD) values for the time of initiation of backswing relative to ball-racket contact by the server and the initiation of foreswing relative to ball-racket contact by the receiver

	M1	M2	M3	F1	F2
Initiation of backswing relative to ball-racket contact by server	240 ms (48)	224 ms (60)	352 ms (110)	272 ms (65)	216 ms (60)
Initiation of foreswing relative to ball-racket contact by receiver	216 ms (80)	200 ms (48)	96 ms (35)	144 ms (35)	176 ms (72)

4 Discussion and Conclusions

This study was the first in which the visual search patterns of highly skilled players were analysed on the tennis court where responses were made to a real rather than filmed opponent. Also, unlike many other investigations in which the relatively obvious differences between experts and novices have been compared, this study was unique in that we attempted to examine the subtle differences in visual search behaviours between highly ranked collegiate players. The results indicated that the higher ranked players initially focused on the arm-racket-shoulder and then tracked the ball as it was tossed to the point of ball contact. Conversely, in the time period immediately before the toss, lower ranked players either focused on the expected ball toss area or followed the ball from toss to apex using visual saccades. The greatest variation in visual search behaviour was observed after ball-racket contact by the server. The higher ranked players had a more consistent smooth-pursuit pattern from service to ball return, implying use of the eye-head movement system to extract ball flight information. Although the lower ranked players' scanning patterns were considerably more scattered and variable, they tended to use anticipatory saccades to place the eye ahead of the ball and then let the ball move across the retina, implying use of the image-retina system (see Haywood, 1984). Although research has not clearly demonstrated the superiority of either system, the consistent use of smooth pursuit tracking by the higher ranked players implicates the more effective use of eye and head movements. However, it is likely that the effectiveness of either system is dependent on ball velocity as well as the player's dynamic visual acuity (DVA). Interestingly, Sanderson (1981) suggested that skilled players may be more 'velocity-resistant' with regard to DVA than less skilled performers, demonstrating a relatively slow deterioration in pursuit tracking ability with increasing ball velocity. Also, research has suggested that DVA performance can be improved following a modest period of training (Long and Riggs, 1991).

Finally, though the data summarised above are of interest to tennis-specific questions, the primary purpose of the study was to establish whether eye-monitoring equipment could be used effectively in a real-world setting. Overall, preliminary findings indicate that the ASL 4000SU system is potentially valuable not only for research, but also for training anticipation, selective attention and ball-tracking skills in tennis.

5 References

Bahill, A.T. and LaRitz, T. (1984) Why can't batters keep their eyes on the ball? **American Scientist**, 72, 249-253.

Goulet, C., Bard, C. and Fleury, M. (1989) Expertise differences in preparing to return a tennis serve: A visual information processing approach. **Journal of Sport and Exercise Psychology**, 11, 382-398.

Haywood, K.M. (1984) Use of the image-retina and eye-head movement visual systems during coincidence-anticipation performance. **Journal of Sports Sciences**, 2, 139-144.

Long, G. M. and Riggs, C.A. (1991) Training effects on dynamic visual acuity with free-head viewing. **Perception**, 20, 363-371.

McLeod, P. (1987) Visual reaction and high-speed ball games. **Perception**, 16, 49-59.

Sanderson, F. H. (1981) Visual acuity and sports performance, in **Vision and Sport** (eds I.M. Cockerill and W.W. MacGillivary), Cheltenham, England: Stanley Thornes, pp. 64-79.

Singer, R.N., Cauraugh, J.H., Chen, D., Steinberg, G.M., and Frehlich, S.G. (1996) Visual search, anticipation, and reactive comparisons between highly-skilled and beginning tennis players. **Journal of Applied Sport Psychology**, 8, 9-26.

Williams, A.M., Davids, K. Burwitz, L. and Williams, J.G. (1993) Visual search and sports performance. **Australian Journal of Science and Medicine in Sport**, 22, 55-65.

17 Perceptions of the direction of multi-dimensional state anxiety during performance in elite and non-elite male tennis players

J. Smith[1] and G. Jones[2]
[1]Centre for Sport and Exercise Sciences, Liverpool John Moores University, Liverpool, UK and [2]Department of Physical Education, Sports Science and Recreation Management, Loughborough University, Loughborough, UK

1 Introduction

A considerable amount of research has examined the area of competitive state anxiety and its effects on performance (Jones, 1995). This research has been associated with the development of the Competitive State Anxiety Inventory-2 (Martens et al., 1990). Despite the inventory's popularity, Jones and Swain (1992) have criticised it for failing to take into account the directionality of the anxiety symptoms.

Directionality is considered by many as an important factor (Jones et al., 1994). Jones et al. (1994) revealed no significant differences in the cognitive and somatic intensity scores of skilled and low skilled athletes; however, skilled athletes did perceive their intensity levels as being more facilitative to performance. Swain and Jones (1996) also noted that directionality was a better predictor of performance than intensity.

More recently, researchers have begun to focus on qualitative methodologies in order to attain a more in-depth understanding of the anxiety-performance relationship (Gould et al., 1992).

This study employed a qualitative approach to explore the anxiety-performance relationship in a sample of male elite and non-elite tennis players. The aim was to identify the perceived direction of *in vivo* anxiety, and how this was thought to mediate performance globally and specifically.

2 Methods

2.1 Subjects

The subjects comprised 8 British tennis players with a mean age of 17 years. Elite (n=4) and non-elite (n=4) players were distinguished by their British rating. The elite players had a British rating of +2/6 (Division 2) or above, with some holding junior world rankings. The non-elite players were competitive club players who had an average British rating of +15/2 (Division 4) and no junior world ranking.

Science and Racket Sports II, edited by A. Lees, I. Maynard, M. Hughes and T. Reilly. Published in 1998 by E & FN Spon, 11 New Fetter Lane, London EC4P 4EE, UK.   ISBN: 0 419 23030 0

2.2 Measures

A standardised format was used for the interview schedule, designed in accordance with Patton's (1980) recommendations. The schedule comprised of five core sections. The main sections focused on *in vivo* state anxiety and were sub-sectioned into cognitive anxiety, somatic anxiety and self-confidence.

A tennis performance list was also developed, categorising basic core skills: percentage of first serve, percentage of second serve, return of serve percentage, number of double faults, number of aces, forehand, backhand, volley, lob, smash and drop-shot/stop volley.

2.3 Procedure and data analysis

Retrospective taped interviews were carried out and the data were subjected to both content and frequency analysis (Côté et al., 1993).

The interviews were transcribed verbatim. Preparation and inductive analysis of data were conducted in accordance with established protocol of Gould et al. (1992). Altogether 150 raw data themes were identified. From these, 41 higher order sub-themes and 6 higher order themes emerged from both the elite and non-elite players. For each section there was one general dimension, namely cognitive anxiety, somatic anxiety and self-confidence.

Triangular consensus was reached with an independent qualitative researcher on all themes. Follow-up deductive analysis provided additional verification of the inductive analysis themes. Comparisons were then made between elite and non-elite themes.

Data obtained from the *in vivo* interview were analysed by descriptive and frequency analysis. A comparative frequency analysis was conducted for the two groups of subjects with regards to the effects of anxiety and self-confidence upon core skills of performance.

3 Results

3.1 *In vivo* cognitive anxiety

For elite players, 25 raw data themes were categorised into 9 higher order sub-themes (HOST), 5 of which were then categorised into the higher order theme (HOT)-"facilitative cognitive anxiety" and four into the HOT "debilitative cognitive anxiety". For facilitative cognitive anxiety, tactical strategy focus was composed of the most raw data themes. Typically these thoughts revolved around the player's own game and ability: "*I used the change of ends to ...analyse what to do*". However, "task irrelevant thoughts": "*I just hoped he'd double fault or something*" was the factor that caused most players to perceive their anxiety as debilitative.

Twelve raw data themes were obtained from the non-elite players. These were organised into eight HOSTs, three under the facilitative HOT and five under the debilitative HOT. Game facilitation under pressure: "*I played the big points better than him more of the time*", was perceived by 50% of the players to be the most influential factor. Half of the players identified opponents' influence (negative), tactical error, and physical rage: "*I got angry and threw my racket*".

3.2 *In Vivo* somatic anxiety

Twenty raw data themes were extracted from the elite players' interviews. Ten HOST's, were equally divided into two HOT, namely "facilitative somatic anxiety" and "debilitative somatic anxiety". Specific timing of positive feeling states, positive feelings states in general, and positive physical states was associated most with the facilitative anxiety. The most detrimental effect upon their anxiety was reported to be the timing of negative feeling states: *"my stomach was upset a little bit in the last game" [of the match]*.

Non-elite players produced twenty one raw data themes, categorised into eight HOST's and equally divided into the two HOT's. Timing of positive feeling states and positive feeling states in general had the greatest effect on facilitative anxiety. Factors most affecting debilitative anxiety were defined as timing of negative physical states: *"I was very tired in the last set. I had a lot of long rallies and my legs went a bit"*, the timing of negative feeling states and negative feeling states in general.

3.3 *In vivo* self-confidence

For the elite players, fourteen raw data themes were organised into eight HOST's. Seven were classified into the HOT of "high self-confidence", whilst the HOT of "low self-confidence" contained only one HOST.

Effects upon positive cognitive states: *"I truly believed deep down that I'd win, and that helped me stay positive"*, and positive states in general were identified as the two major factors influencing high self-confidence. The only factor which contributed to low self-confidence for elite players was the timing of self-belief with negative consequences: *"My self-confidence went down a little bit when I lost the first set"*.

Twenty raw data themes emerged from the non-elite players. Eleven HOST's were developed with eight of these placed into the HOT of high self-confidence. The non-elite players cited effects upon positive cognitive states, positive states in general and timing of positive self-belief as most influential on their high self-confidence: *"Even when he [opponent] was a break up in the second [set], I was still confident"*. Half of the players perceived over-confidence to contribute to errors, with repetition causing low self-confidence: *"I did get over-confident and missed silly shots"*.

3.4 Anxiety and self-confidence effects upon core skill in performance

Table 1. Number of elite and non-elite players affected positively and/or negatively
by the three components of multidimensional anxiety

Core skills of performance	Cognitive anxiety		Somatic anxiety		Self-confidence	
	Elite	Non-elite	Elite	Non-elite	Elite	Non-elite
% of first serves						
Positive effect	4	3	1	0	3	2
Negative effect	4	0	0	3	0	1
% of second serves						
Positive effect	1	0	1	0	1	1
Negative effect	0	1	0	1	0	0
% return of serve						
Positive effect	3	1	1	0	1	0
Negative effect	0	1	0	0	0	0
Number of double faults						
Positive effect	1	0	0	0	0	1
Negative effect	1	1	0	0	0	0
Number of aces						
Positive effect	2	0	0	0	1	1
Negative effect	0	0	0	1	0	0
Forehand						
Positive effect	2	0	0	0	1	0
Negative effect	0	0	0	0	0	0
Backhand						
Positive effect	0	0	0	1	0	0
Negative effect	0	0	1	0	0	0
Volley						
Positive effect	1	0	3	0	0	0
Negative effect	0	0	0	0	1	2
Lob						
Positive effect	0	0	0	0	0	0
Negative effect	0	0	0	0	0	0
Smash						
Positive effect	0	0	0	0	0	0
Negative effect	0	0	0	0	0	1
Dropshot						
Positive effect	1	1	0	0	0	2
Negative effect	0	1	0	0	1	1

Non-elite players reported twice as many core skills being negatively affected by
cognitive anxiety as the elite players. Elite players showed almost three times as
many core skills were positively affected by their perceptions of cognitive anxiety.
Both groups acknowledged that percentage of first serves and return of serve
percentage were most affected by their cognitions, either positively or negatively.

In the non-elite group, three core skills were perceived to be negatively affected by debilitative somatic anxiety, for example, the percentage of first serves was cited by 75% of players. Only one skill was positively affected for facilitative somatic anxiety for the non-elite players (backhand, 25%). Only one skill was negatively affected for debilitative somatic anxiety for the elite players (backhand, 25%) with four skills positively affected by facilitative somatic anxiety, in particular the volley (75%): "*My volleys were really solid because I was feeling pumped up physically*".

Although both groups had five core skills positively affected by high self-confidence, the non-elite players had twice as many skills negatively affected by low self-confidence, namely percentage of first serves, volley, smash and drop shot. Elite players reported percentage of first serves as being most affected in a positive direction (75%): "*The more confident I became, the harder I hit the serve [and] the more it went in*". Non-elite players reported percentage of first serves and drop shots as being most positively affected.

4 Discussion

Elite players elicited more facilitative cognitive and somatic anxiety HOSTs compared to non-elite players. However, somewhat surprisingly the elite players also reported a considerable number of debilitative HOSTs. Indeed, for somatic anxiety an even distribution of facilitative and debilitative HOSTs were generated. Both the elite and non-elite players identified a greater number of high self-confidence HOSTs than low self-confidence HOSTs.

These findings partially support earlier research which suggests elite athletes perceive their anxiety as more facilitative and experience higher self-confidence compared to non-elite athletes (Jones et al., 1994). The generation of an even split between facilitative and debilitative HOSTs for elite players, coupled with non-elite players reporting a number of facilitative HOSTs, suggests that differences between elite and non-elite may not be as clear cut as originally thought.

Perceived direction of anxiety and self-confidence were also noted to have a differentiated impact on the tennis players' core skills. The most affected core skill was the first serve. This could be explained by an examination of the nature and circumstances of the shot. The serve is cited as one of the most important shots in the players' repertoire and the only shot that players can execute in their own time. The pre-serve protocol may allow time for anxiety and/or self-confidence symptoms to manifest themselves, either positively or negatively. Overall, direction of anxiety and self-confidence was perceived to be more detrimental for non-elite than elite players and all players felt that their perceptions of anxiety influenced the execution of certain core skills.

5 Conclusion

This study examined the perceptions of the direction of multidimensional state anxiety amongst tennis players of different skill levels, and the effects upon core skills of performance. Although the small sample size used in the study meant that results could not be generalised to the population at large, it did provide a basis for future research. The study suggested the need to break down performance into core skills, and to allow a deeper understanding of *in vivo* anxiety and self-confidence effects.

This study also demonstrated how a qualitative approach to research can elicit fresh perspectives on the stress and performance relationship.

6 Acknowledgements

The assistance of David Gilbourne with the review of earlier drafts of the manuscript is greatly appreciated.

7 References

Côté, J., Salmela, J. H., Baria, A. and Russell, S. J.(1993) Organising and interpreting unstructured qualitative data. **The Sport Psychologist**, 7 (2), 127-137.

Gould, D., Eklund, R. C. and Jackson, S. A. (1992) 1988 U.S. Olympic wrestling excellence: I Mental preparation, precompetitive cognition and affect. **The Sport Psychologist**, 6, 358-382.

Jones, G. (1995) More than just a game: research developments and issues in competitive anxiety in sport. **British Journal of Psychology**, 86, 449-478.

Jones, G. and Swain, A. (1992) Intensity and direction as dimensions of competitive state anxiety and relationships with competitiveness. **Perceptual and Motor Skills,** 74, 467-472

Jones, G., Hanton, S. and Swain, A. (1994) Intensity and interpretation of anxiety symptoms in elite and non- elite sports performers. **Personality and Individual Differences**, 17, 657-663.

Martens, R., Vealey, R. S. and Burton, D. (1990) **Competitive Anxiety in Sport.** Champaign, III: Human Kinetics.

Patton, M. Q. (1980) **Qualitative Evaluation Methods**. Sage, Beverley Hills.

Swain, A. and Jones, G. (1996) Explaining performance variance: the relative contribution of intensity and direction dimensions of competitive anxiety in sport. **Anxiety, Stress and Coping**, 9, 1-18.

18 The method of research into the speed of specific movements and anticipation in sport under simulated conditions in table tennis

J. Lapszo
University School of Physical Education, Gdansk, Poland

1 Introduction

The movements in ball games or combative sports there is often consist of two separate specific movements performed sequentially. Firstly, a displacement in the direction of the moving ball or opponent (displacement movement) which is followed by contact with it or him/her (target movement). Together, these two movements constitute a sequential movement. The speed and accuracy of sequential movements are related to the anticipation of coincidence, which means that the competitor visually tracks the movement of the opponent or ball, predicts the time or place (or both) at which the opponent or ball will arrive, and executes a coincident response (Belisle, 1963). This anticipation was divided into *place* and *movement coincidence anticipation* (Lapszo and Morawski, 1994). In the first case, the place towards which the ball is moving will be anticipated. In the second case, the anticipation determines the spatial and temporal coincidence of the player's and ball's movement. The place coincidence anticipation is based on the recognition of an *anticipatory stimulus* which constitutes the opponent's movement or the early phase of the ball's path. The final phase of the ball's path can be treated as a *target stimulus*, which is the basis for the movement coincidence anticipation. These anticipatory or target stimuli initiate sequential movements. Sequential movements initiated by anticipatory stimuli are called *anticipatory sequential movements*. The initiation of sequential movements on the basis of the middle or final phase of the ball's path is characteristic of *simple sequential movements*. Place coincidence anticipation is based on memorisation of the way in which the ball was struck and the place where the ball ended up. Memorised experiences of this kind make up an *anticipatory schema*, the essence of which is similar to Schmidt's motor schema (Schmidt, 1975). The process of interpolating the information memorised in the anticipatory schema is the basis of place coincidence anticipation. It requires concentration on the essential details of the opponent's movement, and then switching the attention to the final phase of the ball's path. A smaller capacity for anticipation leads to the subject reacting in the form of simple

Science and Racket Sports II, edited by A. Lees, I. Maynard, M. Hughes and T. Reilly. Published in 1998 by E & FN Spon, 11 New Fetter Lane, London EC4P 4EE, UK.   ISBN: 0 419 23030 0

sequential movements. The speed of these movements is related to genetic speed factors.

The purpose of this paper is to introduce a multi-dimensional method of research into the speed of sequential movements in sport under simulated conditions. The following psychomotor factors were taken into consideration: behavioural fluctuations caused by variations in attention concentration, motivation, arousal (Hull, 1942), the speed of anticipatory and simple sequential movements, and the capability of place coincidence anticipation. These factors were examined as a psychomotor aptitude for sport. A selection procedure based on cluster analysis is also described.

2 Methods

2.1 Subjects
The method is presented on the basis of table tennis. Ten adult male members of the Polish national table tennis team, and 22 children with an average age of 13.15 years and an average of 4.34 years of special training participated in the research.

2.2 Apparatus

2.2.1 The simulatory timer of movement speed and anticipation
The timer consists of a specific simulator, control card and computer. The specific simulator is applied in the investigation of the speed of specific movements in a selected sport and constitutes an exchangeable element of the timer. The simulator for research in table tennis was used in this experiment.

2.2.2 The simulator of play in table tennis
This consists of a stimuli board, a set of sensors and a special table tennis bat (Fig. 1). The speed of seven specific sequential movements can be tested with the simulator. The range of movements was 0.4 - 2.25 m. The anticipatory sequential movements were stimulated by seven constant pairs of lamps (one on the board and another in the sensor), which constituted the anticipatory schema.. Both lamps were switched on sequentially (simulated ball flight). The lamps on the board acted as the anticipatory stimuli, indicating the position of the sensors corresponding to them. In this way, place coincidence anticipation could be taken into consideration. The simple sequential movements were stimulated only by lamps in the sensors, which functioned as the target stimuli.

2.2.3 Measurements
The subject's task was to simulate the striking of the ball at the places indicated indirectly by the lamps on the board (anticipatory sequential movements) or directly by the lamps in the sensors (simple sequential movements). The simulated forehand and backhand strokes were executed by hitting flexible straps attached to the sensors with a table tennis bat equipped with an infra-red transmitter (the construction of the

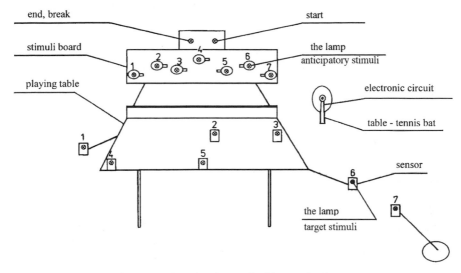

Figure 1. The simulator of table tennis play.

Simulatory Timer of Movement Speed and Anticipation and of the sensors is provided by patent law). The time (in seconds) elapsing from switching on the lamp on the stimuli board (learning process) or in the sensor (speed of anticipatory and simple sequential movements) to the instant of simulating the hitting of the ball was the measure of the speed of particular movements. The sensors identified the instant of the simulated stroke photoelectrically (infra-red receiver), thereby enabling the movements to be performed at maximum speed. The speed of seven different anticipatory and simple sequential movements was investigated in two series (tests) of 17 different measurements. The result of the whole test was the average of these 17 measurements.

2.3 Behavioural fluctuations

2.3.1 The curve of learning
Learning curves were used to investigate behavioural fluctuations. These curves illustrate the process by which the anticipatory schema develops. A test of the speed of anticipatory sequential movements was used to investigate the learning process. This test was repeated many times until the measurements stabilised. The results obtained were approximated by the exponential learning curve. An example of the learning curve is shown in Fig. 2. The following formula of this curve was used:

$$T(p) = (T_{max} - T_p) \times (1 - I_t)^{(P-1)} + T_p \qquad (1)$$

where p - serial number of the trial, T(p) - the result of the test as a function of the trial, T_{max} - the lowest speed of anticipatory sequential movements, I_t -increase in learning (memory) in each trial (computed), T_p - potential speed (the asymptote of the learning curve, computed).

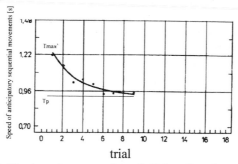

trial

Figure 2. The learning curve for a Polish national team player.

2.3.2 The index of behavioural fluctuations

The changes in attention concentration, motivation and arousal produced dispersal of test results around the learning curve. The statistical parameter R^2 showing the magnitude of this dispersal was used as the index of behavioural fluctuations. If $R^2 = 1$, all the test results lie on the learning curve.

2.4 The speed of anticipatory and simple sequential movements

Two different tests were used to investigate the speed of anticipatory and simple sequential movements. The research lasted 5 days and the tests were repeated twice a day. The ten results obtained for each kind of movement were then averaged in order to obtain the final speed of anticipatory and simple sequential movements.

2.5 Place coincidence anticipation

The increase (as a percentage) in the speed of sequential movements resulting from place coincidence anticipation was treated as an index of this anticipation (I_{pca}). Place coincidence anticipation is based on association of the position of the sensor with a particular lamp (anticipatory stimuli) on the stimuli board. The speeds of the anticipatory (T_{asm}) and simple (T_{ssm}) sequential movements described above were used to calculate the index I_{pca} according to the following formula:

$$I_{pca} = \frac{T_{ssm} - T_{asm}}{T_{ssm}} \times 100\% \tag{2}$$

This shows the extent to which the speed of displacement to the place towards which the ball is moving increases as a result of place coincidence anticipation.

2.6 Selection

The psychomotor factors were investigated in order to check aptitude for sport were correlated with the sporting ranking of the national team players. This group was then divided into six sub-groups (A,B,C,D,E,F) using cluster analysis (multidimensional graduation). The dimensions of this analysis were the speeds of anticipatory and simple sequential movements, and the indices of behavioural fluctuations and anticipation. Each group obtained a rank and in this way the psychomotor ranking was composed. This ranking was then correlated with sporting ranking. Cluster analysis was used to select very talented players and children, and to discover the psychomotor weaknesses of less talented players.

3 Results and Discussion

Table 1. The mean index of behavioural fluctuations (R^2) for men and children

Group tested	N	R^2	SD
men	10	0.84	0.11
children	22	0.78	0.12

SD - standard deviation

The index R^2 was greater than 0.75 (the lower limit of the occurrence of learning). This implies that both groups were able to learn the anticipatory behaviour. The fluctuations in attention concentration, motivation and arousal were less in men (0.84>0.78, less dispersal). These results are in accordance with Nettleton's (1986) research, which indicated the differences in attention flexibility between elite and less-skilled athletes in fast-ball games. The high standard deviation also indicates high individual differences in behavioural fluctuations.

Table 2. The mean speeds of anticipatory (T_{asm}) and simple sequential (T_{ssm}) movements, and the index of anticipation (I_{pca}) for men and children

Group tested	N	T_{asm} (s)	SD	T_{ssm} (s)	SD	I_{pca} (%)	SD
men	10	0.4	0.07	0.55	0.05	27.5	7.5
children	22	0.63	0.09	0.71	0.07	11.1	8.5

SD - standard deviation

Men displayed a much higher speed in both sequential movements and a greater capacity for anticipation. Their speeds of anticipatory and simple sequential movements were higher by 37% and 23% respectively, and their anticipation was two and a half times as good as that of children. The average range of table tennis bat movement from starting position to the sensors was 0.93 m. This means that in each movement the men outstripped the children by an average of 0.34 m in anticipatory and 0.21 m in simple sequential movements. The place coincidence anticipation enabled the men to move 0.26 m towards the flight path of the ball, the children only 0.10 m. The differences in sequential movement speed and anticipation are statistically significant (Student's test, $P < 0.05$), and are probably due to age, period of special training, and level of skills (sporting experience). These findings are in disagreement with those in published investigations, in which the reaction and movement time (Keele, 1982) and anticipation (Meeusen, 1991) were found not to differentiate between highly proficient and less-skilled players. The standard deviations indicate high individual differences in the level of development of the factors investigated in the two groups

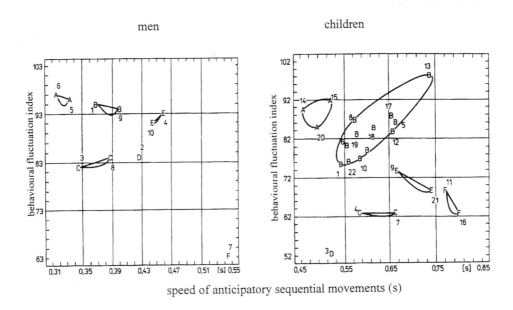

Figure 3. Cluster analysis used in the selection in the groups of men and children.

The results shown in Table 3 indicate that the psychomotor factors tested are at a higher level of development in players with a higher sporting ranking. These factors can therefore be taken into consideration as a pre-disposition for table tennis. The factors were used in selection based on the cluster analysis shown in Fig. 3. Cluster analysis divided both groups tested into very talented players (A), talented (B) and those who have psychomotor deficiencies (C,D,E,F).

Table 3. The correlation coefficents (Cc) between sporting ranking and the speed of movements (T_{asm}, T_{ssm}), the index R^2 and (I_{pca}), and psychomotor ranking (R_p) in men

men	T_{asm}		T_{ssm}		R^2		I_{pca}		R_p	
	Cc	P	Cc	P	Cc	P	Cc	P	Cc	P
sporting ranking	0.89	0.001	0.84	0.002	-0.81	0.002	0.80	0.006	0.89	0.001

T_{asm}, T_{ssm} - speed of anticipatory and simple sequential movements   P - level of significance

4 Conclusions

This method allows four psychomotor factors important in various sports to be measured. These factors differentiate the subjects with respect to age, period of special training, sporting experience, and can be used to predict sporting aptitudes. Cluster analysis allows these predispositions to be used to find the most talented players and can indicate psycho-motor deficiencies in others. The simulatory timer can be used as a diagnostic device in various sports, and also as a training device to practise the speed of specific movements and to improve concentration.

5 References

Belisle, J. J. (1963) Accuracy, reliability and refractoriness in a coincidence-anticipation task. **Research Quarterly**, 34, 271-281.

Lapszo, J. and Morawski, M. J. (1994) Badanie szybkosci sekwencyjnych ruchów docelowych i antycypacji na przykladzie tenisa stolowego. **Oficyna Wydawnicza Politechniki Wroclawskiej**, Wroclaw, pp. 191-194.

Hull, C. L. (1942) Conditioning: outline of a systematic theory of learning. **National Social Study of Education,** 41Yearbook, 61-95.

Keele, S. W. (1982) Component analysis and conceptions of skill. **Human Motor Skills**. Erlbaum, London, pp. 141-159.

Meeusen, H. J. (1991) On simplifying reality: implications for research on individual differences. **Perceptual and Motor Skills**, 73, 1055-1058.

Nettleton, B. (1986) Flexibility of attention in elite athletes. **Perceptual and Motor Skills**, 63, 991-994.

Schmidt, R. (1975) A schema theory of discrete motor skill learning. **Psychological Review**, 7, 225-259.

19 Using performance profiles with a regional junior table tennis squad

C.L. Potter and A.G. Anderson
Department of Physical Education and Sports Studies, School of Sciences, Worcester College of Higher Education, Worcester, UK

1 Introduction

Performance profiling was devised by Butler (1989) and is an application of Kelly's (1955) personal construct theory to sport psychology. Performance profiling encourages input from the athlete in order to gain an in-depth understanding of the perception he/she has of his/her performance. It enables an athlete to identify his/her perceived strengths, weaknesses and areas for improvement. This process serves to enhance the athlete's self-awareness and also facilitates the coach's and sport psychologist's understanding of the athlete's perspective (Butler et al., 1993). The utility value of performance profiling in sport psychology has been consistently reported (Butler and Hardy, 1992; Dale and Wrisberg, 1996; Jones, 1993).

Various models that identify the principles and stages of psychological skills training (PST) have been proposed (Boutcher and Rotella, 1987; Vealey, 1988). These models involve an assessment phase in which the sport psychologist determines which mental skills are to be targeted for intervention. However, Butler and Hardy (1992) recognised that the athlete is relatively passive in this process which may influence the athlete's motivation to participate in and adhere to PST. Instead, by using performance profiling in the assessment phase, the intervention becomes athlete-driven and focuses on areas that are important to the athlete (Jones, 1993).

Whilst it is generally acknowledged that individualised PST is the optimal method of providing sport psychology support (Grove and Hanrahan, 1988), various constraints (for example, financial, practical and temporal) can dictate that workshops in a group setting can be more appropriate (Brewer and Shillinglaw, 1992). To determine the content of workshops, individual performance profiles may be clustered together to identify common constructs for improvement. Importantly, clarification of the terms should be sought from the individuals to ensure the meanings attached to the constructs are also common. Consequently, the intervention in a group setting would focus on areas that the athletes themselves identify as important for improvement. Further, the coach's assessment of each players' performance profile is valuable in verifying areas for improvement (Butler and Hardy, 1992; Dale and Wrisberg, 1996).

Science and Racket Sports II, edited by A. Lees, I. Maynard, M. Hughes and T. Reilly. Published in 1998 by E & FN Spon, 11 New Fetter Lane, London EC4P 4EE, UK. ISBN: 0 419 23030 0

This research aims to demonstrate the value of performance profiling in identifying the perceived strengths and weaknesses of individual Regional Junior Table Tennis players. An additional aim was to examine the individual performance profiles to identify common themes for sport psychology workshops in a group setting. The coach's perceptions of the players' strengths and weaknesses were also investigated to verify the athletes' perceptions.

2 Methods

Sixteen male (n=10) and female (n=6) Regional Junior Table Tennis players, aged between 13 and 16 ($\bar{x} \pm$ S.D.= 15 $\pm$1.03) years completed a performance profile (Butler, 1989) at the Squad Summer Camp (1996) in a group session format, to identify how each player felt about his/her current table tennis performance. The procedure followed that of Butler and Hardy (1992) with some modifications for a group setting.

Players initially worked individually and were asked to *"Write down the qualities or characteristics you think an ideal table tennis player possesses"*. A group "brainstorming" session was then undertaken to allow a broad range of qualities to be identified and shared amongst the group (Butler and Hardy, 1992). To generate the individual profiles, players were then asked to *"Identify the qualities or characteristics you think an ideal table tennis player possesses from the list generated by the whole group"*. These constructs then formed the basis of the performance profile for each individual. Players made ideal assessments (IA) and self-assessments (SA) for each construct. Their strengths and weaknesses were identified from the discrepancies between the IA and SA ratings. The researchers retained the original terms used by each player so the profiles accurately reflected the players' perceptions of table tennis performances (Bannister and Fransella, 1986). To enable the researchers to understand fully the individual profiles, the meaning of the constructs was clarified with the players.

Individual performance profile data were examined to ascertain each players' strengths and weaknesses. To identify sport psychology workshops which may be conducted in a group setting, constructs from the individual performance profiles were collated and common categories emerged. Category names and content were agreed by the researchers. Areas for improvement were identified where 50% or more of the players reported a discrepancy between the IA and SA of greater than or equal to three units on that construct. This criterion for inclusion was also used with the coach's assessment of the players.

3 Results

3.1 Individual analysis

The performance profiles identified the perceived strengths and weaknesses of the players. An example of an individual performance profile (Player A) is presented in Figure 1. The overall composition of the performance profile for Player A included constructs from the areas of *psychology, fitness* and *table tennis specific* factors. Figure 1 shows a discrepancy (1 to 6 units) between the IA and SA for a large number of constructs. Player A identified the constructs *fit* (5 units discrepancy), *stamina* (6 units), *deal with pressure* (3 units), *composed* (4 units) and *focused* (5 units) as requiring improvement. Although the players worked in a group session format, the individual performance profiles comprised different constructs and thus indicated that players were working individually. Nevertheless, common themes, *psychological, fitness* and *table tennis* were evident amongst the players.

3.2 Squad analysis

An audit of the performance profiles of all 16 members of the squad was undertaken. A large percentage of athletes identified a discrepancy of three or more units within the categories *psychology* (100%), *fitness* (100%) and *table tennis specific* (94%). Figure 2 shows a breakdown of the common psychological themes that emerged from the audit and the percentage of athletes who had a discrepancy of 3 or more units between their IA and SA on that theme. Three specific constructs emerged; *concentration, motivation, and emotional control*. In the group 75% of players had a discrepancy of 3 or more units for *concentration*, 63% for *motivation* and 85% for *emotional control*. The *emotional control* construct was further broken down to include *relaxed, composed, deal with pressure, positive attitude* and *control of aggression* constructs. Fifty percent of the players had a discrepancy of 3 or more units for *relaxed*, 69% for *composed*, and 56% for *positive attitude*. Due to the large number of players identifying a discrepancy of three or more, the common constructs identified for sport psychology sessions in a group setting were *concentration, motivation, relaxed, composed* and *positive attitude.*

3.3 Coach analysis

The coach rated each player's performance on the constructs identified in their performance profile. By examining the discrepancies between the coach's rating and the player's ideal rating the researchers were able to assess areas in which the coach perceived the players would need to improve. Specifically, the coach perceived that 44% of players had room for improvement in the area of *concentration*, 13% in the area of *motivation*, 44% in the area of *composure*, 25% in the area of *relaxed* and 69% in the area of *positive attitude*. The coach's assessment partially supported the audit of the individual players' weaknesses. There were discrepancies between how the coach construed some individual players and how individual players construed themselves. For example, the coach rated 54% (range=1-2 units) of constructs higher than player A's self-assessment.

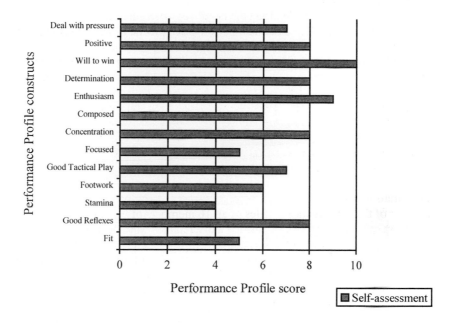

Figure 1. The performance profile showing the self assessments for
Player A, where all ideal assessments were scored as 10.

4 Discussion

4.1 Individual analysis

The performance profile enabled each player to identify perceived strengths and weaknesses relating to his/her table tennis performance (Butler and Hardy, 1992; Butler et al., 1993). The variation of the profiles also indicated the individuality in players' perceptions of the requirements of ideal table tennis players. The players consistently identified *psychological* (for example, *concentration*), *fitness* (for example, *stamina*) and *table tennis specific* (for example, *strong serves*) themes as important in an ideal player. Therefore, the players were aware that an ideal table tennis player would need to be skilled in each of these areas.

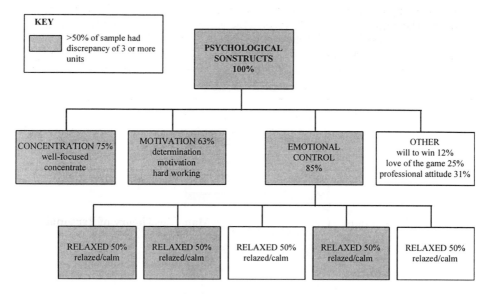

Figure 2. Common psychological themes from all of the performance
profiles and the percentage of the group with a discrepancy
between the IA and SA of three or more on each construct.

4.2 Squad analysis

It was evident from the performance profile data that the players rated themselves
lower than an ideal player by three or more units on a considerable number of
constructs (mean per player = 70%). Thus, the players perceived a large difference
between themselves and an ideal player.

Although individualised PST is thought to be an optimal method, workshops in a
group setting will be more appropriate for these players due to practical, temporal and
financial constraints (Brewer and Shillinglaw, 1992). The examination of all the
performance profiles was valuable in exploring common themes amongst players and
identified areas that were consistently perceived by players as areas for improvement.
The results indicated that by collating this information, the researcher may identify
areas for group sport psychology workshops which are driven by the needs of the
players. Future research must evaluate the effectiveness of the PST in a group setting.

4.3 Coach analysis

The psychological areas identified by the coach partially supported those identified by
the players. Some discrepancies existed between the coach and individual players. In
contrast to the players, the coach did not identify *motivation* as a key area for
improvement. Further discussion between the coach and individual players is required
to identify the cause of these discrepancies (Dale and Wrisberg, 1996).

5 Conclusions

This paper employed performance profiling in an applied setting with table tennis players. The performance profile enabled the perceived strengths and weaknesses of each individual player to be identified. Additionally, the performance profiles of the squad may be collated to identify common areas to be targeted for sport psychology intervention in a group setting. The coach's assessment of players, using the performance profile, is valuable in verifying the areas for improvement. In this study, the coach's assessment partially supported the identification of players' sport psychology requirements, suggesting a need for further discussions. In summary, performance profiles serve as a valuable baseline assessment for the identification of athlete-driven sport psychology intervention.

6 References

Bannister, D. and Fransella, F. (1986) **Inquiring Man-The Theory of Personal Constructs.** London: Croom Helm.

Boutcher, S.H. and Rotella, R.J. (1987) A psychological skills educational program for closed-skill performance enhancement. **Sport Psychology,** 1, 127-137.

Brewer, B.W. and Shillinglaw, R. (1992) Evaluation of a psychological skills training workshop for male intercollegiate lacrosse players. **Sport Psychology,** 6, 139-147.

Butler, R.J. (1989) Psychological preparation of Olympic boxers, in **The Psychology of Sport: Theory and Practice** (eds J. Kremer and W. Crawfords), Belfast: BPS Northern Ireland Branch, pp 74-84.

Butler, R.J. and Hardy, L. (1992) The performance profile: Theory and application. **Sport Psychology,** 6, 253-264.

Butler, R.J., Smith, M. and Irwin, I. (1993) The performance profile in practice. **Journal Applied Sport Psychology,** 5, 48-63.

Dale, G.A. and Wrisberg, C.A. (1996) The use of a performance profiling technique in a team setting: Getting the athletes and coach on the "same page". **Sport Psychology,** 10, 261-277.

Grove, J.R. and Hanrahan, S. J. (1988) Perceptions of mental training needs by elite field hockey players and their coaches. **Sport Psychology,** 2, 222-230.

Jones, G. (1993) The role of performance profiling in cognitive behavioural interventions in sport. **Sport Psychology,** 7, 160-172.

Kelly, G.A. (1955) **The Psychology of Personal Constructs.** Norton, New York.

Vealey, R.S. (1988) Future directions in psychological skills training. **Sport Psychology,** 2, 318-336.

20 Analysis of self-regulation techniques in critical situations in table tennis

D.M. Samulski and F.V. Lima
Federal University of Minas Gerais, Physical Education School, Belo Horizonte-MG, Brazil

1 Introduction

In a high level table tennis competition, many factors could influence the player's performance these factors may be technical, tactical, physical or psychological. The player must control these factors according to the different and specific situations that he/she will face when competing. Critical situations are those which may lead to an increase in psychic stress; at these moments, the player must be able to regulate his/her own behaviour, aiming at mantaining a good level of performance. In the process of self-regulation, the athlete tries to influence his/her own psychic state according to his/her specific performance needs (Samulski, 1992). Nitsch and Hackfort (1979) described "naive" techniques of psychic-regulation as those developed and applied by the athletes through self-experience. The naive techniques could be environmentally and personally oriented; those techniques when personally oriented are divided into two different categories - motor techniques (psychic modification through motor behaviour) and cognitive techniques (psychic modification through a new evaluation of the condition of the problem). These critical situations in table tennis were investigated by Krohne and Hindel (1992), Straub and Hindel (1993) and Hindel (1989) who have identified the techniques that players used to overcome the psychic stress of such situations. The ratio of success in technique in overcoming each critical situation was analysed from the result of the immediate point after each critical situation. It was further used to verify the efficacy of the coping techniques used by the athletes. The present study aimed to investigate the most important critical situations in high level table tennis competitions. It also intended to analyse the self-regulation techniques applied by the athletes, and identify which techniques were more effective in these situations through the result of the immediate two points after each situation. We consider that the performance of the athlete at these points was influenced by the self-regulation techniques applied after the critical situations in a similar way to Hindel (1989) cited above.

Science and Racket Sports II, edited by A. Lees, I. Maynard, M. Hughes and T. Reilly. Published in 1998 by E & FN Spon, 11 New Fetter Lane, London EC4P 4EE, UK.   ISBN: 0 419 23030 0

2 Methods

Five players from the Brazilian national female team took part in this study. They were between 16 and 22 years old and had been training for table tennis for at least 6 years, with national and international experience. The six most important critical situations were chosen by 100 athletes and coaches through the "Critical Situations in Table Tennis" (CSTM) inventory, developed at the Laboratory of Sport Psychology in the Institute of Physical Education -Federal University of Minas Gerais, Brazil. The situations occur when the player loses the point in the following circumstances: easy ball, service, return of service, third ball, long rally point, easy ball in a long rally point. Four national and international competitions were video recorded. The self-confrontation method which allows the athlete to review and describe his/her own behaviour in competition, was used to analyse the critical situations and self-regulation techniques. This method was used also by Hindel (1989), Krohne and Hindel (1990) and Straub and Hindel (1992). In research with players at the 1991 World Championships, 91.3% thought that self-observation through video recording was useful in enhancing their performance, and 85.1% thought it was useful to watch a video of a match they lost badly to study their own behaviour. These self-regulation techniques were classified into motor and cognitive, as described by Nitsch and Hackfort (1979). The present study also identified the combined techniques or those moments when the athlete applies both cognitive and motor techniques together. Also analysed were the percentage frequency of the critical situations and the self-regulation techniques identified and categorized, considering the ratio among: critical situation / self- regulation technique / next 2 points-won or lost. The chi-square test was used to examine the self-regulation techniques, and to determine any statistical differences in the proportion of the next two points. The statistical significance of the results were considered at a level of $P<0.05$.

3 Results and Discussion

Altogether 821 points were analysed and 237 critical situations were identified. It was determined that self-regulation techniques were applied in 105 critical situations (see Table 1). The frequency of application of each technique to each situation was also calculated. The motor techniques of self-regulation were prevalent in 65.7% of all situations; cognitive techniques were applied in 9.5% of the situations and the combination of both motor and cognitive techniques were used in 24.8% of the situations. The comparison of the self-regulation techniques based on the result in the two following points, showed a statistical difference ($\chi^2 = 6.25$; $P<0.05$, df =2), with the cognitive techniques indicating a significantly higher number of positive outcomes than the motor and the combined techniques, which showed no difference (see Table 2).

Table 1. Critical situations analysed

SITUATIONS	N.	%
error in return service	39	37.1%
error in third ball	32	30.5%
error in easy ball	18	17.1%
error in service	7	6.7%
error in a long rally point	5	4.8%
combined error		
(easy ball in a long rally point)	4	3.8%
TOTAL	**105**	**100%**

The critical situations were also divided into two groups of three situations, the first being related to basic errors, which means basic skills for any athlete who competes at international level (service, return to service and third ball) and the second to general errors. In this case results indicated significant diferences in those basic errors ($\chi^2 = 7.24$; $P<0.05$ df = 2), with the motor techniques proving to be less efficient than cognitive or combined techniques (Fig. 1). With the general errors, the motor and the combined techniques showed the higher value of lost points, when compared to cognitive techniques. It was not possible to evaluate the significance of this difference due to the low number of errors in these situations, mainly cognitive techniques. Straub and Hindel (1993) in a similar study, concluded that the motor techniques had little importance in overcoming critical situations in table tennis.

Table 2. Success ratio : Self-regulation techniques / 2 following points

	Points Won	Points Lost
MOTOR	60 / 43.5%	78 / 56.5%
COGNITIVE	14 / 73.7%	5 / 26.3%
COMBINED	26 / 50.0%	26 / 50.0%
TOTAL	**100 / 47.9%**	**109 / 52.2%**

Examples of the most usual motor techniques identified are - slow controlled breathing, self-instructions (through the simulation of the correct skill), walking from side to side, bouncing the ball on the floor repeatedly, successive jumps, head and arm movements. Examples of cognitive techniques are: self-talk, imagery, distraction, re-evaluation of the problem (oriented to the equipment).

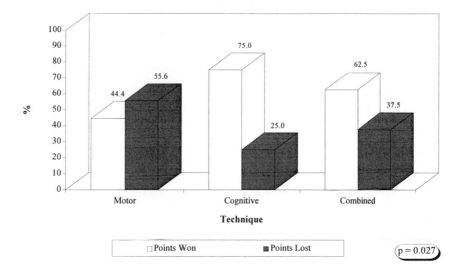

Figure 1. Evaluation of the efficacy of self-regulation techniques after a basic error.

4 Conclusions

The results suggest that the table tennis player should be prepared to use self-regulation techniques when facing critical situations in competition, and, in this present study, the cognitive techniques proved to be more efficient when one considers the immediate result after each critical situation. Despite these results, the Brazilian female athletes analysed, tended to use more motor techniques to achieve the self-regulation, but they did not know that these techniques do not work very well, as demonstrated in the present study.

Based on the results the main suggestions are
1) it is advantageous to use essentially cognitive techniques of self-regulation when facing stressful situations;
2) there is a need for the development of specific self-regulation techniques for overcoming critical situations;
3) the self-confrontation method should be used to analyse the athlete's behaviour in both training and competition.

Other studies must be carried out in order to find out how individual and inter-cultural differences can modify the efficacy of these techniques, as well as, the self-perception of the critical aspects of a table tennis match.

5 References

Hindel, C. (1989) Die Bewältigung kritischer Situationen im Tischtennis. **Sportpsychologie,** 4, 18-25.
Krohne, H.W. and Hindel, C. (1992) Stressbewältigung und sportlicher Erfolg. **Sportpsychologie**, 6, 5-11.
Nitsch, J.R. and Hackfort, D. (1979) Naive Techniken der Psychoregulation im Sport, in **Praxis der Psychologie im Leistungssport**, (eds. H. Gabler et al.) Bartels and Wernitz, Berlin, pp. 299-311.
Samulski, D. (1992) **Psicologia do Esporte: Teoria e Aplicação Prática**, Belo Horizonte, MG. Universitary Press. (In Portuguese).
Straub, S. and Hindel, C. (1993) Bewältigung belastender Wettkampfsituationen im Tischtennis. **Sportpsychologie,** 1, 17-22.
The International Table Tennis Federation. (1991) **Questionary of elite athletes**. World Table Tennis Championships, Chiba, Japan.

21 Technical rehearsal and imagery: a system for enhancing technical skills in table tennis

J. Fallby
Centre for Sport Science, Halmstad University, Halmstad, Sweden

1 Introduction

Many sports demand that competitors have high abilities in technical skills. Table tennis, like many other sports has returned the same practice methods over a long period of time. This work is an attempt to approach the problem from a new angle by combining mental training methods with technical skills practice to produce a new way of developing these table tennis skills.

Similar approaches has been made in this area before with Suinn´s (1972a, 1972b) Visual Motor Behavioural Rehearsal (VMBR) often used as a starting-point. The VMBR method has combined training in controlled emotional anxiety, relaxation and imagery.

Weinberg et al. (1982) found that repeated VMBR training is valuable and even that a single exposure can have positive effects in some situations. Multiple training sessions ensure that participants are involved in a sufficient number of learning trials and that the athletes improve their imagery technique. This technique is of importance in making any progress in technical skills through mental rehearsal (Fallby, 1995). Gray (1990) completed an investigation with racquetball players. He researched the effect of VMBR and videotaped modelling on 24 male students "beginning" players. Two groups were assigned randomly, one to VMBR and videotaped modelling, and the other to VMBR only. The training period was for two weeks and all subjects were tested on forehand and backhand racquetball skills tests before and after the intervention. Results indicated that both groups experienced an increase in performance, but the group with VMBR and videotaped modelling exhibited better performance. These findings correspond to Hall and Erffmeyer`s (1983) findings in basketball.

Zhang et al., (1991) conducted a field study in table tennis with 7 to 10 year-old children in China. The 40 subjects were divided into three groups; group 1 joined the experimental training programme which included relaxation, videotaped observation and imagery, group 2 members were assigned only to observe the same video as group 1, and finally group 3 did not take part in any aspect of the mental training programme (control group). The intervention took 22 weeks and the results were promising. The

Science and Racket Sports II, edited by A. Lees, I. Maynard, M. Hughes and T. Reilly. Published in 1998 by E & FN Spon, 11 New Fetter Lane, London EC4P 4EE, UK. ISBN: 0 419 23030 0

improvement in accuracy and technical quality of the mental training group led the researchers to believe that mental-imagery training can enhance performance in 7 to10 year-old children.

In Sweden, recent research has led to the belief that to teach athletes just "to relax" is not enough. Janson (1995) has, after studies with electromyography (EMG), come to the conclusion that an athlete has to be mentally alert, at his/her "right" arousal level and with physically relevant tension in his/her synergists and relaxation in the antagonistic muscles. Experienced athletes can still have a problem with this, letting the body take control and "just let go with the flow".

With this knowledge a pilot study was conducted at Halmstad University with a new system containing five steps: (1) relaxation, (2) video observation, (3) imagery, (4) physical training, and (5) verbal feedback. Results showed significantly higher forehand top-spin accuracy for the experimental group in comparison to a control group (Fallby, 1995). The purpose of the present study was to investigate further the potential benefits of the technical-mental training system that was applied in the pilot study. The techniques selected for practice were forehand top-spin on backspin from the backhand corner, movement, and forehand top-spin from the forehand corner, this time on top-spin (block).

2 Methods

2.1 Subjects
Three male table tennis players ranked just below Swedish national team standard were asked and volunteered to carry out the present study (Table 1).

Table 1. Characteristics of the subjects

	Case A	Case B	Case C
Age (years)	25	23	25
Years of playing	18	16	18
Practice, hours/week (table tennis)	10-15	14-16	18-20
Years in Premier League, Sweden	10	6	10

2.2 Instruments
The study contained several different instruments to assure a richness of data. There were two different questionnaires, one for technique and one for "touch" of the ball. Both instruments had earlier been used in the pilot study and were handed out here as two separate questionnaires for completion.

The EMG measures were obtained on five different occasions. These measures can not be considered reliable in a physiological perspective due to changes of electrodes between different measures (see for example Clarys and Cabri, 1993). The electrodes were not necessarily placed in exactly the same spot at every measure, and differences could occur between the electrodes. This bias was reduced by a standardised calibration that was worked out for table tennis before starting the study. Three bipolar surface electrodes were used, one on each side of extensor carpi ulnaris approximately

10 cm below the elbow, and a contrast electrode on the elbow. The EMG measures were expressed as a % of maximum voluntary contraction of the agonist muscle during performance (see Table 3).

An exercise was constructed to use at the time of EMG measurements: multi-ball training with one backspin played to the backhand corner, returned by the subject with an aggressive forehand top-spin, and one ball played to the subject's forehand corner (to simulate a block), returned also with an aggressive shot. The same exercise was also used in the multi-ball measurement, but on this occasion the rally began with a short ball in the middle to make it more realistic to the match-play situation.

In conjunction with the EMG measurements, self-assessments of the "feeling" the subject experienced during the performance were made. Subjects were instructed to assess every stroke played when EMG measures were taken on a scale from 1-5, "1" meaning "very bad" and "5" meaning "very good". This which was the same scale as used in all self-assessments in the study.

Multi-ball training was used together with self-assessment of the subject's experience. Every sequence of the training programme was assessed by the subjects on the scale from 1-5. The intervention was finally ended with an interview that was considered the most essential instrument in this study.

2.3 Procedure
Since the purpose of this study was to try out the appropriateness of the system in the field, an A-B-A design was carried out - baseline measure, 9 weeks intervention with three different measures and 3 weeks of returning to baseline ending with the final measure.

To ensure that the relaxation and mental imagery abilities of the subjects were sufficient to take advantage of the system, the intervention started with a theoretical introduction. Subjects were introduced into critical variables in relaxation and imagery on two different occasions. At these meetings they also had the opportunity to try the relaxation and imagery programme that was going to be used in the intervention. A mental training programme was constructed for six weeks, with five practice sessions each week. The ability to visualize was assessed in discussions with the subjects both before and after the intervention together with a test (Bump, 1989). Their ability was then judged to be sufficient, and a baseline measure was obtained.

The intervention with the training-system was executed with two practice sessions a week, besides the traditional training over 9 weeks. Subjects could, together with the coach, decide when to carry out the sessions during the week, with the one exception that they could not use the routine two days in a row. Four further measurements, after baseline 1, were planned at week 3, 6 and 9 of the intervention, and at the end of baseline 2.

2.4 Experimental technique-mental training system
In the progressive relaxation programme the subject listened to a taped voice working its way through different parts of the body, relaxing one muscle after another. The duration of the programme was about 6 min. While still in a relaxed mood, they were asked to open their eyes and observe a videotape with top table tennis players performing forehand top-spins. The subjects had before the recording of the videotape

themselves chosen their favourite players, watched the video and been instructed what cues to focus on and pay attention to. The tape was about 5 min in duration. Following the videotape was a 5 min imagery session where the subjects were instructed to imagine themselves, in a successful way, execute the same technical skills they had seen the top-players perform. In a focused state of mind the subjects then moved from the mental training room to the playing arena, warmed up and began physical practice. Two of them performed traditional exercises with the purpose of training forehand top-spins, while the third subject practised multi-balls with the coach. After around 10 min of practice the coach gave verbal feedback on the subjects performance on this session for about 5 min. This was followed by a change of players so that all of the subjects came to get feedback from the coach at the "multi-ball table", and an equal amount of time to play regular exercises.

3 Results

In the "multi-ball training" the subjects were asked to focus on the feeling of the performance experienced while performing the techniques. This was considered more important than the quantitative number of accurate shots made (Table 2).

Table 2. Accuracy in multi-ball practice (maximum score is 10) and subjective assessment of the feeling experienced during the performance (scale ranging from 1, "very bad" to 5, "very good"). Empty boxes mean that the subject was absent

	1st forehand top-spin			2nd forehand top-spin			Experienced feeling rating		
	Case A	Case B	Case C	Case A	Case B	Case C	Case A	Case B	Case C
Baseline 1	7.0	7.6	5.9	6.9	7.3	6.8	3.2	3.7	3.4
Measure 1	6.4	7.1	6.6	6.8	7.6	7.0	3.3	4.1	3.4
Measure 2	7.0	-	6.6	7.3	-	7.0	3.9	-	3.4
Measure 3	7.5	7.4	7.0	7.9	7.4	7.2	3.9	4.0	3.8
Baseline 2	7.4	8.1	-	9.0	8.5	-	3.9	4.1	-

Qualitative results, using EMG were generated according to Janson`s (1995) protocol described in the introduction. Table 3 explains how the tension in extensor carpi ulnaris, that is an antagonist in the forehand top-spin technique, varied through the study. Two critical points of tension were identified in the exercise that was played; "a" the hit of the ball on the first forehand topspin, and "b" the hit of the second ball at the second top-spin. The subjects were also asked to assess the performance on the two tasks in this exercise.

Table 3. The EMG measurements of the extensor carpi ulnaris (antagonist), given in %
MVC, on the two identified critical points in the exercise played, and the self-
assessment on the performance of the task, (scale ranging from 1 to 5).
Empty boxes mean that the subject was absent

	Case A				Case B				Case C			
	"a"	rating	"b"	rating	"a"	rating	"b"	rating	"a"	rating	"b"	rating
Baseline 1	67.1	3.8	72.7	3.5	86.0	3.9	75.1	4.0	80.7	3.6	78.7	3.6
Measure 1	83.5	3.9	83.3	3.9	68.0	4.5	83.3	4.1	-	-	-	-
Measure 2	67.0	4.3	73.2	3.9	-	-	-	-	40.2	3.9	42.1	3.8
Measure 3	53.0	4.3	52.5	4.2	66.2	3.9	61.2	4.3	72.0	3.8	70.3	3.9
Baseline 2	57.1	4.4	58.4	4.4	92.3	3.9	89.3	4.6	-	-	-	-

A self-assessment task was also given after each meeting when multi-ball and EMG
measures were taken. It was designed to assess the players' technique and "touch" of
the ball in the last three training sessions by means of two different questionnaires.
The questionnaires contained twelve variables, but only three of them were relevant to
the study; forehand top-spin on backspin, (a) down the line, and (b) crosscourt, and (c)
forehand top-spin on block, free. These variables showed a pattern among the three
cases. In self-assessment of the technique the mean increased from 3.67 to 4.33, and
the assessment of the feeling/experience rose from 3.78 to 4.56.

The interview that concluded the study was summarised as follows:

Case study A was very interested in the study itself and had some thoughts that could
be used to develop a technique further. He concluded that he had made progress
during the study by way of safety of the shots practised, in technique, but mostly in his
self-awareness. He was much more aware of the importance of his feeling and
experience of the performance during technical skills practice.

Case study B felt more relaxed in his movements during performance and through that
felt his performance was more consistent, hitting more balls on the table with the same
speed as before. He found the combination of video modelling and imagery inspiring
and motivating and he wanted to try it in combination with competition situations. He
believed that technical skills training in table tennis was outdated.

Case study C found the video modelling good and motivating, but had problems with
imagery at the start of the study. He wanted to integrate video modelling with the
traditional training sessions and thought that a video camera should film the practice
sessions so that the tape could provide visual feedback after training. He found that his
technique had improved during the study and that it had been more enjoyable to
practice with the new training system.

All three subjects were positive about the thought of integrating the training system
into their regular practice. They stressed the importance of the motivation of the coach
and all practical details surrounding the new methods of practising.

4 Discussion and Conclusions

The results of the present study suggest that the technical-mental training system is a promising complement to traditional technical training in forehand top-spin in table tennis. The application of this training system in the field is very appropriate and it could give coaches an alternative in the training and learning situation.

Concerning the quantitative measurements, some results showed inconsistent patterns. First, case A showed a decrease in all measures following baseline 1. This can be explained through heavy weight-training conducted directly before the measures that he thought influenced his behaviour a great deal. Second, case B showed an increase in tension on baseline 2. This suggested that the effect of the training system had disappeared, but the self-assessments and the results with the multi-balls show opposite results. The conclusion from this could be that self-awareness is an important part of technical training. Case B had a better feeling of his technique after participating in the training system. According to Janson's (1995) protocol, his tension should also stay at the lower level. One explanation why this did not occur is that case B had been training for many years with a high tension "built in to" his technique. When the inducement from imagery and relaxation in the training system faded away, so did the relaxed technique. This suggests that a good "education" in the difference between tense and relaxed states during technical performance is of vital importance. Thus, a long-term practice plan on how to replace the tension would be the best way to deal with the situation. The EMG should be included in the plan as a biofeedback instrument. Janson (1995) reported that when a new, more "relaxed", technique is learned the athlete feels a lack of control over the performance. This feeling has to do with the former tension that now is replaced with the relaxed and more "smooth" technique. The result is a non-interference from disturbing thoughts and tensed muscles. The coach of technical skills in table tennis should note the difference between the athletes "feeling", or experience of the performance and the actual physical performance, to reach a more effective learning situation.

Case C did not participate in two of the measurements; this was attributable to the location of this study in the field. Injuries, training camps and other circumstances can be disruptive. One important factor in this context is, before starting a new training method the coach or the researcher should be aware of the practical issues concerning all different aspects. The coach and the athletes should be motivated, accurately introduced to the theoretical and practical details, ready to accept new working conditions during practice, and have all new training equipment needed (VCR, tape recorder, relaxing room, and so on).

The coach has a very important place in the training system, as in all learning and training situations. He should work together with a "resource-person" (sport psychologist or other appropriate person) when introducing this type of training system. This is because of the change that is impending, and the extra work that it entails. It may be dangerous to overload the coach and therefore the theoretical parts of the training system should be introduced by a person that is experienced in sport psychology and the theoretical background.

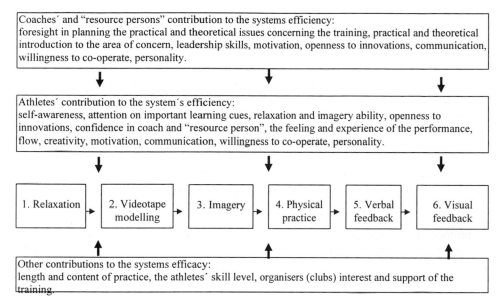

Figure 1. A summary of the mental-technique training (Fallby, 1997).

The importance can be stressed by the example of case C, who did not improve much during the first three weeks of the intervention. Later in the interview he explained that he had problems with the imagery technique. This corresponded to earlier findings that suggested that the imagery technique was crucial for the outcome of the training system (Fallby, 1995).

Two of the subjects suggested that a video camera could be set up during practice sessions to give visual feedback of the performance. This idea was also suggested in a pilot study, but could not be realised in the present study. Visual feedback is an important factor when comparing current with earlier performances. It is important that the coach can edit the tape so that any negative stimulus can be left out. This was supported by McCullagh (1993) who proposed that visual feedback is effective in the correction of technical skills, but not in their detection.

A summary of a promising foundation to start a new approach to technical training is presented in Figure 1. Hopefully it offers a contribution to a growing body of knowledge that shows that technical-mental training is an alternative to traditional technical training.

5 Acknowledgement

The author wishes to thank Fredrik Wetterstrand, CIV, Halmstad University, Sweden, for his help in carrying out the EMG testing.

6 References

Bump, L.A. (1989) **American Coaching Effectiveness Program. Sport Psychology.**
   Human Kinetics, Champaign, IL.
Clarys, J.P. and Cabri, J. (1993) Electromyography and the study of sports movements:
   A review. **Journal of Sports Sciences**, 11, 379-448.
McCullagh, P. (1993) Modeling: learning, developmental, and social psychological
   considerations, in **Handbook of Research on Sport Psychology** (eds R.N. Singer,
   M. Murphey and L.K. Tennant) Macmillan, New York.
Fallby, L.J. (1995) Psychoneuromuscular theory - en studie i praktisk tillämpning av
   mental träning. Halmstad University, **Sport Psychology**, 21-40.
Fallby, L.J. (1997) Teknisk-mental träning: En träningsmodell för att förbättra tekniska
   färdigheter i bordtennis. C-thesis, Halmstad University, **Pedagogy**, 41-60.
Gray, S.W. (1990) Effects of visuomotor rehearsal with videotaped modeling on
   racquetball performance of beginning players. **Perceptual and Motor skills**, 70,
   379-385.
Hall, E.G. and Erffmeyer, E.S. (1983) The effect of visuo-motor behavior rehearsal
   with videotaped modeling on free throw accuracy of intercollegiate female basketball
   players. **Journal of Sport Psychology**, 5, 343-346.
Janson, L. (1995) Avspänd teknik, in **SVEBI:s årsbok** (ed. G. Patriksson)
   Reprocentralen Lund, pp. 63-74.
Suinn, R.M. (1972a) Behavioral rehearsal training for ski racers: brief report.
   Behavior Therapy, 3, 210-212.
Suinn, R.M. (1972b) Removing emotional obstacles to learning and performance by
   visuo-motor behavior rehearsal. **Behavior Therapy**, 3, 308-310.
Weinberg, R.S., Seabourne, T.G. and Jackson, A. (1982) Effects of visuo-motor
   bahavior rehearsal on state-trait anxiety and performance: Is practice important?
   Journal of Sport Behavior, 5, 209-219.
Zhang L-W., Ma Q-W., Orlick, T. and Zitzelsberger, L. (1991) The effect of mental-
   imagery training on performance enhancement with 7-10-year-old children.
   Unpublished Report; Beijing Institute of Physical Education and University of
   Ottawa.

22 Type 'A' behaviour in squash

K. Robertson[1], M. Hughes[2], F. Sanderson[3] and T. Reilly[3]
[1]Division of Sport and Recreation, University of Northumbria at Newcastle, Newcastle, UK; [2]School of Graduate Studies and Continuing Education, University of Wales Institute, Cardiff, UK and [3]School of Human Sciences, Liverpool John Moores University, Liverpool, UK

1 Introduction

The issue of sudden death during racket sports, such as squash, has attracted recent attention (Brady et al., 1989; Visser et al., 1987). It is recognised that all forms of exercise lead to some immediate increase in the risk of sudden death (Siscovick, 1990). There remains a suspicion that the hazard may be greater for squash than for other forms of physical activity such as jogging (Shephard, 1991; 1992). It is unclear whether this is due to the intensity of the required activity, the extreme competitive nature of the sport, or the type of individuals attracted to this mode of exercise.

Shephard (1983) has suggested that if competition, publicity, or pride encourage persistence in the face of warning symptoms, or if participation occurs in conjunction with time pressures, business or social anxieties, then exercise is more likely to have adverse consequences. These properties are reflective of some of the characteristics of the Type A behaviour pattern.

A substantial body of literature has documented the association of Type A behaviour patterns with coronary heart disease (Review Panel, 1981). However, many of the behavioural characteristics displayed by Type A individuals (such as elevated achievement strivings, tendency to deny subjective states including fatigue and pain, and proneness to seek out challenging situations) would seem to provide distinct advantages in contexts such as athletic competition (Carver et al., 1981).

Attempts have been made to analyse the incidence and implications of Type A behaviour in competitive and challenging situations (e.g. Shahidi et al., 1991) but few studies have extended the research environment to include sport competition. Friedman (1979) has cautioned that people with this behavioural characteristic may find severe exercise and competitive sport hazardous. There is a concern that squash may prove an attractive exercise mode for Type A individuals and that this has the potential for adverse health consequences.

The purpose of this paper is to report the findings of two cross-sectional studies on Type A behaviour in squash:
(i)   a profile of Type A behaviour patterns of squash-players at differing standards,

Science and Racket Sports II, edited by A. Lees, I. Maynard, M. Hughes and T. Reilly. Published in 1998 by E & FN Spon, 11 New Fetter Lane, London EC4P 4EE, UK.   ISBN: 0 419 23030 0

(ii)   an investigation into the relationship between physiological health and fitness, and Type A behaviour in male squash-players at differing standards.

2 Methods

The Jenkins Activity Survey - Form E (Jenkins et al., 1974) was distributed to 230 subjects recruited by means of poster advertisements and personal enquiries. The 173 subjects who completed the questionnaire (75% response rate) were allocated to 5 groups contingent upon squash-playing competence as follows:

(i)   Sedentary   (n = 35, 20 male, 15 female; age,   S.D. = 35.0   11.3 years)
(ii)   Recreational (n = 49, 32 male, 17 female; age,   S.D. = 30.3   9.6 years)
(iii)   Club   (n = 49, 35 male, 14 female; age,   S.D. = 33.9   7.9 years)
(iv)   County   (n = 26, 15 male, 11 female; age,   S.D. = 30.8   7.0 years)
(v)   National   (n = 14,   9 male, 5 female; age,   S.D. = 23.9   4.1 years)

In addition to the Type A-B scale, the Jenkins Activity Survey (JAS) can be scored for three independent factors. The three scales have been named Speed and Impatience, Job-involvement and Hard-driving. Since the focus of this study was competitive behaviour, only the Type A and Hard-driving scales were considered relevant. Normative scores are calculated by a linear transformation of raw scores to a mean of 0.0 and a standard deviation of 10.0. Positive scores therefore indicate Type A tendencies.

A sample of 31 voluntary male subjects from the squash-playing groups were further tested for selected physiological measures. Due to small numbers, the county and national groups were collapsed into an Elite group. Subject distribution was as follows:

(i)   Recreational   (n = 11, age,   S.D. = 36.4   7.4 years)
(ii)   Club   (n = 10, age,   S.D. = 34.6   6.3 years)
(iii)   Elite   (n = 10, age,   S.D. = 29.8   7.8 years)

Anthropometric measurements were taken for body mass (Avery scales) and skinfold thickness (Harpenden skinfold calipers). Body composition was assessed by the summation of four skinfolds (Durnin and Womersley, 1974).

Cardiorespiratory fitness was determined by means of a submaximal ergometer test. Individuals with Type A characteristics have been found to underestimate perceived exertion and are more likely to ignore fatigue signals that pre-empt voluntary termination of exercise (Carver et al., 1976), thus exposing themselves to the possible risk of over-exertion. In this study, the index of aerobic capacity was taken to be the oxygen uptake (VO_2) corresponding to a heart rate of 170 beats.min[-1]. Oxygen consumption was measured using an on-line gas analysis system (P.K. Morgan, Rainham) and heart rate was recorded using a three-lead electrocardiogram during a graded treadmill test. The VO_2-170 value was determined by interpolation of the oxygen consumption and heart rate regression line.

Coronary risk was assessed by means of subjects' blood lipid profiles. Venous blood samples were collected, following a 12 hour fast, by a qualified phlebotomist and were subsequently analysed by reflective photometry at Wallasey General Hospital. Both total cholesterol and high density lipoprotein fraction were measured.

3 Results and Discussion

In order to control for the age differences and the unequal male: female ratios within the groups, a one-way analysis of covariance (ANCOVA) was performed with age and sex as covariates. A Least Significant Difference multiple comparison test was employed to determine differences between each sample mean.

3.1 Type A Scores

Results from the initial cross-sectional study revealed that no significant difference existed between the club, recreational and sedentary subjects on the JAS subscales (Table 1). Based on the normative scoring method of the JAS, approximately 49% of subjects in the sedentary and club groups were classified as Type A. The percentage of Type A subjects in the recreation group was somewhat lower at 35%. These results do not suggest that Type A individuals are specifically attracted to squash as an exercise mode.

The County group members were found to have significantly higher Type A than both the Recreational ($P < 0.01$) and Sedentary groups ($P < 0.05$). The competitive element of the Type A behaviour pattern is reflected in the Hard-driving scale of the JAS. On this subscale the County group scored significantly higher than the Sedentary, Recreational and Club groups ($P < 0.05$; $P < 0.001$; $P < 0.05$ respectively). In addition, approximately 73% of subjects within the county group were classified as Type A. Although the National group was found not to differ from any of the other subject groups in terms of their absolute JAS scores, 64% of the subjects were classified as Type A. These results indicate a prevalence of Type A individuals in the higher competence groups that may be explained by a self-selection process whereby the characteristics required for competing at higher levels are those displayed by Type A individuals. This has the potential for adverse health consequences.

3.2 Physiological profiles

Comparative results displayed in Table 2 demonstrate a similarity in body mass for the three groups. The recreational and club groups were found to possess above average total skinfold thicknesses. Significant differences were noted between the recreational players and the elite group ($P < 0.05$).

Table 1. Comparative results for the Jenkins Activity Survey

Group	Percentage Type A	Type A Mean (S.D.) [normative]		Hard-driving/ Competitive Mean (S.D.) [normative]	
Sedentary	48.6%	225.37_a (78.65) [- 0.16]		139.14_a (43.62) [0.03]	
Recreational	34.7%	206.94_a (60.66) [- 2.51]		129.00_a (31.49) [- 2.20]	
Club	49.0%	$229.24_{a,b}$ (72.27) [0.32]		142.33_a (39.55) [0.87]	
County	73.1%	260.58_b (77.70) [4.32]		162.73_b (52.85) [5.35]	
National	64.3%	$245.71_{a,b}$ (64.07) [2.37]		$151.93_{a,b}$ (37.04) [2.99]	

Note: Columns with different subscripts are significantly different

Table 2. Physiological characteristics of male squash-players

Variable	Recreational (n = 11) Mean (S.D.)		Club (n = 10) Mean (S.D.)		Elite (n = 10) Mean (S.D.)		ANCOVA
Body Mass (kg)	72.56	(7.6)	71.29	(5.6)	71.92	(6.0)	n.s.
Sum of Skinfolds (mm)	46.4	(17.7)	40.3	(8.3)	29.3	(9.0)	$P < 0.05$
VO_2 - 170 (ml.min^{-1}.kg^{-1})	42.81	(5.23)	48.70	(7.16)	58.81	(7.53)	$P < 0.01$
Total Cholesterol (mmol.l^{-1})	5.71	(1.24)	5.71	(0.68)	4.43	(1.21)	$P < 0.05$
Total HDL Cholesterol (mmol.l^{-1})	1.29	(0.30)	1.42	(0.35)	1.35	(0.22)	n.s.
Total Cholesterol/ HDL Ratio	4.61	(1.32)	4.24	(1.06)	3.32	(0.80)	n.s.

The most significant difference between the groups was their aerobic capacity as measured by VO_2 (ml.min^{-1}.kg^{-1}) at 170 beats.min^{-1}. This aerobic capacity index progressively increased as the group standard increased. Thus, the Elite group scored significantly higher than both the Club ($P < 0.01$) and Recreational players ($P < 0.001$).

In accordance with their more favourable aerobic capacity values, the Elite group also possessed significantly less plasma cholesterol than the other groups (both $P < 0.05$). However, no differences were observed in the amount of high density lipoprotein (HDL) contained within this sample nor on the total cholesterol: HDL ratio. The results for the Recreational and Club groups exceed the threshold (4.0 mmol.l[-1]) for very low risk of CHD, but only marginally (Williams et al., 1979). Overall, the squash-playing sample demonstrated a very positive physiological health profile.

In order to determine the relationship between the physiological measures and Type A behaviour, a correlation matrix was calculated (Table 3). Although the correlation values are moderate, some significant relationships were identified. The VO_2-170 measure was found to correlate with a tendency to display Type A ($r = 0.447$, $P < 0.05$) and hard-driving and competitive behaviour ($r = 0.403$, $P < 0.05$). It seems that the fitter squash players are more likely to display overt competitive and Type A behaviours. These are primarily subjects within the upper competence group.

Table 3. Correlation matrix of physiological measures and Type A scores

	Mass	Skinfold	VO_2-170	Chol.	HDL	Chol/HDL
Type A	-0.261	-0.289	0.447*	0.074	0.436*	-0.286
Hard-driving	-0.137	-0.349	0.403*	0.026	0.429*	-0.335

* $P < 0.05$

The more positive HDL levels were displayed by subjects with Type A tendencies ($r = 0.436$, $P < 0.05$). Similar relationships existed between HDL scores and the Hard-driving subscale ($r = 0.429$, $P < 0.05$).

The Type A behaviour pattern has been linked retrospectively and prospectively with CHD (Review Panel, 1981). Yet in the present study, subjects with higher Type A scores possessed more favourable HDL profiles which paradoxically protects against the occurrence of CHD (Castelli et al., 1977). This is in conflict with previous findings (Glass, 1977) and may be explained by the following:

(a) the physiological mechanism for the link between the Type A behaviour pattern and CHD may not be serum cholesterol. Heart disease refers to a collection of disease endpoints that may vary greatly i.e. angina pectoris, coronary insufficiency, myocardial infarction. It is possible that psychological factors could have a greater impact on one disease condition than on another (Booth-Kewley and Friedman, 1987). Numerous studies have demonstrated that Type A individuals display larger episodic increases in catecholamines when confronted with challenging or stressful tasks than their Type B counterparts (e.g. Shahidi et al., 1991). Thus, arousal of the sympathetic nervous system may play a more important role in the formation of CHD than serum cholesterol profiles.

(b) the threat that Type A behaviour poses to cardiac health may be attenuated by cardiorespiratory fitness. It has been noted that increased levels of physical fitness are associated with more favourable blood lipid profiles (Seals et al., 1984). Participation in regular exercise has been shown to improve the coronary risk profile of subjects as well as reducing Type A tendencies. Although the competitive nature of squash may negate the expected reduction in Type A scores associated with exercise involvement, the improvements in physiological status seem to have a counterbalancing effect.

(c) the specific behavioural aspects of the Type A pattern may be advantageous in sport contexts and may be exhibited in this context without having negative implications for health. Although the athletes in the present sample were found to possess the behaviour characteristics of the Type A pattern, elite athletes in general display physiological contra-indicators to CHD. It is questionable whether the terms Type A and coronary-prone should be used interchangeably (Matthews et al., 1982)

4 Conclusions

This study has revealed no evidence to suggest that Type A individuals are naturally attracted to squash. The results did, however, indicate a prevalence of Type A behaviour amongst the higher competency groups, suggesting a self-selection mechanism. Higher Type A scores for these subjects were not associated with greater cardiac risk as measured by blood lipid profiles. The relationship between Type A behaviour and heart disease in athletes is an important area for future research.

5 Acknowledgements

This study was funded by the Health Promotion Research Trust

6 References

Booth-Kewley, S. and Friedman, H.S. (1987) Psychological predictors of heart disease: A quantitative review. **Psychological Bulletin**, 101, 343-362.

Brady, H.R., Kinirons, M., Lynch, T., Ohman, E.M., Tormey, W., O'Malley, K. and Horgan, J.H. (1989) Heart rate and metabolic response to competitive squash in veteran players: Identification of risk factors for sudden cardiac death. **European Heart Journal**, 10, 1029-1035.

Carver, C.S., Coleman, A.E. and Glass, D.C. (1976) The coronary-prone behaviour pattern and the suppression of fatigue on a treadmill test. **Journal of Personality and Social Psychology**, 33, 460-466.

Carver, C.S., De Gregorio, E. and Gillis, R. (1981) Challenge and Type A behaviour among intercollegiate football players. **Journal of Sport Psychology**, 36, 361-366.

Castelli, W.P., Doyle, J.P. and Gordon, T. (1977) HDL cholesterol and other lipids in coronary heart disease. **Circulation**, 55, 767-772.

Durnin, J.V.G.A. and Womersley, J. (1974) Body fat assessed from total body density and its estimation from skinfold thickness. **British Journal of Nutrition**, 32, 169-179.

Friedman, M. (1979) The modification of Type A behaviour in post-infarction patients. **American Heart Journal**, 97, 551-560.

Glass, D.C. (1977) **Behaviour Patterns, Stress and Coronary Heart Disease**. Eslbaum, Hillsdale, New Jersey.

Jenkins, C.D., Rosenman, R.H. and Zyzanski, S.J. (1974) Prediction of clinical coronary heart disease by a test for the coronary-prone behaviour pattern. **New England Journal of Medicine**, 23, 1271-1275.

Matthews, K.A., Krantz, D.S., Dembroski, T.M. and MacDougall, M. (1982) Unique and common variance in Structured Interview and Jenkins Activity Survey measures on the Type A behaviour pattern. **Journal of Personality and Social Psychology**, 42, 303-313.

Review Panel on Coronary-prone Behaviour and CHD (1981) Coronary prone behaviour and coronary heart disease: A critical review. **Circulation**, 63, 1199-1215.

Seals, D.R., Allen, W.K., Hurley, B.F., Dalsky, G.P., Ehsani, A.A. and Hagberg, J.M. (1984) Elevated high-density lipoprotein cholesterol levels in older endurance athletes. **American Journal of Cardiology**, 54, 390-393.

Shahidi, S., Henley, S., Willows, J. and Furnham, A. (1991) Type A behaviour pattern: The effect of competition on heart rate and performance on a driving game. **Journal of Personality and Individual Differences**, 12, 1277-1282.

Shephard, R.J. (1983) Identifications of individuals at high risk. **Proceedings of the Exercise, Health and Medicine Symposium**. Sports Council, London, 49-51.

Shephard, R.J. (1991) Cardiac risks of racquet sports (Editorial). **Canadian Journal of Sports Sciences**, 16, 6-7.

Shephard, R.J. (1992) Death on the squash court? (Editorial). **Canadian Journal of Sports Sciences**, 17, 152.

Siscovick, D.S. (1990) Risks of exercising: Sudden cardiac death and injuries, in **Exercise, Fitness and Health: A Consensus of Current Knowledge** (eds C. Bouchard, R.J. Shephard, T. Stephens, J.R. Sutton and B.D. McPherson). Human Kinetics, Champaign, Ill., 707-713.

Visser, F.C., Mihciokur, M., Van Duk, C.N., den Engelsman, J. and Roos, J.P. (1987) Arrhythmias in athletes: Comparison of stress test, 24 h Holter and Holter monitoring during the game in squash players. **European Heart Journal**, 8, 29-32.

Williams, P., Robinson, D. and Bailey, A. (1979) High-density lipoprotein and coronary risk factors in normal men. **Lancet**, 1, 72-75.

23 The psychological skills of Britain's top young squash players

C.A. Mahoney[1] and M.K. Todd[2]
[1]Department of Sports Studies, Roehampton Institute London, UK
and [2]Department of Physical Education and Sports Studies,
Worcester College of Higher Education, Worcester, UK

1 Introduction

Squash in Britain is one sport which has experienced success at all levels over the last 25 years. During this time senior males and females have won major titles and team events and more recently the junior teams have also done well, though the consistency of success has been far from evident. This success can be attributed to the determination of individual players rather than any real structure in sport development. However, since 1993 a Sport Science Support Programme, funded by the Sports Council in England, has been in place to allow access to sport science provision in physiology and psychology for Nationally ranked players at various age groups and in open competition. Australian squash has for over 13 years had access to such provision, and in that time it has maintained a very high profile in world squash, consistently winning major individual and team competitions, with several players consistently ranked in the world's top 10 males and females. This is undoubtedly due, in part, to a highly structured coaching and development programme and the benefit of an Institute of Sport which has provided full support for sport sciences, sports medicine and other services.

The use of psychology in British sport is still not well received. At the last three Olympic Games, Britain has taken one, seven and nine sport psychologists, respectively, this compared with the 1988 US athletics team who took 14. While there is no direct correlation between the use of psychological skills training (PST) and winning, such programmes have been valued as part of the learning process (Vealey, 1994) and have been shown to enhance cognitive processing in sport (Vealey, 1988; 1994).

In squash the use of PST has remained relatively low key, apart from the highly publicised involvement of Graham Jones with Lisa Opie when she won the British Open in 1991. Given the level of research world-wide which now accepts the value of PST programmes and the integration of psychology into sport (Beauchamp et al., 1996; Murphy, 1995; Weinberg and Comar, 1994) it is surprising that a sport such as squash, which often draws its clientele from a professional background, has been slow

Science and Racket Sports II, edited by A. Lees, I. Maynard, M. Hughes and T. Reilly. Published in 1998 by E & FN Spon, 11 New Fetter Lane, London EC4P 4EE, UK.   ISBN: 0 419 23030 0

to encompass such initiatives. This study sought to determine the baseline level of psychological skills in professional junior ranked players resident in Britain.

2 Methods

The thirteen players involved in this study were all ranked in English Junior Under 19 ranking lists at the time of testing, with only one player ranked outside the top 10 for their gender. Each player was a current junior professional squash player (mean age±S.D. 16.7±1.5 years) and part of the National Training Scheme organised and run by the Squash Rackets Association under the control of their National Coach, team physiologist and fitness trainers. Following descriptions of what would be involved and assurances of confidentiality, verbal informed consent was gained from the players, and then each completed the Psychological Skills Inventory for Sports revision 5 (PSIS R-5; Mahoney, 1989) in a non-competitive setting to establish baseline data.

The PSIS R-5 assesses cognitive strategies to control anxiety, confidence, concentration, mental preparation, motivation and team focus. The questionnaire consists of 45 items using a 5-point Likert response scale in which Mahoney (1989) reported an internal consistency with a split-half correlation coefficient at 0.567 and Spearman-Brown coefficient of 0.724. Other authors (White and Croce, 1992; White, 1993) reported Cronbach alpha reliability coefficients for the six subscales ranging from $r = 0.69$ to $r = 0.77$ and $r = 0.69$ to $r = 0.84$ respectively. Bull (1990) found acceptable reliability for the anxiety management and confidence subscales and claimed the results lent construct validity to these dimensions.

Data were analysed using a range of simple statistics, one-way ANOVA with gender as the independent variable, correlation and by using visual interpretation of graphical representation of PSIS R-5 data.

3 Results

The completed questionnaires included responses from 6 female players and 7 male players. Since the players were already categorised as elite players the intention was not to differentiate them on ability but to establish what mental strategies identified from the questionnaire appeared to be important in squash, or may be in need of further development.

The results from the PSIS R-5 questionnaire have been summarised in Table 1, and show the percentile scores for each of the six factors previously identified within the questionnaire. The final column is for comparison with previously established data by Mahoney (1989) of characteristics in elite sport.

Table 1. Mean (±SD) player responses to PSIS R-5 self report questionnaire

Characteristics	Males (n=7)	Females (n=6)	All (n=13)	Mahoney (1989) (n=28)
Age (years)	17.1 ± 1.2	16.2 ± 1.7	16.7 ± 1.5	>14
Anxiety AX (%)	56.1 ± 6.1	49.2 ± 18.1	52.9 ± 13.0	58.2 ± 15.7
Concentration CC (%)	57.1 ± 19.1	45.8 ± 8.7	51.9 ± 15.7	61.6 ± 21.9
Confidence CF (%)	67.9 ± 12.7	47.7 ± 15.5	58.6 ± 17.0	69.7 ± 17.7
Mental Preparation MP (%)	50.0 ± 8.0	48.6 ± 11.4	49.4 ± 9.3	46.0 ± 10.8
Motivation MV (%)	61.7 ± 19.6	54.8 ± 13.3	58.5 ± 16.7	61.1 ± 17.8
Team Focus TF (%)	67.4 ± 9.6	70.8 ± 7.6	69.0 ± 8.6	59.3 ± 11.9

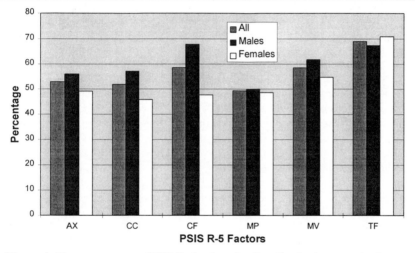

Figure 1. Factor scores on PSIS R-5 subscales for elite junior squash players.
AX=anxiety, CC=concentration, CF=confidence, MP=mental preparation, MV=motivation, TF=team focus

One way ANOVA with gender as the independent variable showed a significant difference between males and females in confidence ($F_{1,12}$ = 6.68, P<0.05). This can be clearly seen in Figure 1 though no other significant differences were established between the groups.

Figure 2 is a visual comparison of ranking with the average score from each of the 6 factors on PSIS R-5 (ranking has been multiplied by 5 to give magnitude for plotting). This averaging technique has been used by Mahoney (1989) to give a mean scale score (MSS) as an impression of overall mental strategy behaviour in sport. While there was no statistically significant relationship between ranking and MSS, their is an obvious inverse relationship between ranking and MSS (see Figure 2), as expected.

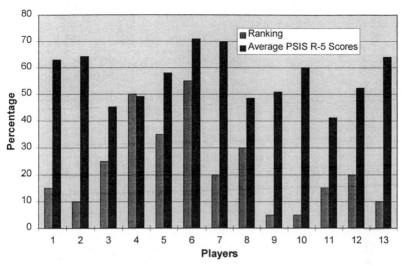

Figure 2. Player ranking (x5) and average PSIS R-5 scores.

4 Discussion

This study has managed to throw some light on the self-reported nature of the mental skills inherent in elite junior squash players. While these players have not been exposed to an intensive on-going PST programme, they have had limited exposure to the use of psychology in sport and access to a sport psychologist. This study has highlighted the difficulties in establishing information on the mental skills of players in any sport and raised further questions related to the evaluation of baseline levels and the efficacy of programmes to develop mental strategies for sport (Mahoney and O'Leary, in press). The PSIS R-5 has however, been described as a tool potentially suitable to use in pre- and post-intervention studies to determine improvement (Singer et al., 1993).

The results quite clearly show a gender difference for confidence, a result shown in the research of others (Lirgg, 1992; Stewart and Corbin, 1988; Petruzzello and Corbin, 1988). In addition, it is clear from Table 1 that the self-reported female's mental skills are much lower than that reported by Mahoney (1989) of elite performers in America and from European research (Morrison and Mahoney, 1996; Mahoney et al., 1996). The normative nature of the PSIS R-5 subscales suggests players who score more than the 50 percentile are above average. Female squash players are clearly below this threshold except in motivation where they score very highly. While this study sought to establish baseline data as part of a needs analysis, it is reasonable to speculate as to why these variations are so apparent. Cause and effect are unknown from this study; nevertheless the findings could be the result of, cultural variations as described by Cox & Liu (1993), squash players lacking appropriate mental skills when compared with other sports, the mental demands of squash differing from those of other sports or female squash players, while more motivated, lack elite performance mental skills

5 Conclusions

The study has shown that cognitive skills can be discriminated using questionnaires like PSIS R-5. This information has value as part of needs analysis and in establishing a performance profile which should be integrated into the initial stages of any cognitive intervention.

The study has served to highlight a number of important issues surrounding the preliminary development of PST programmes, and suggests cultural variations (at least in responses of females) need to be considered as a significant determinant in studies of this type. The PSIS R-5 is sufficiently sensitive to discern differences between groups based on gender and gives valuable information related to the mental skills of elite junior squash players.

Since the PSIS R-5 questionnaire was developed in America, for elite American athletes and Mahoney (1989) has stated it is still in its developmental infancy, there is a strong need to develop a British and/or European version which takes into account cultural variations between Britain/Europe and America, especially the differences between British English and American English. On this basis it is reasonable to suggest PSIS R-5 should be critically reviewed in this context with a view to producing a population specific variation, something which has yet to be completed in a valid and reliable manner.

6 References

Beauchamp, P.H., Halliwell, W.R., Fournier, J.F., and Koestner, R. (1996) Effects of cognitive-behavioural psychological skills training on the motivation, preparation, and putting performance of novice golfers. **The Sport Psychologist**, 10, 157-170.

Bull, S.J. (1990) The psychological skills inventory for sports: A preliminary investigation. **Journal of Sport Psychology**, 8, 82-83.

Cox, R.H., and Liu, Z. (1993) Psychological skills: A cross-cultural investigation. **International Journal of Sport Psychology**, 24, 326-340.

Lirgg, C.D. (1992) Girls and women, sport and self-confidence. **Quest**, 44, 158-178.

Mahoney, M.J. (1989) Psychological predictors of elite and non-elite performance in Olympic weightlifters. **International Journal of Sport Psychology**, 20, 1-12.

Mahoney, C.A., MacIntyre, T. and Moran, A. (1996) Mental skills in Ireland's top sports performers. **The Irish Psychologist**, 23, 46.

Mahoney, C.A. and O'Leary, O. (in press). Measuring cognitive enhancement: cross cultural variations and the link with psychological skills training. **BPS Publication.**

Morrison, Z.A. and Mahoney, C.A. (1996) A multisport comparison of psychological skills. **Journal of Sports Sciences**, 14, 41 (abstract).

Murphy, S.M. (1995) Introduction to sport psychology interventions, in **Sport Psychology Interventions** (ed. S.M. Murphy), Human Kinetics, Champaign, Ill, pp. 1-17.

Petruzzello, S.J. and Corbin, C.B. (1988) The effects of performance feedback on female self-confidence. **Journal of Sport and Exercise Psychology,** 10, 174-183.

Singer, R.N., Murphey, M. and Tennant, L.K. (eds) (1993) **Handbook of Research on Sport Psychology**. Macmillan Publishing Company, New York.

Stewart, M.J. and Corbin, C.B. (1988) Feedback dependence among low confidence preadolescent boys and girls. **Research Quarterly for Exercise and Sport**, 59, 160-164.

Vealey, R.S. (1988) Future directions in psychological skills training. **The Sport Psychologist**, 2, 318-336.

Vealey, R.S. (1994) Current status and prominent issues in sport psychology interventions. **Medicine and Science in Sport and Exercise**, 26, 495-502.

Weinberg, R.S., and Comar, W. (1994) The effectiveness of psychological interventions in competitive sport. **Sports Medicine**, 18, 406-418.

White, S.A. (1993) The relationship between psychological skills, experience, and practice commitment among collegiate male and female skiers. **The Sport Psychologist**, 7, 49-57.

White, S.A., and Croce, R.V. (1992) Nordic disabled skiers and able-bodied skiers: an exploratory analysis of the psychological skills inventory for sport (PSIS, R-5). **Clinical Kinesiology**, 45, 7-9.

24 Stress and arousal in elite youth badminton players: a reversal theory perspective

J. Hudson
Sport Science, School of Social Sciences, University of Teesside, Middlesbrough, UK

1 Introduction

Understanding the complex relationship between arousal and sports performance remains a primary concern within sport psychology. For instance, Kerr (1987) stated that there is a consensus amongst sport psychologists that the relationship between arousal and performance is critical to elite level sport. One approach which has been employed to investigate this phenomenon is "reversal theory" (Kerr, 1987). Only those proposals of reversal theory that are examined in this study are discussed here and a more comprehensive review can be found in Apter (1989). Reversal theory suggests that level of arousal *per se* is less important for performance than the individual's own interpretation of his/her arousal level - a proposal that contradicts earlier models of the arousal-performance relationship, for example, the "inverted-U hypothesis" (Yerkes-Dodson, 1908, cited by Kerr, 1987). According to Kerr (1990), sports performance will be detrimentally affected by discrepancies between the athlete's perceived arousal and the level that he/she would prefer to experience, that is, if the athlete feels more or less aroused than he/she would like to.

Arousal discrepancy is thought to result in unpleasant emotions and subsequently, stress - known as tension stress (Males and Kerr, 1996). Further stress is created by coping efforts directed at alleviating this tension stress - this is referred to as effort stress. It is likely that insufficient or excessive effort stress, in relation to experienced tension stress, will not alleviate the tension stress but will further exacerbate the situation. This has prompted Males and Kerr (1996) to claim that discrepancies between effort and tension stress will result in poor sports performance.

Empirical substantiation of these proposals is currently emerging: for example Cox and Kerr (1989) revealed that skilled and winning squash players reported less pre-match arousal discrepancy than did novice and losing players. Using intra-individual comparisons of elite male slalom canoeists' performances over a season, Males and Kerr (1996) found that all the subjects' best performances were preceded by no arousal discrepancy. However, only one subject reported a significant arousal discrepancy prior to his worst performance and only one subject reported a significant discrepancy between tension and effort stress prior to their worst performance.

Science and Racket Sports II, edited by A. Lees, I. Maynard, M. Hughes and T. Reilly. Published in 1998 by E & FN Spon, 11 New Fetter Lane, London EC4P 4EE, UK.   ISBN: 0 419 23030 0

Biddle and Hill (1992) have demonstrated the importance of considering subjective performance outcomes (the individual's own assessment of his/her performance) in sport psychology research. However, Cox and Kerr (1989) and Males and Kerr (1996) measured only objective performance outcomes (performance finishing time or position). Considering this, and the equivocal support for the reversal theory proposals outlined above, it seems that further empirical inquiry is required into these proposals across a range of sports contexts, performers and outcomes. This is particularly important if reversal theory is to be used as a framework for sport psychology interventions as Kerr (1993) suggested it can be. Therefore, using a sample of elite youth badminton players, this study investigated the following hypotheses: pre-game arousal discrepancy is associated with poor objective and subjective performance outcomes, and, pre-game discrepancy between tension and effort stress is associated with poor subjective and objective performance outcomes.

2 Methods

2.1 Subjects
Subjects were 7 male and 9 female youth badminton players whose ages ranged from 13 to 19 years with a mean age of 14.9 years (S.D.=± 1.6 years). Relative to their age group, 8 were international standard, one was a national standard player, 6 were county or regional standard and one player failed to provide this information. All players were attending a week long 'High Performance Badminton Camp' at a United Kingdom university. Data reported here were collected during a tournament held on the final evening of the camp.

2.2 Instruments
The measurement instrument consisted of various sub-components. The modified Tension Effort Stress Inventory [TESI] (Svebak, 1993), as used by Males and Kerr (1996), assessed perceived internal and external tension and effort stress. The modification made by Males and Kerr (1996) was to add two scales of the Telic State Measure [TSM] (Svebak and Murgatroyd, 1985, cited by Moles and Kerr, 1996) to assess the individual's levels of preferred and felt arousal.

Perceived internal tension stress was assessed using the following item: *In relation to your next game, how much pressure, stress, challenge or demand do you feel under from your own body/self?* and, for effort stress: *In relation to your next game, how much effort do you think you're putting up to cope with the pressure, stress, challenge or demand you feel from your own body/self?* Items relating to external tension and effort stress replaced *your own body/self* with *other factors.* Perceived and preferred arousal levels were assessed using the following items, respectively, *Please estimate how aroused (worked up) you feel right now* and, *Please estimate how aroused (worked up) you would prefer to feel right now.* Subjects responded using a 7 point Likert scale anchored with *1=low* and *7=high* on the TSM items and *1=no pressure* and *7=very much pressure* on the TESI items. Males and Kerr (1996) combined these state measures in this way and suggested that the validity of each questionnaire was unlikely to be compromised simply by presenting the measures in the same questionnaire, which have been used in a number of previously published studies (Males and Kerr, 1996). Likert scale measures of performance satisfaction have also been used in a number of previously published studies (for example, Biddle and Hill, 1992). Objective performance outcomes were recorded as win or lose and subjective performance outcomes were recorded as the individual's level of satisfaction with his/her performance. These were indicated by subjects' responses to the question: *How satisfied are you with the way you just played?* which were recorded on a 7 point Likert scale, anchored by *1=very satisfied* to *7= not at all satisfied.*

2.3 Procedure
Informed consent was obtained from all subjects and from coaching staff at the 'High Performance Badminton Camp' who were acting in *loco parentis.* Prior to warming up for the tournament, subjects were instructed on how and when to complete the questionnaire. The athletes were divided into two teams which competed against each other throughout the tournament (this was not part of the experimental manipulation). Each player could play a maximum of three games: a singles, a doubles, and, a mixed doubles match. Points were awarded to each team on the basis of the outcome of each game (this was not part of the experimental manipulation) and the winning team was the one with the most points at the end of the tournament. Due to the number of players attending the camp it was not possible for every player to play three games, therefore 13 played a total of three games and 3 played only two, meaning that complete data sets were not available for all subjects.

Subjects completed the measurement instrument at the following times throughout the tournament: before their first game; after their first game; after their second game, and, after their third game

3 Results

3.1 Subjective outcome and arousal discrepancy
Arousal discrepancy was determined by calculating the absolute difference between the subjects' reported levels of preferred and felt arousal. Two groups were formed based on the subjects' reported levels of satisfaction: 'satisfied' was indicated by a rating from 1-3 on the subjective performance scale described above and 'dissatisfaction' by a rating from 4-7. A Wilcoxon Matched Pairs Signed Ranks test indicated significantly greater arousal discrepancy when players were satisfied with their performance than when they were dissatisfied [$Z=-2.8966$, $P<0.01$ (2-tailed probability)].

3.2 Objective outcome and arousal discrepancy
A Wilcoxon Matched Pairs Signed Ranks test indicated no significant differences in arousal discrepancy when players won compared with when they lost [$Z=-0.2213$, $P>0.05$ (2-tailed probability)].

3.3 Subjective outcome and stress discrepancy

Stress discrepancy was indicated by calculating the absolute difference between the subjects' reported tension and effort stress - one for internal stress discrepancy and one for external stress discrepancy. 'Satisfied' and 'Dissatisfied' groups were formed as above. A Wilcoxon Matched Pairs Signed Ranks test indicated greater external stress discrepancy when players were dissatisfied with their performance than when they were satisfied that approached traditional alpha levels [Z=-1.8743, P=0.06 (2-tailed probability)]. A Wilcoxon Matched Pairs Signed Ranks test indicated no significant differences in internal stress discrepancy between 'satisfied' and 'dissatisfied' players [Z=-0.5112, P>0.05 (2-tailed probability)].

3.4 Objective outcome and stress discrepancy

A Wilcoxon Matched-Pairs Signed Ranks tests revealed no significant differences between the internal and external stress discrepancies reported prior to games that were won and those that were lost. [For internal stress discrepancy, Z=-0.9308, P>0.05 (2-tailed probability) and for external stress discrepancy, Z=0.00, P>0.05 (2-tailed probability)].

4 Discussion

Results of this study lend only partial support to the first hypothesis. Contrary to predictions, but in support of Males and Kerr's (1996) findings, poor objective performance outcomes were not associated with pre-game discrepancy between felt and preferred arousal levels in these elite youth badminton players. However, in line with predictions, significantly less pre-game arousal discrepancy was reported when players were satisfied with the way they had played than when they were dissatisfied. This supports Biddle and Hill's (1992) contention of the importance of subjective performance outcomes. Also supported here was Kerr's (1987) suggestion that the athlete's own interpretation of their arousal is central to the relationship between arousal and performance in sport.

These findings also offered only partial support for the second hypothesis investigated. Contrary to predictions, pre-game internal or external stress discrepancy was no greater prior to games that were lost than prior to those that were won. Internal stress discrepancies were no greater when players were dissatisfied than when they were satisfied with the way they played. However, external stress discrepancies were significantly greater when players were dissatisfied with the way they had played. This may indicate that these athletes were unable to cope with perceived stress from external sources which could have adversely affected personal performance satisfaction. These dissatisfied players reported greater perceived effort than tension stress. External sources of stress may be particularly salient for these athletes who may then exert greater effort stress than is needed to cope with perceived external tension stress. In so doing, effort may be directed away from performance, resulting in performance dissatisfaction. It is also possible that the athletes' coping efforts were misdirected which again may have influenced reported levels of performance satisfaction.

5 Conclusions

Interventions aimed at helping athletes to manage arousal levels and so gain maximal satisfaction from their sporting experience should be based around the individual's currently preferred level of arousal. This is particularly important in minimising attrition from youth sport as the athlete may be achieving objective success, but not personal satisfaction, and therefore may no longer want to participate in the sport. Subsequent research should investigate this suggestion and should identify and explain reasons why arousal discrepancy appears to influence subjective but not objective performance outcomes. To extend the current line of inquiry, future research should examine whether or not performance satisfaction is underpinned by perceptions of optimal levels of felt arousal in relation to desired levels of arousal.

Future empirical inquiry should identify external sources of stress and interventions that can help young athletes to cope with them to maximise the positive affect which can be gained from sports participation.

In summary, it appears that reversal theory offers a potential framework for understanding the relationship between arousal, stress and sports performance and for guiding interventions that seek to maximise the athlete's performance achievements and satisfaction. Further research in this area is clearly required.

6 References

Apter, M. J. (1989) **Reversal Theory: Motivation, Emotion and Personality.** Routledge, London.

Biddle, S.J.H., and Hill, A. B. (1992) Attributions for objective outcome and subjective appraisal of performance: Their relationship with emotional reactions in sport. **British Journal of Social Psychology,** 31, 215-226.

Cox, T., and Kerr, J.H. (1989) Arousal effects during tournament play in squash. **Perceptual and Motor Skills**, 69, 1275-1280.

Kerr, J.H. (1987) Structural phenomenology, arousal and performance. **Journal of Human Movement Studies,** 13, 211-229.

Kerr, J.H. (1993) An eclectic approach to psychological interventions in sport: Reversal theory. **The Sport Psychologist,** 7, 400-418.

Males, J.R., and Kerr, J.H. (1996) Stress, emotion, and performance in elite slalom canoeists. **The Sport Psychologist,** 10, 17-36.

Svebak, S. (1993) The development of the Tension and Effort Stress Inventory (TESI), in **Advances in Reversal Theory** (eds J.H. Kerr, S. Murgatroyd and M.J. Apter), Swets Zeitlinger, Amsterdam, pp. 189-204.

Svebak, S., and Murgatroyd, S. (1985) Metamotivational dominance: A multimethod validation of reversal theory constructs. **Journal of Personality and Social Psychology,** 48, 913-919.

Yerkes, R.M., and Dodson, J.D. (1908) The relation of strength of stimulus to rapidity of habit formation. **Journal of Comparative Neurology of Psychology,** 18, 4, 459.

Part Five

Medical, Biomechanical and Technical Aspects of Racket Sports

25 Is the inhibition of smashing and serving movements due to anatomical variations?

J.P. Clarys, E. Barbaix and P. van Roy
Department of Experimental Anatomy, Vrije Universiteit Brussel, Belgium

1 Introduction

All muscles crossing the glenohumeral joint (art. Humeri) participate with high intensities and combine spurt and shunt functions in all overhand movements i.e. above 90° abduction with rotation (Shevlin et al., 1969 ; Jobe et al., 1983, 1984 ; Clarys et al., 1992). They consist of a series of thorax, back, shoulder and intrinsic arm muscles and are particularly trained to reinforce throwing, pitching, smashing and serving movements. In combination with this reinforcement, there is a high level of stabilisation and precision. Most of these overhand ballistic movements are combined with constant or intermittent gripping, resulting in an almost perfect electromyograph (EMG) synchronisation of the shoulder, upper arm and forearm flexors and extensors (Toyoshima et al., 1971 ; Clarys and Cabri, 1993 ; Cheng et al., 1988).

The forward motion of the arm and shoulder girdle becomes clear through the activity of the M. pectoralis major, M. latissimus dorsi and M. biceps brachii with the latter very active half-way through the swing movement and ending with a dynamic contraction of M.triceps brachii prior to ball impact and beyond. In other words, the M. triceps and all forearm and wrist extensors continue their activity in the full extension range of the arm movement. These extensors have to be activated to counteract the wrist flexion torque caused by the finger tendons, as demonstrated by Snijders et al.(1987). They work in harmony with the upper arm extensors and the M. latissimus dorsi and the other shoulder rotators (Basmajian and De Luca, 1985 ; Clarys and Cabri, 1993).

From these findings one can safely assume the presence of a high level of co-contraction during movements such as thowing, pitching, smashing and serving (Rouard and Clarys, 1995). These co-contractions between both flexors and extensors and spurt and shunt muscles could explain : (a) the neuromuscular control in delaying the significant EMG signs of fatigue at various regimes of intermittent gripping (Hägg and Milerad, 1997) and (b) the mechanism of stabilisation and torque generation in the wrist, elbow and shoulder joints at the moment of ball- racket impact, resulting in executions of a powerful and precise serve and/or smash.

Often these different motor control and skill qualities are disturbed in throwing and racket sport athletes. The result is either a decrease in precision or a decrease in force, or both. A series of pain and compression syndromes collected within the terminology

Science and Racket Sports II, edited by A. Lees, I. Maynard, M. Hughes and T. Reilly. Published in 1998 by E & FN Spon, 11 New Fetter Lane, London EC4P 4EE, UK.   ISBN: 0 419 23030 0

of "Thoracic outlet syndrome" (TOS) and "Instability syndromes" are most often, pointed out as the cause of the disturbance in motion.

The thoracic outlet syndrome and shoulder instability provoke well known and partly similar sensations, often described by the athlete as "my arm feels dead... I have no strength in my arm... I feel pins and needles in my arm..." Athletes with shoulder instability and thoracic outlet syndrome share one or more of the following phenomena:- arm-hand weakness, loss of strength, intermittent pain, a burning sensation, limb stiffness, paraesthesia, overall discomfort in arm and shoulder and possibly sweating and swelling of the hand. In relation to pathogenesis, shoulder instability can be arthrological or muscular in origin. The problem frequently arises in movements such as abduction combined with extension and extreme humeral rotation. The cause of TOS may be neurological, vascular or a combination of the two, but will be enhanced by muscular and/or bony structures. On the other hand, approximately 20% of the population have anatomical anomalies such as cervical ribs or a long cervical transverse process, first rib anomalies, hypertrophy or anomalies of the scalene or the omohyoid muscles, hypertrophic callus after fracture of the clavicle and post-stenotic aneurysms of the subclavian artery (Roos, 1971; Tyson and Kaplan, 1975).

The purpose of this study is to increase the knowledge of the function anatomy and kinesiology of the shoulder joint muscles, including the axilla, with the study of the topography and function of an anomalous muscular arch crossing the axilla. In particular, the aim is to use data from Clarys et al. (1996) and interprete their relevance to racket players.

2 Clinical Anatomy

The classical causes of TOS are compression of the brachial plexus between the scalene muscles (Fig. 1A), and either a cervical rib, an anomalous transverse process or an anomalous first rib, or an anomalous slip of the scalene muscles assing in between parts of the plexus. The thoracic outlet syndrome can also be caused by compression of the neurovascular elements of the axilla between the clavicle and the first rib (Fig. 1B) or by compression between the thoracic wall and the coracoid process with its attaching pectoralis minor tendon (Fig. 1C).

In addition to the three classical compression points surgeons sometimes refer to a constriction by a fibromuscular string, but do not define it. This string is the muscular arch of the axilla forming a bridge between the latissimus dorsi and the pectoralis major. According to EMG studies, these two muscles work in perfect co-ordination (co-contraction) during the extension phaze of the smashing or serving arm prior to ball impact.

The muscular arch of the axilla also known as the Arch of Langer, can be described as a muscular slip passing from latissimus dorsi and joining the M. pectoralis major to insert on to the lateral border of the intertubercular sulcus of the humerus, passing medially and anteriorly to biceps brachii, coracobrachialis, the axillary artery surrounding veins, and the median, ulnar and radial nerves and medial cutaneous nerve of the forearm. The origin of the arch is generally a fibrous thickening of the anterior

aponeurosis of latissimus dorsi near the musculotendinous junction ; in some cases a slip of muscle fibres gradually separates from the main body of latissimus dorsi. The muscle itself can either be a well developed thumb-shaped muscle (Fig. 2) or a fibromuscular band or string (Fig. 3). It tends to insert on the tendon of pectoralis major or between this muscle and the intertubercular sulcus. Some fibres often pass to the aponeurosis of the biceps brachii and/or coracobrachialis or to the covering of the intertubercular sulcus. The arch is innervated by a branch of the medial pectoral nerve or by a separate branch from the ansa pectoralis (Birmingham, 1889 ; Tobler, 1902 ; Kasai and Shiba, 1977). The arch can be visualized in lean athletes(Fig. 3)
It is assumed that the contraction of the arch is initiated (or provoked) by the contraction of the co-contracting latissimus dorsi and pectoralis major muscles.

A contraction of the muscular arch can influence blood flow in the basilic vein (Fritsch, 1869). However, it is likely that the contraction of the arch produces compression of all the neuro-vascular structures in the axilla or around the brachial artery. The only other report of a possible role of the arch in TOS is found in a post-mortem description of a muscular arch of the axilla in two patients who had exhibited neuro-vascular symptoms in the forearm and hand (Schramm and von Keyserlingh, 1984). More recently, Serpell and Baum (1991) described the arch's possible role in the aetiology of lymph oedema and suggested that it should be considered in the differential diagnosis of axillary swellings. The authors believed that compression can occur under certain dynamic circumstances and indeed of all neuro-vascular structures at the entrance of the medial bicipital groove (sulcus bicipitalis medialis). It is unlikely that compression is caused by contraction of the arch, alone. Arm motion simulations show that compression occurs when the arm is held in abduction (above horizontal) with simultaneous external rotation.

Increased abduction (to vertical) increases the compression. In this position the insertions of latissimus dorsi and pectoralis major move laterally over the humerus. The angle between both muscles is narrowed and the stretched muscles move closer to each other (Clarys et al., 1996). This corresponds with the arm position of smashing and serving prior to impact. The mechanism of the compression leading to TOS and instability syndromes is (dynamically) demonstrated on cadaveric material in Fig. 4 with a simple abduction and limited rotation.

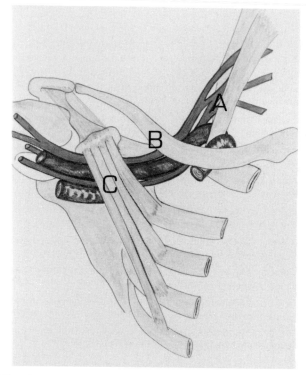

Fig. 1   The three compression locations of TOS
A. between the Mm scaleni
B. between the clavicula & the 1st rib
C. between the M. pectoralis minor & underlying bony structures

3 Echo Graphic (in situ) and Cadaveric (ex-vivo) Quantification of the Axillary Arch

The muscular arch of the axilla (Arch of Langer) was visualized for the first time through echography (Clarys et al., 1996). A Sonoace 81 echo-graphic device with a linear 7.5 MHz probe was used for the quantification (in vivo) of 1321 healthy-sporting-military personnel (1179 male and 142 female soldiers).

The Arch of Langer was found in 8.48 % of the subjects - 99 male and 13 female, generally bilaterally (5.75%). In some cases, the form and shape were quite different on both sides. Unilateral arches were twice as frequent on the left side as on the right side. There were no significant differences between genders in the frequencies. A detailed survey is shown in Table 1. The total number of subjects with arches was 112, but 188 arches in total were found (2642 axillae) corresponding to an incidence of 14.5%.

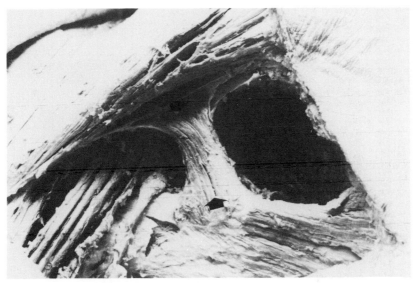

Fig. 2   A large thumb-shaped axillary arch

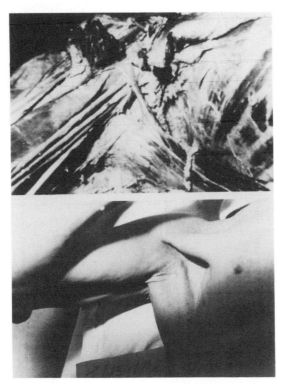

Fig. 3   A fibromuscular string shaped axillary arch (ex-vivo and in situ)

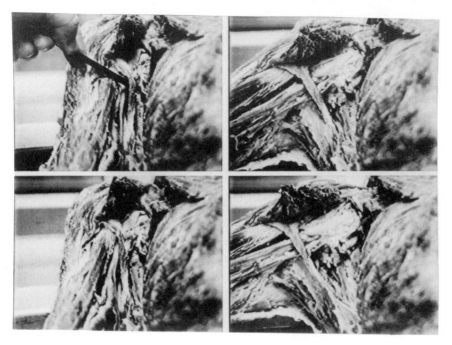

Fig. 4 The axillary arch creates compression of all neurovascular structures in
abduction movements of the arm above horizontal

Table 1. Distribution of axillary arches

	Male	Female	Total
Number of subjects	1179	142	1321
Bilateral	68	8	76
	5.77%	5.63%	5.75%
Left only	20	4	24
	1.70%	2.82%	1.82%
Right only	11	1	12
	0.93%	0.70%	0.91%
Total	99	13	112
	8.39%	9.15%	8.48%

Fourteen cadaver studies have dealt with the axillary arch. Together with the dissection room findings of the authors, Table 2 lists the number of arches found and their percentage of occurrence. Omitting the minimum and maximum value, the average incidence (N=13 studies) is about 11%. Concerning both the in-vivo and ex-vivo data, it seems correct to state that about 10% of the population, and thus of the athletic population can have an axillary arch.

Table 2. The cadaver findings of the axillary arch (of Langer)

Author year	Number of Arches	Number of subjects	Percentage	Population
Kasai & Shiba (1977)	10	88	11.36	Japanese
Krause (1880)	7	100	7.00	Caucasian
Langer (1846)	1	4	25.00	Caucasian
Le Double (1897)	6	95	6.31	Caucasian
MacAlister (1875)	1	16	6.25	Caucasian
Meckel (1816)	1	30	3.33	Caucasiërs
Nishi (1953)	?	?	11.70	Japanese
Perrin (1871)	7	29	24.14	Caucasian
Princeteau (1892)	25	208	12.02	Caucasian
Schramm & von Keyzerlingk (1984)	9	60	15.00	Caucasian
Struthers (1854)	8	105	7.62	Caucasian
Serpell & Baum (1991)	4	2000	0.2	Caucasian
Wagenseil (1927)	?	?	27.00	Chinese
Wood (1868)	6	102	5.88	Caucasian
Clarys et al. (1996)	16	183	9.70	Caucasian

Mean (N=13)   11.1

4 Conclusions

Thoracic outlet syndrome (TOS) is a complex clinical syndrome, the cause of which is generally thought to be a compression of neuro-vascular structures between scalene muscles, the clavicle and the first rib or behind the coracoid process. The presence of a muscular arch of the axilla could give rise to a fourth compression when the arm is simultaneously held in external rotation and abduction (from horizontal to vertical).

The possible presence of this anatomical variation should be considered in the differential diagnosis of thoracic outlet and shoulder instability syndromes. About 10% of racket sports players could see their serve, smash, and grip quality decrease because of the "unknown" presence of an axillary arch, since all in vivo and ex vivo data support this interpretation.

5 References

Basmajian, J.V.and De Luca, C.J. (1985) **Muscles Alive**, 5th edn. ch. 9, Williams and Wilkins, Baltimore, pp. 224-228.

Birmingham, B.A. (1889) The homology and innervation of the Achselbogen and Pectoralis quartus, and the nature of the lateral cutaneous nerve of the thorax. **Journal of Anatomy and Physiology**, 23, 206-223.

Cheng, S. Cheng, L. Gao, X Ke, Z and Li, Y (1988) An analysis on the biomechanics of softball pitching, in **International Series on Biomechanics, Volume 7-B Biomechanics XI-B** (eds G. de Groot, A.P. Hollander, P.A. Huijing and G.J. van Ingen Schenau), Free University Press, Amsterdam, pp.805-809.

Clarys, J.P. Barbaix, E. Van Rompaey, H. Caboor, D.and Van Roy, P. (1996) The muscular arch of the axilla revisited its possible role in the thoracic outlet and shoulder instability syndromes. **Manual Therapy**, 1, 133-139

Clarys, J.P. and Cabri, J. (1993) Electromyography and the study of sports movements: A review. **Journal of Sports Sciences**, 11, 379-448.

Clarys, J.P. Cabri, J.and Teirlinck, P. (1992) An electromyographic and impact force study of the overhand water polo throw, in **Biomechanics and Medicine in Swimming** (eds D. Maclaren, T. Reilly and A. Lees), E. & F.N. Spon, London, pp.111-116.

Fritsch, H. (1869) Abnorme Muskelbundel der Achselhohle. **Arch Anat. Physiol. und Wissensch**. Medicin, pp. 367-371.Hägg, G.M.and Milerad, E. (1997) Forearm extensor and flexor muscle exertion during simulated gripping work - an electromyographic study. **Clinical Biomechanics**, 12, 39-43.

Jobe, F.W. Tibone, J.E. Perry, J.and Moynes, D. (1983) An EMG analysis of the shoulder in throwing and pitching. A preliminary report. **American Journal of Sports Medicine**, 11, 3-5.

Jobe, F.W. Moynes, D. Tibone, J.E. and Perry, J.(1984) An EMG analysis of the shoulder in pitching. A second report. **American Journal of Sports Medicine**, 12, 218-220.

Kasai, T.and Shiba, S. (1977) True nature of the muscular arch of the axilla and its nerve supply. **Acta Anatomica Nippon**, 52, 309-336.

Krause, W. (1880) **Handbuch der menschlichen Anatomie, Anatomische varietäten, Tabellen etc.3**. Band. Hahn'sche Buchhandlung, Hannover.

Langer, C. (1846) Ueber die Achselbinde und ihr verhältnis zum Latissimus dorsi. **Oesterreichish Mediciner**, Wochenschrift 15 & 16, 454.

Le Double (1897) Traité des variations du système musculaire de l'homme, 1, 197-202, 2, 17-32.

MacAlister, A. (1875) Additional observations on muscular anomalies in human anatomy. **Transactions of the Royal Irish Academy of Science**, 25, 1-130.

Meckel (1816) **Handbuch der Anatomie des Menschen**. Bd. II p. 402, cited in Tobler 1902.

Nishi, S. (1953) Miologio de la Japano, Statistika raporto pri muskol-anomaliojce japanoj. III. Muskoloj de trunko. (1) **Gumma Journal Medical Science**, 2, 109-121.

Perrin, J.B. (1871) Notes on some variations of the pectoralis major, with its associate muscles seen during sessions 1868-69, 69-70 at King's College, London, **Journal of Anatomy and Physiology** 5, 233-240.

Princeteau (1892) Note pour servir à l'histoire des anomalies musculaires du creux de l'aisselle. **Soc. de Biol. Comptes Rendus hebdomadaire des Séances et Mémoires**, 44, 202-206.

Roos, D.B. (1971) Experience with the first rib resection for thoracic outlet syndrome. **Annals of Surgery**, 173, 429-442.

Rouard, A.H.and Clarys, J.P. (1995) Co-contraction in the elbow and shoulder muscles during rapid cyclic movements in an aquatic environment. **Journal of Electromyography and Kinesiology**, 5, 177-183.

Schramm, U.and von Keyserlingk, D. (1984) Studien uber latissimusbogen des Oberarmes. **Anatomische Anzeigen Jena**, 156 : 75-78.

Serpell, J.W.and Baum, M. (1991) Significance of Langer's axillary arch in axillary dissection. **Australian and New Zealand Journal of Surgery**, 61, 310-312.

Shevlin, M.G. Lehmann, J.F.and Lucci, J.A. (1969) Electromyographic Study of the Function of some Muscles crossing the Glenohumeral Joint. **Archives Physical Medicine & Rehabilitation**, 50, 264-270.

Snijders, C.J. Volkers, A.C.W. Michelse, K. and Vleeming, A. (1987) A provocation of epicondyalgia lateralis (tennnis elbow) by power grip or pinching. **Medicine Science in Sports and Exercise**, 19, 518-523.

Struthers (1854) **Anat and phys.observ.** Edinburgh, in Tobler, 1902.

Tobler, L. (1902) Der Achselbogen des Menschen. **Morpholg. Jahrburch**, 30, 453-507.

Toyoshima, S. Matsui, H.and Miyashita, M. (1971) An Electromyographic study of the Upper-arm muscles involved in throwing. **Research Journal of Physical Education**, 15 (2), 103-110.

Tyson, R.R. and Kaplan, G.F. (1975) Modern concepts of diagnosis and treatment of the thoracic outlet syndrome. **Orthopedic Clinics of North America**, 6, 507-519

Wagenseil, F. (1927) Muskelbefunde bei Chinesen. Verh. Ges. physische Antropologie, 1927. **Anthropol. Anz., Stuttgart**, 2, 42-51.

Wood, J. (1868) Variations in human myology observed during the winter session of 1867-68 at King's College, London. **Proceedings of Royal Society of London**, 17, 483-525.

26 The importance of the speed of ball flight for the performance of junior tennis players

K. Mantis, A. Kambas, E. Zachopoulou, N. Grivas and
P. Kontos
*Democritus University of Thrace, Department of Physical Education
and Sport Science, Komotini, Greece*

1 Introduction

Scientists have focused on studing the profile of tennis, in order to provide coaches with help in finding solutions concerning training practices (Galber and Zein, 1984). In that regard, data collection concerning technique, taking into account elements of biomechanics, anatomy, physical and co-ordinating abilities, is of great importance, since this information is immediately applicable (Gabler et al., 1986). Research has clearly shown that the game of tennis is highly demanding in coordination and skill, based on the quantified data mentioned in the literature (Mantis et al., 1996a). Contact times between ball and racket during impact of 0.005 and 0.003 s; speed of racket motion in various strokes of up to 150 km.h^{-1}; frequency of ball revolutions (up to 150 rad.s^{-1}) and load of the strings on impact (between 8.2 - 31.7 kg) have been reported (Gabler et al., 1986). These researchers have also reported total contact time between ball and racket in a game averaging 490 strokes (1.9 s), as well as ball flight velocities between 57-86 km.h^{-1} during rallies, reaching up to 300 km.h^{-1} on service.

According to Knauf (1986) and Schoenborn (1981) the elements relate to athletic success and allow the optimization of performance. It is of interest to know, whether the performance rankings, and any corresponding modifications to the above mentioned parameters would be significantly related, so that the evaluation of one variable may lead to conclusions concerning another (Mantis et al., 1996b).

The purpose of the present study was to measure the velocity of the ball during flight for basic tennis strokes, in boys of the youngest category (below 12 years of age) and investigate its relation with a child's national (Greece) ranking, which is used to indicate his/her ability.

Science and Racket Sports II, edited by A. Lees, I. Maynard, M. Hughes and T. Reilly. Published in 1998 by E & FN Spon, 11 New Fetter Lane, London EC4P 4EE, UK. ISBN: 0 419 23030 0

2 Methods

2.1 Subjects
Eight junior players, aged 11 and 12 (mean = 11.09, S.D. = 1.01 years), participated in the study. The subjects were ranked in the top 8 in their category in Greece during the period of the measurements.

2.2 Measuring apparatus
The calculation of the speed of ball flight was measured with the RADAR GUN PSK II PROSPEED (Decatur Electronics, IL, USA). It had been tested and found to oscilate at 4951   5 Hz at 70°F. It will cause a Doppler traffic radar transmittion at 24/50 GHz to display 110.6 km.h^{-1}.

2.3 Procedures
The measurements were carrying out during the 2nd official junior 1996 Championship Games. The Games were played on clay courts. Each subject was measured for the speed of ball flight in the following strokes : 1st service (SE1), 2nd service (SE2), forehand (FO) and backhand (BA). Twenty (20) strokes for each player and each stroke were measured.

3 Results

A correspondance analysis has been used. This statistical technique is a form of factor analysis, which receives quantitative data, for example classes of variables which are grouped in relation to subjects. In this study, the variables had values as given in Table 1.

Table 1. Classes of variables

	Mean ± S.D. (km.h^{-1})	min (km.h^{-1})	max (km.h^{-1})
SE1	78.87 ± 12.11	65	125
SE2	62.87 ± 14.59	38	90
FO	73.37 ± 11.50	45	97
BA	68.98 ± 13.60	42	92

On the other hand, the classes concern the number of player ranking, for example : class 1=player No1, class 2=player No2, class 3=player No3 and so on.

The correspondance analysis results, showed that the pattern of the data points, was described mainly by three axes, whose eigenvalues are shown in Table 2.

Table 2. Eigenvalues of factor axes

axis	eigenvalue	variance (%)	cumulative variance (%)
1	.062	60.33	60.33
2	.026	24.65	84.98
3	.008	8.70	93.68

The first axis comprised of two groups of variables. In first group were, the following: the player ranked as #1, with average ball speed at first service (SE1A), the player ranked as #5, with low ball speed at forehand (FOL), the player ranked as #6, with average ball speed at backhand (BAA) and the player ranked as #8, with average ball speed at 2nd service (SE2A) (Table 3).

Table 3. Classes of variables of the first group of the first axis

variable	class	coor*	con*	cos*
SE1A	1	-.23	12.0	.68
FOL	5	-.30	25.8	.94
BAA	6	-.52	21.0	.97
SE2A	8	-.56	32.2	.92

*coor:co-ordinate, con:absolute participation, cos:cosine

In the second group on the other side of the axis were: the player ranked as #2, with average ball speed at 1st service (SE1A), the player ranked as #5, with high ball speed at forehand (FOH), the player ranked as #7, with high ball speed at backhand (BAH) and the player ranked as #3, with low ball speed, at 2nd service (SE2L) (Table 4).

Table 4. Classes of variables of the second group of the first axis

variable	class	coor*	con*	cos*
SE1A	2	.39	21.4	.62
FOH	5	.37	27.0	.90
BAH	7	.29	15.6	.68
SE2L	3	.33	15.3	.95

*coor:co-ordinate, con:absolute participation, cos:cosine

The second axis comprised of two groups of variables. At the one side of the axis, the following appeared : the player ranked as #4, with average ball speed at 1st service (SE1A), the player ranked as #6, with low ball speed at forehand (FOL), the player ranked as #7, with average ball speed at 2nd service (SE2A) and the player ranked as #8, with average ball speed at backhand (BAA) (Table 5).

Table 5. Classes of variables of the first group of the second axis

variable	class	coor*	con*	cos*
SE1A	4	-.15	13.5	.28
FOL	6	-.78	55.7	.67
SE2A	7	-.14	9.5	.91
BAA	8	-1.55	54.8	.83

*coor:co-ordinate, con:absolute participation, cos:cosine

On the other side of the axis, the following appeared : the player ranked as #1, with high ball speed at 1st service (SE1H), the player ranked as #4, with low ball speed at 2nd service (SE2L), the player ranked as #6, with average ball speed at 2nd service (SE2A) and the player ranked as #8, with average ball speed at forehand (FOA) (Table 6).

Table 6. Classes of variables of the second group of the second axis

variable	class	coor*	con*	cos*
SE1H	1	.23	20.7	.28
SE2L	4	.08	5.7	.67
SE2A	6	.24	18.7	.32
FOA	8	.11	4.8	.38

*coor:co-ordinate, con:absolute participation, cos:cosine

The third axis comprised two groups of classes of variables. In first group, the following participated: the player ranked as #5, with average ball speed at 2nd service (SE2A) and average ball speeds at forehand (FOA) and the player ranked as #8, with average ball speed at 1st service (SE1A) (Table 7).

Table 7. Classes of variables of the first group of the third axis

variable	class	coor*	con*	cos*
SE2A	5	-.41	78.5	.84
FOA	5	-.11	17.5	.33
SE1A	8	-.11	12.7	.84

*coor:co-ordinate, con:absolute participation, cos:cosine

In the second group were: the players ranked as #3,6 and 8, with low ball speeds at 1st service (SE1L) (Table 8).

Table 8. Classes of variables of the second group of the third axis

variable	class	coor*	con*	cos*
SE1L	8	.08	15.3	.84
SE1L	6	.19	30.4	.57
SE1L	3	.11	13.8	.38

*coor:co-ordinate, con:absolute participation, cos:cosine

4 Discussion and Conclusions

The information contained in the data description of the three factor axes, is not completely clear. However, it is sufficient to conclude that the velocities of the strokes analysed are not enough to account for the top 8 players' rankings, that comprised the sample of this research. In this sense, high forehand, backhand or service velocities do not appear to be decisive factors, since they are grouped in relative disorder, and lack any regular progression. The elements needed to describe the final performance of the players, as reflected in points in a given ranking table, should concern not only quantitative data on strokes, but also other quantitative variables such as physiological and biomechanical parameters, or qualitative variables such as technical and tactical parameters, that would describe the players' rankings, with greater accuracy. Nevertheless, the use of RADAR GUN PSK II PROSPEED, for the determination of ball speed at various strokes, can be of significant help to the coaches, as the information provided is indirectly related to execution techniques, as well as other parameters involved in the training process. It can also contribute towards a suitable form of training, whose purpose is the improvement of the coefficients of the parameters investigated.

5 References

Gabler, H. and Zein, B. (1984) **Tennis-Technik**, Ingrid Czwalina, Ahrensburg bei Hamburg.
Gabler, H., Schoenborn, R., Scholl, P. and Weber, K. (1986) Deutscher Tennis Bund, **Tennis-Lehrplan 5, Training und Wettkampf,** München-Wien-Zürich.
Knauf, K. (1986) **Biomechanische Grundlagen des Tennis**, in Tennis-Technik (eds H. Gabler and B. Zein), Ingrid Czwalina, Ahrensburg bei Hamburg.
Mantis, K., Grivas, N., Kambas, A. and Zachopoulou, E., (1996a) **Coaching in the Developmental Phase** (GR), Univ. Press, Komotini.

Mantis, K., Zachopoulou, E., Kambas, A., Kontos, P. and Grivas, N. (1996b) **Speed of ball flight in tennis,** 4th International Congress on Physical Education & Sport, Komotini, Greece.

Schoenborn, R. (1981) **Die neue Teniispraxis**, Falken-Verlag GmbH, Niederhausen 1981.

27 Knowledge based system for the simulation of decision-making of the serve-return phase in tennis: the LIFT system

A. Pizzinato, G. Denis, G. Vachon and F. Kohler
Faculté du Sport, Villers les Nancy, France

1 Introduction

The importance of the service in winning matches is one of the major factors in today's competitive tennis. Considering the velocity of serves, between 191 km.h^{-1} and 206 km.h^{-1} for the best professional tennis players in 1991 (Parier, 1992), the receiver must plan the response before the opponent actually hits the ball. This characteristic has been discovered by observing sudden preparatory adjustements in the receiver at the time of the opponent's stroke (Keller et al., 1987). In order to put this behaviour into practice, the player supposedly uses cues from the server before the ball is put into motion (Keller, 1985), which allows him to foresee its future trajectory (Jones and Miles, 1978). In order to complete this research, a series of studies was devoted to determine the nature of the information used by the receiver to dispel uncertainty about the opponent's serve. Collected cues regarding the position of the ball, the racket and the server at the time of the stroke are selected as pertinent to the identification of the nature and direction of the serves (Goulet et al., 1988, 1989). It appears that none of the cited works clearly show how these cues are used. The collecting of cues about the server's behaviour is not the only information category the receiver can use to plan the response. The use of a probability type of approach underlines the fact that the choice of strong first serve and a softer second serve is not systematically the best one throughout the whole course of a match (Bartoszynki and Puri, 1981; Norman, 1985). Lastly, the quality of the serve also seems to vary according to the court surface (Hughes and Clarke, 1995). However, these data remain very individual and cannot be perceived by the receiver as they are.

An artificial intelligence type of approach allows us to clarify not only the nature of the information to be taken into account in receiving the serve but also the relationship between the various pieces of information. The direction is similar to that of works aimed at exploiting human knowledge in tactical problem solving in sport, and especially works dealing with the understanding and simulating of decision-making in squash (Sarrazin et al., 1983, 1986) or works dealing with assistance in tactical decision-making in rugby (Singer et al., 1994) and sailing (Gouard, 1993). This

Science and Racket Sports II, edited by A. Lees, I. Maynard, M. Hughes and T. Reilly. Published in 1998 by E & FN Spon, 11 New Fetter Lane, London EC4P 4EE, UK. ISBN: 0 419 23030 0

approach is situated within a conceptual framework of the extracting of expert knowledge in the considered domain.

The purpose of this study was to describe the conception and the development of a knowledge based system named LIFT (In french, LIFT stands for Logique Informatique pour la Formalisation des connaissances en Tennis) which allows the simulation of the receiver's decision-making during a tennis match.

2 Methods

2.1 Knowledege acquisition

The acquisition of knowledge was achieved by discussion with an expert, a tennis coach in charge of the technical and tactical training of the best young players in the Lorraine Tennis League. The interviews were led by a knowledge engineer who had also built the logical program which the system runs on. Later on, the use of video recordings of matches between four national-level adult players helped the expert to clarify and refine the formerly established knowledge. These recordings can also be used to check the coherence of the model. During this phase, the expert was confronted with the answers given by the computer program. The knowledge acquisition phase required thirty 2-hour sessions. Twenty per cent of this time was devoted to the refining of the knowledge through observation of the recordings.

2.2 Knowledge representation

Two categories appear: knowledge which the deductions are based on, also named the facts, and knowledge allowing inferences. For example, the type of toss and the type and court are considered as facts. The system also processes the facts it deduces thanks to functions showing the dependence of one fact on others. For example, the function noted Type_Serve = f(Toss) indicates that the fact "type of serve" is linked to the fact "type of toss". Fundamentally, these functions present the same characteristics as the production rules of expert systems. The execution of a function enables one to give each fact a value, systematically accompanied by a likelihood coefficient. This coefficient reflects the degree of certainty of the expert concerning the considered fact.

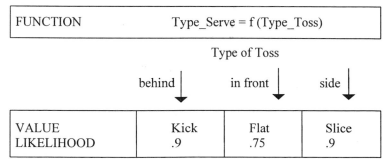

Figure 1. Representation of the function Type_Serve.

Three types of functions are used:- functions reflecting the experience of the expert (61), functions reflecting the logic of the rules of tennis (10) and functions reflecting the analysis of previous situations (27). Regarding the latter, the expert also defines typical situations he would like to record on the computer. Thus, we used a matrix type of representation with its own interrogation language.

2.3 Computer implementation of the system

A computer implementation of the system was made in order to show how it worked in real time and to measure the coherence between the model and the expert. Two hundred video recordings of serve-return phases from actual matches were tested. This implementation also allowed the expert to re-adjust certain rules of operation.

3 Results

3.1 Knowledge available

Three categories of knowledge are handled by the expert. First, there is knowledge established before the beginning of the match. It concerns the players (right or left-handedness, weaknesses and strengths), the estimation of the speed of the surface, the usual service strategies (serving an ace, serving on the opponent's weak stroke or surprising him with a fake), the technique of the different kinds of serves (flat serve, kick serve, sliced serve) and then the most significant points scored associated with the pressure level they put the players under.

The second type of knowledge comes from collecting information on the server. It concerns his relative position to the centre mark and the type of toss he is using.

Lastly, there is knowledge coming from the analysis of events that took place during the match, such as the most frequently used types of serve, the zones usually played by the server into the service court and the effectiveness of the strokes when the player returns the serves.

3.2 The "LIFT" system

The LIFT system goes through three phases which are organised into a hierarchy. The system successively looks for: the server's strategy, the area aimed at by the server and the type of serve.

The knowledge and rules on which this simulation is based, evolve during the match. Two periods become obvious. At the beginning of the match, the system proposes a decision based on knowledge established before the match. It first distinguishes the type of serve and proposes a first range of possible strategies after evaluating their likelihood. The one that gets the highest value is chosen. The type of surface, the type of toss, the right or left-handedness of the players, and the score, constitute the elements of calculation for this likelihood. For the second serve, the chosen strategy is mostly serving on the opponent's weak stroke. During that period, the backhand will be chosen as the weak stroke, unless it is known otherwise before the match.

During the match, the system bases its estimations on knowledge coming from the analysis of events which have occured. The system goes through a process which leads to a characterisation of the technical and tactical behaviours of the server which is as precise as possible. The search for probable strategies takes into account the decision made by the server during the previous playing phases.

3.3 Coherence check

The first type of measurement allowed us to find out that the computer program was faithful to the model and was used as a reference for the remainder of the evaluation. Regarding the comparaison between the model and the expert, the results obtained showed 77% reproducibility.

4 Discussion

The construction of the LIFT system showed that there was no one model for the returner's decision-making. Two models are thus brought to light. The first, theoretical one, is used by the receiver to make decisions at the beginning of the match. The second, optimal one, then takes over. While its nature is less clear than that of the first one, its decision-making relies on the server taking into account his/her real behaviour during the match.

During the match, the system also shows the existence of two shortcuts in the receiver's reasoning. The first one relies on the tendency of servers to repeat a winning strategy. The second one consists in trying to detect the server's possible fakes, thanks to incoherences noticed between the situation and the type of toss. The recognition of those two patterns enables the system to produce a decision which is better suited to the situation.

The system has two drawbacks, as stressed by the coherence check. First, it has trouble differentiating a technical mistake in the server from an unusual tactical choice. The logic of the server's behaviour is the basic postulate the system relies on in order to simulate the decision-making process. Second, despite the amount of knowledge provided, the proposed system is not yet able to take into account more subjective information such as exhaustion or pressure brought about by the importance of the match.

5 Conclusions

In its current version, the LIFT system stressed the fact that the decision-making process of the receiver relies on knowledge from very different origins. However, it must be noted that the LIFT system does not try to explain the real receiver's decision-making process, but only provides a model for simulating complexity of decision-making.

The system can also be used by tennis coaches who wish to improve the effectiveness of their players in returning serves. First of all, the system is used along with a video recording in order to characterize the actual behaviour of the servers.

Then, for each serve-return phase, the coaches compare the decisions made by the system with the decisions actually made by the servers. Finally, when a returning mistake is detected, the coaches show the players the information that the system used to produce the proper response to the situation. This provides the players with a feedback which allows them to understand better their mistakes. Thus, the system enables one to show the players which cues are relevant and how to use them in order to make more efficient decisions when returning the ball.

6 References

Bartoszynski, R. and Puri, M.L. (1981) Some remarks on strategy in playing tennis. **Behavorial Science**, 26, 379-387.

Gouard, P. (1993) Conception et mise en oeuvre d'un centre expert de navigation, in **Sport et Informatique**, INSEP, Paris,pp. 4.

Goulet, C. Bard, C. and Fleury, M. (1989) Expertise differences in preparing to return a tennis serve: A visual information processing approach. **Journal of Sport and Exercise Psychology**, 11, 382-398.

Goulet, C. Fleury, M. Bard, C. Yerles, M. and Michaud, D. (1988) Analyse des indices visuels prélevés en réception de service au tennis. **Canadian Journal of Sport Science**, 13, 79-87.

Hughes, M. and Clarke, S. (1995) Surface effect on elite tennis strategy, in **Science and Racket Sports** (eds T. Reilly, M. Hughes and A. Lees), E. & F.N. Spon, London, pp. 272-277.

Jones, C.M. and Miles, T.R. (1978) Use of advance cues in predicting the flight of a lawn tennis ball. **Journal of Human Movement Studies**, 4, 231-235.

Keller, D. (1985) Comportement préparatoire et adaptation au tennis. **Revue des Sciences et Techniques des Activités Physiques et Sportives**, 11, 54-63.

Keller, D. Goetz, M. and Hennemann, M.C. (1987) Ajustements spécifiques en sports de balle. **Revue des Sciences et Techniques des Activités Physiques et Sportives**, 15, 31-38.

Norman, J.M. (1985) Dynamic programming in tennis - when to use a fast serve. **Journal of Operational Research** Society, 36(2), 75-77.

Parier, J. (1992) **Technopathies du tennis**. Laboratoires CIBA-GEIGY, Paris.

Sarrazin, C. Alain, C. and Lacombe, D. (1986) Simulation study of a decision-making model of squash competition phase two: testing the model through the use of computer simulation. **Human Movement Science**, 5, 373-391.

Sarrazin, C. Lacombe, D. Alain, C. and Joly, J. (1983) Simulation study of a decision-making model of squash competition, phase one: the analysis of the protocol, **Human Movement Science**, 2, 279-306.

Singer, B. Soubie, J.L. and Villepreux, P. (1994) Apports de l'intelligence artificielle pour l'acquisition et la représentation des connaissances en sports collectifs. **Science et Motricité**, 21, 27-38.

28 A qualitative 3D analysis of forehand strokes in table tennis

J. Kasai and T. Mori
Japanese Table Tennis Association, Tokorosawa City, Saitama, Japan

1 Introduction

Table tennis players have various styles and use different techniques for striking the ball. The style and technique of highly skilled players are different from less skilled players. Typically the speed of shot is greater (126 km.h^{-1}), there is more ball spin (7,500 - 9,000 rev.s^{-1}) which produce more demanding ball trajectories, and there is a need for greater levels of control and timing (Kasai, 1982; Yamaoka, 1975; Kasai, 1993). Detailed information concerning the 3D characteristics of technique in table tennis is lacking. It was the purpose of this study to define selected 3D kinematic characteristics of a forehand smash of highly skilled table tennis players.

2 Methods

Six subjects were used for this study. Three were highly skilled table tennis players with more than 10 years playing experience while the other three were non-skilled players who did not practice daily. Two video cameras (operating at 50 Hz) were set up with their optical axes approximately perpendicular to each other so that one camera viewed the rear of the player while the other viewed the striking arm. Calibration of the 3D space was achieved using a calibration pole which was positioned vertically in 16 different locations on the floor so that the measuring volume was 3.0 m x 3.0 m x 2.2 m. The 3D co-ordinates were reconstructed using the Direct Linear Transformation method. A 21-point model defining 14 body segments (feet, lower legs, upper legs, hands, lower arms, upper arms, torso and head) was used for the kinematic analysis.

In order to maintain constant conditions for the subject, a skilled coach fed the ball to the subject at a rate of 30 shots per minute with light top spin. Ten shots hit by the subject were filmed and the best short shot and best long shot were used for analysis.

Science and Racket Sports II, edited by A. Lees, I. Maynard, M. Hughes and T. Reilly. Published in 1998 by E & FN Spon, 11 New Fetter Lane, London EC4P 4EE, UK.   ISBN: 0 419 23030 0

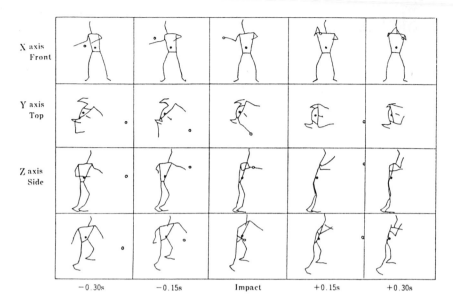

Figure 1. Positions for a skilled player performing a short shot. A black circle shows the subject's centre of gravity. A white circle shows the ball.

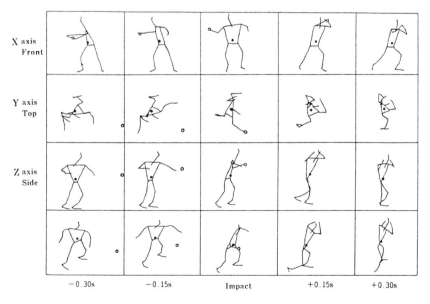

Figure 2. Positions for a skilled player performing a long shot. A black circle shows the subject's centre of gravity. A white circle shows the ball.

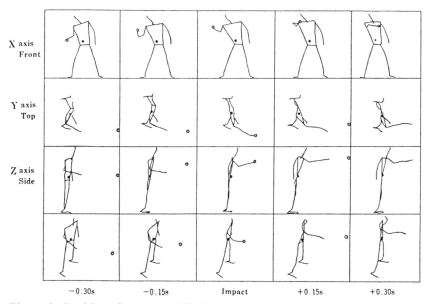

Figure 3. Positions for a non-skilled player performing a short shot. A black circle shows the subject's centre of gravity. A white circle shows the ball.

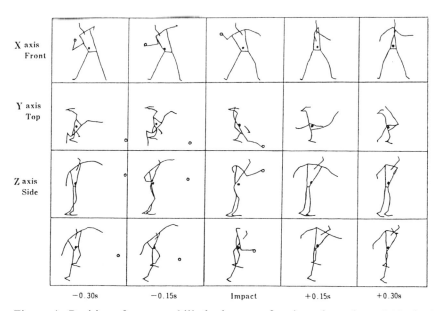

Figure 4. Positions for a non-skilled player performing a long shot. A black circle shows the subject's centre of gravity. A white circle shows the ball.

3   Results and Discussion

Typical forehand strokes are given for one skilled and one non-skilled subject performing short (Figures 1 and 2) and long strokes (Figures 3 and 4). Body positions are shown from 0.3 s before to 0.3 s after impact. In each figure, the view along each of the three axes is given as well as a general view from a convenient viewing angle.

The skilled player performing a short stroke (Figure 1, front view) demonstrates several features of technique which are used to enhance the performance of the shot. Although there is only a small twist of the shoulders and trunk away from the ball in the preparation phase, there is evidence of a further counter twist of the shoulders (top view). The non-hitting arm is flexed and held close to the body. As the stroke progresses, the shoulders and hips twist towards the ball while the non-hitting arm moves across the chest in an opposite direction. This counter-movement will provide a better action for the hitting arm through the action-reaction principle (Hay, 1985). From the side view, this subject has both knees bent during the pre-impact phase and which extend during the impact and follow through. This suggests that the knee extension is used to control and add speed to the shot. Further, the legs are placed one in front of the other to give greater body stability and to allow the trunk to lean forward more on impact and during the follow through phase.

In contrast, the non-skilled player demonstrates little use of the shoulder counter-rotation with respect to the hips (top view, Figure 2), little use of the non-hitting arm and little knee flexion. The subject tilts the shoulders in order to lower the hitting arm, rather than to use the knees. The legs are close together and there is little lean into the shot at impact.

For the long stroke shot, the skilled player continues to demonstrate a marked trunk rotation (Figure 3, top view) and also demonstrates the same use of the non-hitting arm, knee bend and foot placement. In contrast, the non-skilled player shows the same lack of these features as noted for the short shot. Similar observations were made on the other two subjects used in this study.

The underlying technique employed by the skilled and non-skilled players appears to remain unchanged even during strokes of a similar type which require different detailed movement characteristics. This suggests that attention should be paid to technical competence during the early years of developing of the skills of table tennis players.

4   Conclusions

This qualitative analysis of the table tennis forehand stroke based on 3D motion analysis has highlighted important characteristics of technique which are used by the skilled player. These basic characteristics of technique remain observable even when the requirements of the stroke changes markedly. It is concluded that this approach can be used to identify weaknesses in technical performance of table tennis players.

5 References

Hay, J. G. (1985). **The Biomechanics of Sports Technique**. Prentice-Hall, Englewood Cliffs, NJ.

Kasai, J. (1982). Research of forehand smash strokes in Table Tennis(1) -speed and accuracy. **WASEDA University Physical Education Research Bulletin**,14, 25-33.

Kasai., J. (1993). Table Tennis -The speed of the ball and the number of the rotation. **Japanese Journal of Sports Sciences**, 12, 372-378.

Yamaoka, H. (1975). Science of Table Tennis –speed. **New Physical Education**, 48, 653-657.

29 An experimental investigation into the influence of the speed and spin by balls of different diameters and weights

Z. Xiaopeng
The Chinese Table Tennis Association, National Research Institute of Sports Science

1 Introduction

As table tennis has developed and players' techniques have improved, the ball's speed and spin in competitive matches have become too fast for ordinary spectators to appreciate. Moreover, the number of rallies for each point have decreased in duration, apparently leading to a loss in spectators' interest in table tennis matches.

In order to regain spectator interest, the International Table Tennis Federation has made some rule changes such as restricting the use of two-sided rubber on the racket, changing the ball's colour from white to yellow, and introducing some new regulations for service. These measures do not seem to have been effective in improving the attractiveness of table tennis to the spectators.

Recently, the ITTF suggested that if the ball's diameter increased 2 mm from 38 mm to 40 mm, the ball's speed and spin might be reduced and rallies would be longer, thus making table tennis matches more interesting for spectators. In order to obtain suitable scientific data on these points, the ITTF entrusted the Sport Science Committee of the Chinese Table Tennis Association to carry out experimental investigations into the influence of the ball's diameter and mass on its speed and spin during table tennis play.

2 Methods

2.1 Instrumentation
All tests were conducted during October 1996 at the Table Tennis Training Centre in Beijing. A PD-1 Dynamic Spin Test Instrument was used to measure ball spin. This can display and print the results simultaneously. The manufacturer's estimate of accuracy is that it is better than 3%.

A 2D Motion Analysis System (Peak 5, Colorado Springs, USA) was used to obtain images of ball and player movement at a sample frequency of 120 Hz. The camera was placed 1m to the side of the subject. The balls used were Double Happiness orange, black and white balls of diameter 38 and 40 mm, and of masses 2.5 g and 2.8 g. Three balls were used:- Ball A (38 mm, 2.5 g); Ball B (40 mm, 2.8 g); and Ball C

Science and Racket Sports II, edited by A. Lees, I. Maynard, M. Hughes and T. Reilly. Published in 1998 by E & FN Spon, 11 New Fetter Lane, London EC4P 4EE, UK.   ISBN: 0 419 23030 0

(40 mm, 2.5 g). A fourth ball D (Wittaker, Japan) was used for the bounce test. This had a diameter of 44 mm and a mass of 2.24 g.

2.2 Subjects
Three subjects were used to conduct the trials. Two were females (aged 18 and 14 years) who used a pen hold and shake hand grip respectively, and one male (age 23) who used a pen hold grip. All players had a racket with an inward pimple. To ensure the consistency of the striking strength, pre-experiment training was carried out.

2.3 Procedures
The players performed 10 forehand attack and 10 smash shots with 3 different balls. The average speed was calculated from the video recordings for all balls hit.

The players performed 50 loop shots with 3 different balls in each ball category, i.e. 150 loops in total. The average spin was calculated as the spin of all loops for each type of ball. The height of the bounce was also recorded.

Statistical analysis was conduced using Student's t test. The level of significance was set at $P<0.05$.

3 Results

The results of the speed tests are given in Tables 1 and 2 for the forehand smash and attack shots respectively. The forehand smashes for balls B and C were slower than ball A, although only ball C was significantly different ($P<0.05$) from the speed of ball A. Similar results are found for the forehand attack shot (Table 2).

Table 1. Comparison of the speeds of forehand smashes

Ball	diameter (mm)	mass (g)	velocity m.s^{-1}	t	P	Reduction %
A	38	2.51	17.8	AB = 1.9	> 0.05	BA = 4
B	40	2.79	17.0	BC = 7.6	< 0.05	CB = 9
C	40	2.49	15.4	AC = 5.6	< 0.05	CA = 13

Table 2. Comparison of the speeds of forehand attack shots

Ball	diameter (mm)	mass (g)	velocity m.s^{-1}	t	P	Reduction %
A	38	2.51	10.6	AB = 1.0	> 0.05	BA = 2
B	40	2.79	10.4	BC = 2.6	< 0.05	CB = 6
C	40	2.49	9.8	AC = 5.7	< 0.05	CA = 8

The results of the spin test are given in Table 3. Both balls B and C rotate significantly more slowly than ball A ($P<0.05$).

Table 3. Comparison of ball spin for the loop spin shot

Ball Group (n=3)	diameter (mm)	mass range (g)	spin (rev.s⁻¹)	t	P	Reduction %
A	38	2.51-2.54	133.5	AB = 3.5	< 0.05	BA = 13
B	40	2.65-2.80	116.5	BC = 1.8	> 0.05	CB = 10
C	40	2.40-2.53	105.8	AC = 5.6	< 0.05	CA = 21

The results of the bounce response of the balls are given in Table 4. Balls in group B had a higher spin and lower bounce height than balls in group C.

Table 4. Comparison of ball bounce height

Ball	diameter (mm)	mass (g)	bounce height (mm)	t	P
A	38	2.51	24.6	AB = 0.6	> .05
B	40	2.79	24.5	BC = 7.0	< .05
C	40	2.49	23.8	AC = 4.7	< .05
D	44	2.24	23.6		

The striking strength was found to affect ball performance. The smash shot had a higher percentage reduction than the attack shot (Table 5).

Table 5. Striking speed comparison on the percentage reduction for different strengths

	BA %	CA %	CB %
Forehand smash	4	13	9
Forehand attack	2	8	6

4 Conclusions

The tests showed that the speed and spin of the larger balls were slower than the smaller lighter balls. If the larger balls were adopted in the game, they would make the rallies longer and potentially the matches more attractive to spectators.

Part Six

Notational Analysis of Racket Sports

30 The application of notational analysis to racket sports

M. Hughes
Centre of Notational Analysis, UWIC, Cardiff, UK

1 Introduction

Downey (1973) initiated research in notational analysis of sport when he published his systems for tennis and badminton which, although providing a fund of ideas used by other analysts, were never actually used to gather data due to their complexity. Nevertheless the idea of recording actions in sport was appealing, and Reilly and Thomas (1976) used notation analysis to record the different ambulatory modes and durations of soccer players by their playing position, and linked these data to further kinesiological characteristics of the athletes measured under laboratory conditions. Sanderson and Way (1979) and Sanderson (1983) used a system based upon Downey's work to analyse the importance of tactics in squash. Hughes (1985) computerised Sanderson and Way's system, making adjustments to it necessary because of the limited memory of the microcomputer available at that time, the layout of the keyboard and finally for a concern for accuracy for defining player position. The system was used to define the patterns of play for differing standards of players, analyse the tactics used at each level and the technical deficiencies at the lower levels of play. Each of these researchers have used notation to analyse sport in different ways.

The areas of applications of notation have been defined a number of times, but since notation has advanced and developed, that these purposes can now be extended to cover:-

1. tactical evaluation;
2. technical evaluation;
3. analysis of movement;
4. development of a database and modelling, and
5. educational use for both coaches and players.

Most research using notation, or indeed any practical applications working directly with coaches and athletes, spans more than one of these purposes.

Of the racket sports, squash has received the most attention. This is probably due to both the simple nature of the game making it ideal as a starting point in developing

Science and Racket Sports II, edited by A. Lees, I. Maynard, M. Hughes and T. Reilly. Published in 1998 by E & FN Spon, 11 New Fetter Lane, London EC4P 4EE, UK.   ISBN: 0 419 23030 0

notation systems, and the coincidence that a number of the early researchers (Sanderson, 1983; Hughes, 1985; Sharp, 1986) were involved in this sport.

2 The Applications of Notation

2.1 Tactical evaluation

The definition of tactical patterns of play in racket sports has been a profitable source of research. The maturation of tactics can be analysed at different levels of development of a specific sport, usually by means of a cross-sectional design. The differing tactics used at each level of development within a sport inevitably depend upon technical development, physical maturation and other variables. The 'maturation models' have important implications for coaching methods and directions at the different stages of development in each of the racket sports. These tactical 'norms' or 'models', based both upon technique and tactics, demonstrate how the different applications, defined above, can overlap.

Sanderson and Way (1977) used symbols to notate 17 different strokes, as well as incorporating court plans for recording accurate positional information. The system took an estimated 5-8 hours of use and practise before an operator was sufficiently skilful to record a full match in real time. In an average squash match there are about 1000 shots and an analyst using this system will gather over 30 pages of data per match. Not only were the patterns of rally-ending shots (the Nth shot of the rally) examined in detail, but also those shots that preceded the end shot , (N-1) to a winner or error, and the shots that preceded those, (N-2) to a winner or error. In this way the rally ending patterns of play were analysed. Not surprisingly, processing the data for just one match could take as long as 40 hours of further work. Sanderson (1983) used this system to gather a data-base and showed that squash players demonstrate the same patterns, winning or losing, despite the supposed coaching tenet of '....if you are losing change your tactics'. The major emphasis of this system was on the gathering of information concerning 'play patterns' as well as the comprehensive collection of descriptive match data. Sanderson felt that 'suggestive' symbols were better than codes, being easier for the operator to learn and remember. The main disadvantages of this system, as with all long-hand systems, were the time taken to learn the system and the large amounts of data generated, which in turn needed so much time to process.

Hughes (1985) modified the method of Sanderson and Way so that the hand-notated data could be processed on a mainframe computer. Eventually, the manual method was modified so that a match could be notated in-match at courtside directly into a microcomputer. Summary data were presented during the match, between games, and a complete analysis, based on the ideas of Sanderson (1983) could be completed later. Due to difficulties with the speed of the game and the computing storage capacity, only one player was notated. Hughes (1985; 1986) established a comprehensive database on different standards of squash players and examined and compared the differences in patterns of play between recreational players, county players and nationally ranked players, using the computerised notational analysis system he had developed. The method involved the digitisation of all the shots and court positions, which were entered via a standard QWERTY keyboard.

Analysis of the frequency distribution of shots showed that the recreational players were not accurate enough to sustain a tactical plan, being erratic with both their straight drives and their cross-court drives. They played more short shots, and although they hit more winners they also hit more errors. The county players played a simple tactical game, keeping the ball deep and predominantly on their opponents' backhand, the weaker side of most players. They hit significantly more winners with straight drives. Their short game, consisting of boasts, drops and rally-drops, although significantly less accurate than the nationally ranked players, was significantly more accurate than that of the recreational players. The nationally ranked players, because of their far greater fitness, covering ability and better technique, employed the more complex tactics, using an 'all-court' game. Finally, the serves of the county players and the recreational players, because of shorter rallies, assumed greater importance than the serves of the ranked players.

Hughes and Clarke (1995) used a computerised notation system to analyse the differences in the playing patterns of players on grass at Wimbledon, to those of players at the Australian Open, on a synthetic surface. They found differences in performance between the two surfaces, particularly with the time the ball was in play. This averaged about 10% for the synthetic surface (14 min in an average match of just over 2 hours) whilst it was as low as 5% on grass (7 min in an average match of just over 2 hours).

An unusual application of computerised notation was that by Hughes and Tillin (1994), who notated the levels of aggression by female players at Wimbledon. Each shot was given a score from a scale of aggression, determined by pace, placement and from where the ball was taken. The scale was from '1' - for a totally defensive soft shot, to '7' - for an all-out, attacking shot for the line from an attacking position. 'Aggression', in terms of attacking play, was then correlated with the game and match scores to examine whether the successful players were more or less aggressive on the critical points in a game, or in the critical games of a set. Generally players were less aggressive on the critical stages of the match, but that on critical points the player who was losing attacked more. Play was found to be progressively more aggressive as each set continued.

These research results in the main were linked with analysis of tactics. The interesting theme emerging from this recent research is that the tactical models defined are changing with time, as players become fitter, stronger, faster, bigger and equipment changes, particularly in rackets which have become lighter and more powerful. Over a period of less than 15 years the length of rallies in squash, for elite players, has decreased from about 20 shots to just over 14 shots per rally (Hughes and Knight, 1995; Hughes and Robertson, 1997). An excellent review (Croucher, 1996) of the application of strategies using notational analysis of different sports outlines the problems, advantages and disadvantages associated with this function.

2.2 Technical evaluation
A quantitative definition of where technique fails or excels has very practical uses for coaches, in particular, and also for sports scientists aiming to analyse performance of players at different levels of development. Many of the items of research listed on tactics, in the previous section, serve also as examples of defining levels of technical ability and their use and function.

Taylor and Hughes (1998) compared the patterns of play of elite under-19 players from Britain to those from Europe and North America. Any definition of the tactical patterns of play inevitably starts with the distributions of winners and errors; which in turn show the technical strengths and weaknesses of the respective groups of players. The British players had technical deficiencies on their backhand playing groundstrokes whereas the European players were not as good as the British players when volleying. The Americans had more all round technical ability, adapting easily to different surfaces and different tactics. There were significant differences found in the patterns of play of the British players compared to the other two groups. This was attributed, in part, to better technical grounding given to the European and North American players. A large contribution to these differences was attributed to the types of surfaces on which the British players practise more often. These are mostly fast surfaces encouraging a 'serve and volley' game, precluding a sound technical game over all the court.

Many coaches seek the template of tactical play at the highest level for preparation and training of both elite players, and also for developing players who aspire to reach the highest position. Particular databases, aimed at specific individuals or teams, can also be used to prepare potential opponents for match play. Hughes and Robertson (1998) aimed to utilise computerised notation systems to create, firstly, a structural archetype of the game of squash at the elite level, and then to extend this to a tactical model of the game.

Nine matches of elite players were analysed using a comprehensive computerised notation system (Hughes and Knight, 1995) which was used post event from video. The computerised notational analysis was used to create a template of the modern squash game of elite male players. These templates were then used to design simple hand notation systems to complement these models of performance - these are currently being used with squads of players of different ages. It was suggested that similar models, and complementary hand notation systems, could be constructed for the elite women's game, and also for different levels of performance in squash. This modelling of technical attainment could be replicated in other sports.

2.3 Movement analysis

Reilly and Thomas (1976) recorded and analysed the intensity and extent of discrete activities during match play in soccer. With a combination of hand notation and the use of an audio tape recorder, they analysed in detail the movements of English first division soccer players. They were able to specify work-rates of the different positions, distances covered in a game and the percentage time of each position in each of the different ambulatory classifications. Reilly has continually added to this base of data enabling him to define clearly the specific physiological demands in not just soccer, but all the football codes (Reilly, 1996). This work by Reilly and Thomas has become a standard against which other similar research projects can compare their results and procedures.

Hughes et al. (1989) designed a tracking system that enabled the use of the immediacy of video, and, by using mixed images on the same VDU screen, accurate measurements of the velocities and accelerations of the players, usually associated with film analysis. A `Power Pad ' was used to gather positional data along with the time base. The image of the playing area representation on the Power Pad was captured by a video camera and mixed with that of the subject tape. The images of the two 'playing areas' were carefully aligned, by precisely matching the line markings on both the real court and the representational one. This enabled the subject, and the tracking stylus on the bit pad, to be both viewed at the same time. By keeping them synchronised, an accurate tracing of the movements of the player was possible in real time. A careful validation of the system showed its accuracy and the short learning time required by operators.

Hughes and Franks (1991) utilised this system and applied it to squash comparing the motions of players of differing standards. They presented comparative profiles for four different standard of players, spanning from club players to the world elite. The profiles consisted of analyses of distance travelled, and the average velocities and accelerations during rallies. The distance travelled during rallies by both recreational and regular club players was surprisingly short, the mean distance being approximately 12 m for both top club players and recreational players. Hughes and Franks made suggestions about specific training drills for the sport. They used their system to comment on the reasons why Jahangir Khan had dominated squash for so long. Khan was the 1989 World Champion, for the seventh time - his profile was compared to the top six in the world (which data included his own profile). All the data clearly showed the vast physical advantage that he had over the best athletes in the world at this sport, particularly his average acceleration during a rally which was almost 50% higher than that of his rivals.

In tennis, players often 'run round' a shot so as to hit the ball on their favoured side. This is never done at elite level in squash or badminton because of the speed of the game at the highest levels. This inefficient movement would be expected to have a deleterious effect upon the recovery of the player back to a central position on the court. Hughes and Moore (1998) investigated whether these inefficient movements have an effect on the 'end-of-rally' results. A hand notation system was designed to record the relevant aspects of movement and footwork patterns that would satisfy the aims of the study. The system defined successful footwork patterns in 'serve and volleys', pre-shot (skipchecks, ready positions), during impact (ground contact) and in recovery (speed of change of direction). It was found that efficiency of movement in tennis was far higher than expected, but when players did run or jump through their shots this placed pressure on them which resulted in their frequent loss of the rally. This study could be extended to match-play by women and also the analysis itself could include sequences of these movements.

Modelling movement has created a better understanding of the respective sports, it has enabled specific training programmes to be developed to improve the movement patterns, and fitness, of the respective athletes.

2.4 Development of a database and modelling
Once notational analysis systems are used to collect amounts of data sufficiently large enough to define 'norms' of behaviour, then all the ensuing outcomes of the work are based upon the principles of modelling. Franks (1997) explained very practically how modelling performance in sport can be achieved and how it can be applied in the real world of competitive sport.

Alexander et al. (1988) used the mathematical theory of probability to analyse and model the game of squash. Mathematical modelling can describe the main features of a game such as squash and can reveal strategical patterns to the player. They suggested that squash is an example of a Markov chain mathematical structure, i.e. a series of discrete events each having associated probability functions:

The probability that A wins a rally when serving is   *Pa*
The probability that A wins a rally when receiving is   *Qa*

The probability that B wins a rally when serving is   *Pb = 1 - Qa*
The probability that B wins a rally when receiving is   *Qb = 1 - Pa*

If two opponents are of the same standing then   *Pa, Pb, Qa, Qb = 0.5*

The probability that A winning a point when serving is the sum of each winning sequence of rallies:

$Pa = 1/2 + 1/2^3 + 1/2^5 + 1/2^7 + \ldots = 2/3$ *(geometric series)*

Pa wins 9-0 = $(2/3)^9$ = 0.026

If A is stronger player with Pa = 2/3 and Qa = 3/5 then:

Probability that A wins when serving is 5/6; when receiving is 1/2.
Probability of A being in a serving state is 3/4.

The probability of winning a game is the sum of all the probabilities of each possible score, i.e. sum of p (9-0), p (9-1) . . . . p (9-8), p (10-9).

The model ignores such factors as off-days, fatigue, and so on. By presenting all these associated probabilities, Alexander et al. were able to compute the potential benefits of winning the toss, so as to serve first, - a surprisingly large advantage. They recommended strategies for players having to choose how to 'set' the game, when the score reaches 8-8, depending on the respective skill and fitness levels.

'Point-per-rally' scoring was introduced to most senior international tournaments because it was believed to promote more 'attacking' play, shorter rallies and hence make the game more attractive. A computerised notation system, utilising a graphical user interface, was used by Hughes and Knight (1995) to examine the differences in the game of squash when played under 'point-per-rally' scoring as opposed to the more traditional English scoring. The rallies were slightly longer on average with point-per-rally scoring, not significantly so, and there were more winners but no increase in the errors - this being attributed to the lower height of the 'tin' under these new rules.

McGarry and Franks (1994) created a stochastic model of championship squash match-play which inferred prospective results from previous performance through forecasting shot response and associated outcome from the preceding shot. The results were restricted as players produced the same patterns of responses against the same opponent (P>0.25) but an inconsistent response was found when competing against different opponents (P<0.25). This contradicts earlier work by Sanderson (1983) who found that squash players played in the same patterns against different opponents, whether winning or losing, but this may well be a function of the finer degree to which McGarry and Franks were measuring the responses of the players. These results led to further analysis by these authors (McGarry and Franks, 1995) of behavioural response to a preceding athletic event and they again found the same results. They confirmed that sport analysis can reliably assume a prescriptive application in preparing for future athletic competition, but only if consistent behavioural data can be established. The traditional planning of match strategies from *a priori* sport information (scouting) against the same opponent would otherwise seem to be an expedient and necessary constraint.

Hughes and Clarke (1995) analysed the differences between the playing patterns of players at Wimbledon, on grass, and those of players at the Australian Open, on a synthetic surface and created empirical models of play at the elite level on both surfaces. Hughes (1995) analysed the scoring structures in tennis and squash, using the phrase 'activity cycles' and 'critical points' to describe events leading to exciting points in each system. In tennis these activity cycles last about 3 mins and the scores were always close because of the nature of the system. Hughes recommended a new scoring system in squash to try to make the game more attractive. He recognised the need to shorten the cycles of play leading to 'critical' points in squash - currently it takes about 15-20 minutes to reach a game-ball - by having more, shorter games, more critical points will arise and this will raise the levels of excitement and crowd interest. Badminton has the same problems with its scoring systems and the ensuing activity cycles. He also demonstrated quatitatively that there is also an imbalance in the game when the winner of a rally is given the serve at the start of the next rally - the lesser player is being penalised. Analysis of the effects of rule changes in sport has frequently been the subject of research in notational analysis usually by creating statistical norms or models of performance pre- and post-rule changes. This kind of work is relatively unusual in being proactive rather than reactive.

2.5 Educational applications
Schmidt (1975) compiled extensive research and found that feedback, if presented at the correct time and in the correct quantity, played a great part in the learning of new skills and the enhancement of performance. Recent research, however, has shown that the more objective, i.e. quantitative, the feedback the greater effect it has on performance (Salmoni et al., 1984).

Many studies have been completed on the patterns of play and rally ending outcome of the game of squash (Hughes, 1985 ; Hughes, 1986; Hughes and Knight, 1995; McGarry and Franks, 1996), but the study of feedback and its effect upon performance has received little attention. Brown and Hughes (1995) studied the differing effects that qualitative and quantitative feedback had on the performance of junior squash players. The study found no change in the overall group performance ($P<0.01$) and only one of the individual subjects showed a slight improvement ($P<0.05$). Their study design was limited by the fact that they used adolescent players and they felt that their results were compromised by the effects of maturation.

Murray et al. (1998) examined the effect that detailed quantitative feedback has on the performance of elite and sub-elite standard squash players. By providing accurate and detailed feedback from a computerised squash analysis system and observing matches after the feedback provision, it was possible to gauge temporal transitions in the performers' patterns of play and winner/errors distributions. The subjects also completed Sports Psychological Skills Questionnaires (S.P.S.Q.) to make it possible to evaluate changing psychological states over the feedback provision period.

Two different standard groups of players were selected. An elite group (N=4), all of which were ranked in the top 10 senior in Wales, and a sub-elite group (N=4), all ranked between 10-30 senior in Wales. Both groups in this study reacted positively to the feedback provided. The sub-elite group showed a greater change in performance, but the small change in the performance of the elite players could be argued to have had as great an effect on match results. However, in order to gauge the exact effect of feedback alone, complete control conditions would be needed in order to minimise the effect of other external variables. This experimental design is difficult because working with elite athletes precludes large numbers of subjects.

The sub-elite performers displayed more significant improvements ($P<0.05$) in specific shot types. Arguably, this is representative of the relatively easy task of improving performance when at a lower level of competence. It is clear that the intrapersonal nature of the elite group had an impact on the study. This should be noted by coaches working with such groups in the future. The psychological states of the subjects also had an effect on their performance, be it positive or negative, and evidently further research into this area would improve the status and understanding of the competitive squash coach. In this study quantitative feedback induced a significant temporal transition in performance levels of both groups. The findings were consistent with earlier research on the effect of quantitative feedback (see Salmoni, Schmidt and Walter, 1984).

Hughes and Robertson (1998) are using notation systems (see section 2.2) as an adjunct to a spectrum of tactical models that they have created for squash. The hand notation systems are used by the Welsh national youth squads, the actual notation being completed by the players for the players. It is believed that by getting the players to do the notation, their tactical awareness is heightened.

3 Conclusions

The examples given in this paper are not intended to be a comprehensive review of notational analysis of racket sports but rather a series of examples from publications that are very familiar to the author. The applications defined in this paper are not new but are the extension and distillation of ideas refined over the last 15 years. The value of these applications can be judged by the growth of notational analysis as an area of sports science support for competing national teams and individual athletes.

4 References

Alexander, D., McClements, K. and Simmons, J. (1988) Calculating to win. **New Scientist**, 10 December, 30-33.

Brown, D. and Hughes, M.D. (1995). The effectiveness of quantitative and qualitative feedback on performance in squash, in **Science and Racket Sports**, (eds T. Reilly, M. Hughes and A. Lees), E. and F. N. Spon, London, pp. 232-236.

Croucher, J. S. (1996) The use of notational analysis in determining optimal strategies in sports, in **Notational Analysis of Sport - I and II**, (ed. M. Hughes), UWIC, Cardiff, pp. 3-20.

Downey, J.C. (1973) **The Singles Game**, E.P. Publications, London.

Franks, I.M. (1997) Use of feedback by coaches and players, in **Science and Football III**, (eds T. Reilly, J. Bangsbo and M. Hughes), E. and F.N. Spon, London, pp. 267-278.

Hughes, M.D. (1985) A comparison of patterns of play in squash, in **International Ergonomics** (eds I.D. Brown, R. Goldsmith, K. Coombes and M.A. Sinclair). Taylor and Francis, London, pp. 139-141.

Hughes, M.D. (1986) A review of patterns of play in squash at different competitive levels, in **Sport Science** (eds J. Watkins, T. Reilly and L. Burwitz), E. and F.N. Spon, London, pp. 363-368.

Hughes, M.D. (1994) A time-based model of the activity cycles in squash, with different scoring systems, and tennis, on different surfaces. **Journal of Sports Sciences, 13**, 85.

Hughes, M.D. (1995) Using notational analysis to create a more exciting scoring system for squash, in **Sport, Leisure and Ergonomics** (eds G. Atkinson and T.Reilly), E. & F. N. Spon, London. pp. 243-247.

Hughes, M. and Clark, S. (1995) Surface effect on elite tennis strategy, in **Science and Racket Sports** (eds T. Reilly, M. Hughes and A. Lees). E. & F. N. Spon, London. pp. 272-277.

Hughes, M.D. and Franks, I.M. (1993) A time-motion analysis of squash players using a mixed-image video tracking system. **Ergonomics, 37**, 23-29.

Hughes, M.D. and Knight, P. (1995) A comparison of playing patterns of elite squash players, using English scoring to point-per-rally scoring, in **Science and Racket Sports** (eds T. Reilly, M. Hughes and A. Lees), E. & F.N. Spon, London, pp.257-259.

Hughes, M.D. and Moore, P. (1998) Movement Analysis of Elite Level Male Serve and Volley Tennis Players, in **Science and Racket Sports II** (eds A. Lees, I. Maynard, M. Hughes and T. Reilly), E. & F.N. Spon, London.

Hughes, M.D. and Robertson, C. (1998) Using computerised notational analysis to create a template for elite squash and its subsequent use in designing hand notation systems for player development, in **Science and Racket Sports II** (eds A. Lees, I. Maynard, M. Hughes and T. Reilly), E. & F.N. Spon, London.

Hughes, M.D. and Tillin, P. (1996) An analysis of the attacking strategies in female elite tennis players at Wimbledon. **Journal of Sports Sciences, 13,** 86.

Hughes, M.D., Franks, I.M. and Nagelkerke, P. (1989) A video-system for the quantitative motion analysis of athletes in competitive sport. **Journal of Human Movement Studies, 17**, 212-227.

McGarry, T. and Franks, I.M. (1994) A stochastic approach to predicting competition squash match-play. **Journal of Sports Sciences, 12**, 573-584.

McGarry, T. and Franks, I.M. (1995) Modeling competitive squash performance from quantitative analysis. **Human Performance, 8,** 112-129.

McGarry, T. and Franks, I.M. (1996). In search of invariant athletic behaviour in sport: An example from championship squash match-play. **Journal of Sport Sciences, 14,** 445-456.

Murray, S., Maylor, D. and Hughes, M. (1998) The effect of computerised analysis as feedback on the performance of elite squash players, in **Science and Racket Sports II** (eds A. Lees, M. Hughes, T. Reilly and I. Maynard), E. & F.N. Spon, London.

Reilly, T. and Thomas, V. (1976) A motion analysis of work-rate in different positional roles in professional football match-play. **Journal of Human Movement Studies, 2,** 87- 97.

Reilly, T. (1996) **Science and Soccer**. E. & F.N. Spon, London.

Salmoni, A.W., Schmidt, R.A. and Walter, C.B. (1984). Knowledge of Results and Motor Learning: A review and reappraisal. **Psychological Bulletin, 95,** 355-386.

Sanderson, F.H. (1983) A notation system for analysing squash. **Physical Education Review, 6,** 19-23.

Sanderson, F.H. and Way K.I.M. (1977) The development of an objective method of game analysis in squash rackets. **British Journal of Sports Medecine, 11,** 188

Schmidt, R.A. (1975). A schema theory of discrete motor skill learning theory. **Psychological Review, 82,** 225-260.

Sharp, R. (1986) Presentation: Notation Workshop in the Commonwealth Games Conference on Sport Science. Glasgow.

Taylor, M. and Hughes, M. (1998) A comparison of play of the top Under 18 junior tennis players in the world and Britain, in **Science and Racket Sports II** (eds A. Lees, I. Maynard, M. Hughes and T. Reilly). E. & F.N. Spon, London.

31 Analysing championship squash match-play as a dynamical system

T. McGarry, M.A. Khan and I.M. Franks
School of Human Kinetics, University of British Columbia, Canada

1 Introduction

The aim of sport analysis is to augment the subjective observation of the coach by providing empirical data gathered through the use of systematic observation techniques. This is necessary since human observation is an active process that is subject to error in information recall, as seen in studies of eyewitness testimony in both criminal acts (Wells and Loftus, 1984) and sport performance (Franks and Miller, 1986). The latter is the case even when identification of the key sports behaviours have been primed beforehand through observation training (Franks and Miller, 1991).

Systematic observation techniques have been used to analyse championship squash match-play for signature features of sport behaviour, in particular invariant shot responses to various preceding behavioural events (e.g.,McGarry and Franks, 1996). The results showed that invariant behavioural responses were dependent in part on the level of analytic detail and, also, on the individual player. Thus both invariant and variant shot responses have been found in squash match-play from statistical analysis. This finding, coupled with the anecdotal likening of a badminton rally to a dance in which both partners maintain synchrony until a false step leads to subsequent disruption (Downey, 1993), led to the consideration of squash competition as an open system that intermittently transits between bouts of invariant (stable) and variant (unstable) behaviour. A perceptual analysis subsequently confirmed that squash competition can be independently perceived by different observers to transit between these two system states (McGarry et al., 1996).

We posit squash competition as an open (living) system that proceeds in accord with dynamical principles in order to account for these different system states. We explain, in brief, the dynamical basis of self organisation from an example of human rhythmic coordination (see Haken et al. [1995] for further detail). If the frequency of flexion-extension of the right index finger and left index finger is increased while in anti-phase (i.e. one finger flexes while the other finger extends), then a transition to in-phase (i.e. both fingers flex and extend at the same time) is observed. In contrast, no transition from in-phase to anti-phase occurs at any frequency. The order parameter describes the relation between the constituent units of the system, that is, the system behaviour,

Science and Racket Sports II, edited by A. Lees, I. Maynard, M. Hughes and T. Reilly. Published in 1998 by E & FN Spon, 11 New Fetter Lane, London EC4P 4EE, UK. ISBN: 0 419 23030 0

and the control parameter moves the system through its state space; it does not determine behaviour. In this example, the phase relation is the order parameter and frequency is the control parameter.

Importantly, a dynamical system transits between stable states via instability rather than, as we have posited for squash competition, between stable and unstable states. These self organising behaviours arise as a result of change in the non-linear coupling(s) between the individual oscillators. Thus, we begin by considering squash competition as a pair of non-linearly coupled oscillators, not least since each player oscillates around the T-position (T) as he(she) competes for control of the rally. A candidate order parameter that describes squash competition in this light is the phase relation that exists between the two players, specifically, the position of each player in their cyclical motion to and from the T with respect to each other. The experimental scaling of a control parameter is not possible in this study, given its observational focus, although a change in the order parameter should still be seen if, as posited, the system transits between different system states. Since a dynamical analysis requires a formal demonstration of a non-linear change in the order parameter as a result of scaling in the control parameter, this study provides a first attempt at analysing squash competition as a dynamical system.

2 Methods

A graphics tablet (Kurta, XLP1212), calibrated to the squash court dimensions, was connected to the serial port of a Zenith 386 microcomputer, thus enabling on-line x-y coordinate data collection via a hand held stylus. A Special Effects Generator (Panasonic, WJ-5500) was used to superimpose the signals from the video cassette recorder (Panasonic, NV 8350) and the video camera (Panasonic, WV-3900), the latter being situated such that the court dimensions were superimposed on the video image. Thus, the x-y data for each player were collected in real time from videotape by perceptually tracking a player's movement on court with the hand held stylus.

2.1 Data collection
The x-y coordinates of the pen were sampled at 10 Hz. Data collection began with the touch down of the pen on the graphics tablet, coincident with the instant that the server first contacted the ball with the racket. Data collection stopped at the end of the rally, effected by breaking the contact between the pen and the graphics tablet. Data from the server for each rally in a single game from the 1988 Canadian Men's Open Championship were collected independently by the first author and the second author. The procedure was repeated four days and two days later, respectively. Pearson product moment correlation coefficients (r) for the radial position data (i.e. the distance from a player's location on court to the T at any instant) show that both intra-rater and each pairwise inter-rater reliability measure for each rally (n=36) exceeded r=.8. These results show that the data collection process is both reliable and objective. (It was necessary to phase advance the second author's data for some rallies in order to accommodate the phase shift that was incurred at the start of data collection. This was not the case for the first author.) The first author then collected data for both the server

and the receiver from four rallies. These rallies, selected on the basis of prior good perceptual agreement, showed either; (a)no system transition, (b)a transition from a stable state to an unstable state and (c)a single shot perturbation in an otherwise stable rally. Data collection was repeated for each server and receiver before proceeding to the next rally for an intra-rater reliability check. Intra-rater reliability coefficients ranged from r=.935 to r=.995.

2.2 Data analysis
The x-y data for the server and the receiver were synchronized in time and the radial distance of each player from the T, as well as the absolute distance between both players, were then calculated for each synchronous data pair. The radial data are the distance from a player to the T and the absolute data are the distance between the two players at any instant respectively. The radial data and absolute data were each twice treated to a seven point moving average filtering process. The first twelve data items were thus discarded from each rally.

3 Results and Discussion
The radial data for both the server (bold) and the receiver (normal) for the first four rallies are presented in Figure 1a-1d. The absolute data for the corresponding rallies are presented in Figure 2a-2d. The data from Figure 1a-1d are suggestive of a stable anti-phase system that intermittently transits from this stable state. Figure 1a, for example, shows that the system quickly settles in anti-phase. The synchrony between the maxima and minima indicate that the two players oscillate around the T in an anti-phase relation. In other words, while one player is nearest to the T, the other player is furthest from the T and vice versa. Note that each maxima can reasonably be interpreted as a shot on that player's part. Note also that the first observed maxima for the server is actually his(her) second shot and, consequently, the third shot in the rally sequence. Thus, system instability, as inferred from the loss of synchrony in the radial data (Fig. 1a), occurs at about shot 7 in the rally sequence and continues until the end of the rally.

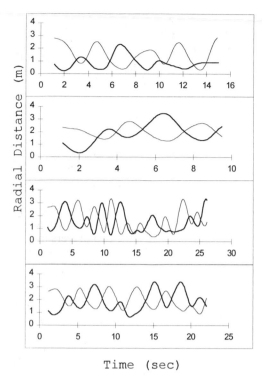

Figure 1a-1d. Radial distance for the server (bold) and the receiver (normal) for (top to bottom) rallies 10, 36, 37 and 42 respectively.

A rally need not show system transition. Figure 1b, for example, shows that the system is anti-phase stable throughout the rally, an interpretation that agrees with the perceptual analysis from independent observation. Figures 1c and 1d, on the other hand, show a transition from anti-phase stability at some time in the rally and, also, a subsequent return to that same stable state afterwards. Thus, it seems that the behaviour of the system is predisposed to an anti-phase relation, on to which system perturbations, or fluctuations, are intermittently and briefly written.

The description of championship squash match-play as a dynamical system requires an order parameter be identified that satisfactorily expresses the relation between the system components, in our case the two players. This relation should be observed to change as a non-linear result of the scaling of a control parameter. This study does not allow for the experimental manipulation of a control parameter although a non-linear change in the order parameter is still expected. A candidate order parameter is the location of one player on court with respect to the other player. This might be expressed in the phase relation (Fig. 1a-1d), or as the absolute distance between the two players (Fig. 2a-2d). We examine these data for evidence of a non-linear change in system behaviour if squash match-play is to be satisfactorily described as a dynamical system.

The data presented in Figure 2a-2d do not support the above hypothesis. While it is of interest to note that the rally with no perturbations, as identified from perceptual analysis (Fig. 2b), is the most stable, as per the order parameter, there is no shift between system states in the other rallies. This result affords one of two possibilities; either absolute distance fails as an order parameter to adequately describe the system dynamics or the system itself is not subject to the dynamical principles of spontaneous pattern formation. Each of these possibilities will now be addressed in turn.

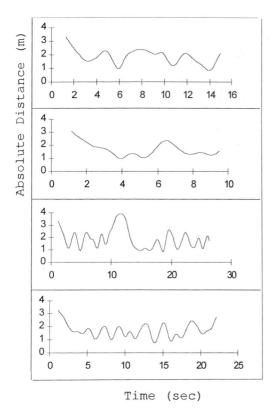

Figure 2a-2d. Absolute distance between the server and receiver for (top to bottom) rallies 10, 36, 37 and 42, respectively.

First, the use of absolute distance to express a relation between the two players might not be reasonable. For example, the oscillatory exchange between the two players in the same corner of the court (e.g. a straight drive exchange) would result in an oscillation in absolute distance (cf. Figure 2c and 2d) since each player would pass the other as one moves to and the other moves from the T. Alternatively, the exchange between the two players in opposite corners of the court (e.g. a cross court boast and cross court lob exchange) would result in a reasonably stationary value of absolute distance because as one player approaches the T in a particular direction, the other player leaves the T in the same direction. The exchange between the two players to adjacent corners would result in an oscillation in absolute distance over time. Thus, absolute distance fails to adequately express the spatial relation that exists between the two players. Identifying a suitable order parameter remains an outstanding issue if championship squash match-play is to be shown to adhere to dynamical principles of self organisation.

Second, it might be that squash competition adheres to physical principles of self organisation other than those of dynamical pattern theory. Homeokinetic theory (e.g.,Soodak and Iberall, 1978), for example, has been developed to explain how order emerges as a result of self regulation in accord with physical law in open systems. African termites, for example, build nests by depositing nest material, initially at random, together with a pheromone (see Kugler and Turvey, 1987). The pheromone (scent) increases the likelihood of attracting other termites and, hence, further nest deposits. The nesting behaviours thus adhere to a basic cyclical function; (a) increasing scent concentration, (b) increasing likelihood of nest deposit and (c) increasing nest deposit, that continues until a nest is built. Of relevance to sport competition is that the nest proceeds in accord with physical law but is always unique in its particular construction. It might be that sport competition yields to similar self organising physical principles that underlie athletic behaviour.

4 Conclusions

Sports scientists are still trying to satisfactorily describe sport competition at the level of behaviour although it is through the development of theory that the system will eventually be explained. The physics of open systems might well be a valuable contributor in this regard. The intent, of course, is that theory informs practice. The reverse also holds in that practice informs theory. The ongoing research program so far would suggest that (a)the empirical behavioural data are not equally informative, (b)the important data are readily subject to direct perception and (c)a different system description of sport competition might be profitable.

5 References

Downey, J. (1993) Match analysis of badminton. Presented at the **First World Congress of Science and Racket Sports**, Liverpool, UK. July.

Franks, I.M. and Miller, G. (1986) Eyewitness testimony in sport. **Journal of Sport Behaviour**, 9, 38-45.

Franks, I.M. and Miller, G. (1991) Training coaches to observe and remember. **Journal of Sports Sciences**, 9, 285-297.

Haken, H., Kelso, J.A.S. and Bunz, H. (1985) A theoretical model of phase transitions in human hand movements. **Biological Cybernetics**, 51, 347-356.

Kugler, P.N. and Turvey, M.T. (1987) **Information, natural law, and the self-assembly of rhythmic movement**. Hillsdale, New Jersey, Lawrence Erlbaum Associates, Inc.

McGarry, T. and Franks, I.M. (1996) In search of invariant athletic behaviour in sport: An example from championship squash match-play. **Journal of Sports Sciences**, 14, 445-456

McGarry, T., Khan, M.A. and Franks, I.M. (1996) Analyzing championship squash match-play: In search of a system description, in **Proceedings of The Engineering of Sport** (ed. S.Haake), Rotterdam, Balkema, pp.263-269.

Soodak, H. and Iberall, A. (1978) Homeokinetics: A physical science for complex systems. **Science,** 201, 579-582.

Wells, G. and Loftus, E. (1984) **Eyewitness Testimony: Psycho-logical Perspectives.** Cambridge University Press,Cambridge

32 Using computerised notational analysis to create a template for elite squash and its subsequent use in designing hand notation systems for player development

M. Hughes[1] and C. Robertson[2]
[1]Centre for Notational Analysis, UWIC, Cardiff, UK and
[2]National Coach, Welsh Squash Rackets Federation, Penarth, UK

1 Introduction

Creating a database of a competitive sport and extracting from that database a tactical model of the game is one of the most desirable outcomes of notational analysis. Many coaches seek the template of tactical play at the highest level for preparation and training of elite players, and for developing players who aspire to reach the highest levels within the game. Particular databases, aimed at specific individuals or teams, can also be used to prepare potential opponents for match play. The aim of this work was to utilise computerised notation systems to create, firstly, a structural archetype of the game of squash at the elite level, and then to extend this to a tactical model of the game. The second aim was to develop hand notation systems for use by coaches and players, with the intention of providing not only immediate feedback to the competing players but also an educational tool for those players using the systems.

2 Development of Database and Models

Five matches of elite players (ranked in the world top 20) were videotaped at the finals of the 1996 British Open. All these matches were analysed using a comprehensive computerised notation system (Hughes and Knight, 1995) which was used post-event. Chi-square and t-tests were used to test for significant deifferences when approprite. A summary of the template of the game is shown in Table 1, more details are shown in the Tables 2-9 and Figs. 1-4.

2.1 The general patterns of the game at elite level

The length of the rallies agrees with recent research (Hughes and Knight, 1995), but differs from other earlier research (Hughes, 1985) - this is attributed to lighter rackets with increased power. In the tactical model a performance indicator, the ratio of winner to errors, W/E (Sanderson, 1983), showed significant differences ($P<0.01$) between the profiles of all the different categories of shots of winning players and

Science and Racket Sports II, edited by A. Lees, I. Maynard, M. Hughes and T. Reilly. Published in 1998 by E & FN Spon, 11 New Fetter Lane, London EC4P 4EE, UK. ISBN: 0 419 23030 0

losing players at elite level. The highest ratios of W/E for both sub-sets of players was for the cross-court drive; the lowest ratio, of those shots that were played with significant frequency, were the boast and the straight drive. The shots that had the highest frequencies of errors were the straight drive and the straight drop.

Table 1. This model is based upon data taken from 5 matches involving players who were in the top 20 in the world at the time (1995-96 season)

	1089
Average number of shots/match	
Average number of shots/game	351.2
Average number of rallies/game	26
Mean rally length (19" tin)	13.52
Mean rally time	21s
Time between rallies	10s
Average number of winners/game - winning player	9 (8.9)
Average number of errors/game - winning player	5 (4.7)
Average number of winners/game - losing player	6 (6.2)
Average number of errors/game - losing player	6 (6.3)

Table 2. Analysis of winners and errors for winning and losing players
The totals for the winners and errors in the columns are for 5 matches

Shot	WINNING PLAYERS			LOSING PLAYERS		
	Winners	Errors	W/E Ratio	Winners	Errors	W/E Ratio
Drive (D)	23	22	1.05	20	29	0.69
Drop (d)	41	21	1.95	32	24	1.33
Boast (B)	8	9	0.89	8	19	0.42
Lob (L)	1	7	0.14	2	10	0.2
Volley Long (VL)	9	2	4.5	2	0	-
Volley Short (VS)	22	9	2.44	19	14	1.36
Volley Boast (VB)	0	1	0	0	1	0
Cross Drive (cD)	29	1	29	11	2	5.5
Cross Drop (cd)	12	6	2	6	5	1.2
Cross Lob (cL)	3	1	3	0	4	0
Cross VL (cVL)	2	1	2	4	1	4
Cross VS (cVS)	10	4	2.25	8	2	4
TOTAL	160	84	1.90	111	114	0.97

2.2 Distribution of serves

Only four of the matches (416 rallies) were analysed, due to administrative problems, but it was felt that there was sufficient data to normalise the patterns of serving. There were 167 hard serves, 100 medium pace serves and 149 lob serves.

The data showed that in almost all rallies the server won a higher proportion of rallies except for when handout hit a cross drive return. Because a straight return to length moves the server all the way across the court and into a backhand corner, this is the most desirable shot, particularly a volley when possible. Perhaps as a tactical option the cross-drive will wrong foot the server and reverse the pressure. When these returns are expressed as percentages then these trends are more clearly demonstrated (see Fig. 1).

Table 3. The type of service returns and the subsequent outcomes of the rallies

	Returns and who won the rally			
	Server	Handout	Let	
VD	43	41	20	104
D	46	35	22	103
cVD	46	43	19	108
cD	11	19	9	39
VS	16	11	11	38
Others	27	7	4	38
Total	**189**	**156**	**85**	**430**

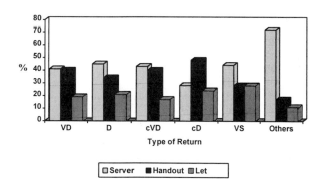

Figure 1. The types of service returns expressed as percentages of the possible outcomes.

2.3 Distribution of long and short shots

There was no difference ($P>0.05$) in the distribution of long and short shots between winners and losers at this level. As expected the length dominates the tactics of the game, with short shots as the tactical option of a 'loose' shot. The average number of shots per match under these different categories, for the 10 elite players, are shown below.

Table 4. The frequency per match of long and short shots for elite players (N=10)

Av/match/player	Total shots	%	Approx. Fraction
Straight Long	232	43	2/5
Cross Long	167	31	1/3
Straight Short	82	15	1/6
Cross Short	61	11	1/10

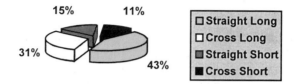

Figure 2. The frequency of long and short shots for elite players (N=10)

2.4 Distribution of volleys

There was no difference in the distribution of volleys between winners and losers at this level (P>0.05). The aggregate of ten players are presented below.

Table 5. Frequency of volley types for elite players (N=10)

Volleys Mean/match/player	Total shots	% (with respect to volleys only)	Approx. Fraction
Straight Long	30	32	1/3
Cross Long	34	36	1/3
Straight Short	20	22	1/5
Cross Short	9	10	1/10
Total	**93**	**18.7% of total**	**1/5**

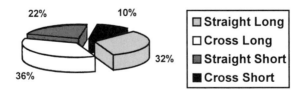

Figure 3. Distribution of volleys for elite players (N=10)

2.5 Awareness of the position of the opponent when playing a short shot
These analyses were completed to assess the patterns of 'short play' in the elite game and also the tactical significance of the position of the opponent when taking the ball to the front of the court.

Table 6. The frequency of short shots for elite players (5 matches)

Short shots			
Shot	**Frequency**	**Per game**	**%**
Drop	273	12.40	36
Volley drop	160	7.27	21
Boast	118	5.36	15
Cross drop	53	2.41	7
Kill	52	2.36	7
Volley kill	37	1.68	5
Cross volley kill	27	1.23	4
Volley Boast	27	1.23	4
Cross volley drop	16	0.73	2
TOTAL	**716**	**32.55**	**100**

Table 7. The position of the opponent when a short shot is played

Position of opponent			
	Shots	**per game**	**%**
Level	211	9.60	29.51
Behind	239	10.86	33.33
In front	266	12.09	37.16
Total	**716**	**32.55**	**100**

The greatest percentage of short shots were played when the opponent is in front of the striking player, this will be due to a combination of the large number of shots played from the back of the court together with the intention to wrong-foot the opponent.

2.6 Awareness of opponent when volleying
Effective volleying in squash is necessary to dominate the central areas of the court, keep the opponent at the back of the court and to sustain pressure.

2.7 Tactical responses in the front and back corners of the court
The four corners in the squash court are the four natural targets for all shots. How players play out of these areas is of fundamental importance to match tactics. The analysis of responses to long and short shots by opponents produced a clear tactical hierarchy of shots from those particular parts of the court - the elite players resorting in the main to one of three or four tactical 'best options' (Shot percentages less than 5% are not shown).

2.8 Summary

Seven models, and nine associated notation systems, were developed that encompassed all parts of the game from serve and return to awareness of the opponent when playing a short shot or long shot, from patterns of volleying to responses to short or long shots.

Table 8. The frequency of volleys for elite players (5 matches)

Shot	Volleys		
	Frequency	Per game	%
Long	115	5.75	23.5
Cross long	203	10.15	41.5
Short	138	6.90	28
Cross short	28	1.40	6
Volley Boast	6	0.30	1
TOTAL	490	24.50	100

Table 9. The position of the opponent when a volley is played

	Position of opponent		
	Shots	per game	%
Level	154	7.70	31.43
	134	6.70	27.35
In front	202	10.10	41.22
Total	490	32.55	100

`RESPONSE TO A SHORT SHOT
(a shot landing in the front quarter of
the court)

RESPONSE TO A LENGTH
(a shot landing in the back quarter of
the court)

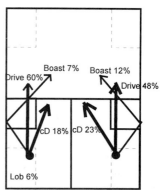

Figure 4. Patterns of shots played by elite players from the corners of the court.

3 Development of the Systems

All these tactical models were used as a basis for creating nine systems for notating squash in-match in a simple, visual way, that require little or no data processing. The tactical ideas on which the systems are based are listed :-

- Service and return
- Positioning of shot - Straight-long or -short, cross-long or -short
- Winners and errors
- Winners and errors - and rally length
- Volleys
- Response to a short shot
- Response to a long shot
- Awareness of opponent when volleying
- Awareness of opponent when playing short.

Space prevents a complete demonstration of these systems but an example of the service and return is shown in Fig. 6; this is one of the more complex systems but even so, the data collection sheet acts as a visual presentation of the patterns of play, any processing is easy. There is a deliberate tactical progression within this list of systems and it has been found that this progression is useful when using the systems with squads of players that are of different standards. This list of systems offers two or more systems that could be used for a squad session, no matter what the theme of the session may be. The systems are designed to be used by the players, for the players, and are all visual and therefore can provide immediate feedback. Learning time for the players is minimal, particularly when they operate in pairs. This use of the systems by the players has an extra benefit for them, as it heightens their awareness of the importance of the tactical reason for the particular system. The ideas behind the systems and progressions of tactical development involved in the systems can easily be extended to other racket sports.

4 Conclusions

Computerised notational analysis was used to create a template of the modern squash game of elite male players. Simple hand notation systems were designed to complement these models of performance - these are currently being used with squads of players of different ages. It is suggested that similar models could be constructed for the elite women's game, and also for different levels of performance. This modelling of performance could be replicated in other sports.

ANALYSIS SYSTEM FOR SERVE AND RETURN

The type of serve is categorised as : Hard (h); Medium (m); Lob(L)

The return of serve types are:-

Drive (D) - other sub-categories: Volley (V)
Drop (d)   Cross (c)
Boast (b)   e.g. cVd - cross volley drop
Lob (L)   Vb - volley boast
Kill (k)

For winner of the rally enter 'S' for server or 'R' for the returner of serve

Court position:-

1	2	3	4
5	6	7	8
9	10	11	12
13	14	15	16

Rally	Type of serve (h, m, or L)	Side Wall? (Y or N)	Pos. return taken (1 - 16)	Type of Return	Pos. return bounces or Volley	Winner of Rally (S or R)
1						
2						
3						
4						
5						

Figure 6. An example of one of the hand notation systems - the service and return system (Normally the sheet will have 30 rows - usually this will be enough for one game).

5 References

Hughes, M. (1985) A comparison of the patterns of play in squash, in **International Ergonomics '85** (eds I.D. Brown, R. Goldsmith, K. Coombes and M.A. Sinclair), Taylor and Francis, London, pp. 139-141.

Hughes, M. and Knight, P. (1995) in **Science and Racket Sports** (eds T. Reilly, M. Hughes and A. Lees), E. & F. N. Spon, London, pp. 257-259.

Sanderson, F. (1983) Developing a hand notation system for squash. **Physical Education Review**, 6, 19-23.

33 A preliminary investigation into the provision of computerised analysis feedback to elite squash players

S. Murray, D. Maylor and M. Hughes
Centre for Notational Analysis, UWIC, Cardiff, UK

1 Introduction

The effect of feedback provision has been at the centre of psychological research for many years. Schmidt (1975) reported that feedback, if presented at the correct time and in the correct quantity, played a great part in the learning of new skills and the enhancement of performance. Recent research (Salmoni et al., 1984) has shown that the more objective, i.e. quantitative, the feedback, the greater the effect that it has on performance. Many studies have been completed on the patterns of play and rally ending outcome of the game of squash (Hughes, 1985, 1986; Knight and Hughes, 1995; McGarry and Franks, 1996), but the study of feedback and its effect upon performance has received little attention. Brown and Hughes (1995) studied the differing effects that qualitative and quantitative feedback had on the performance of junior squash players.

The aim of this study was to provide detailed quantitative feedback to elite, and sub-elite, standard male squash players and monitor its effect on performance. By providing accurate and detailed feedback from a computerised squash analysis system and observing matches after the feedback provision, it was possible to gauge any temporal transition in the performers' patterns of play and winner/errors distributions. No research has been completed on the effect of feedback on psychological states of athletes - in an effort to gain some preliminary data, Sports Psychological Skills Questionnaires (S.P.S.Q., Butler et al., 1993) were administered over the period that feedback was provided.

It was predicted that the players would produce a significant increase in total winners played and a decrease in total errors played. It was also expected that differing psychological states would have a direct impact upon performance levels. If detailed quantitative feedback appeared to be a factor affecting performance then a case could be established for a controlled experimental study.

Science and Racket Sports II, edited by A. Lees, I. Maynard, M. Hughes and T. Reilly. Published in 1998 by E & FN Spon, 11 New Fetter Lane, London EC4P 4EE, UK.   ISBN: 0 419 23030 0

2 Methods

2.1 Subjects
Two different groups of male players were selected, an elite group (N=4), all members of which were ranked in the top 10 senior in Wales, and a sub-elite group (N=4), all ranked between 10-30 senior in Wales. A group case study design was used.

2.2 Apparatus and Data Processing
The software used to input data was designed by Hughes (1985) and was validated by Brown and Hughes (1995). The display on the computer split the court into 16 cells permitting a positional entry of the rally ending shot, type of shot played, a winner or error decision, identification of player, and the number of shots in the rally. The distribution of winners and errors was analysed and used as an index of performance.

2.3 Procedure
Each of the subjects' play was recorded during a series of competitive matches (N=4 for each player) at the start of the study (T1). These matches were aggregated by the software and detailed analyses performed for each player; these formed the basis of the initial feedback. Over the next eight weeks , match-play for each of the players was video-taped and computerised analysis and video feedback provided, combined with specific on court practises and training (designed around findings of T1). Each of the players had regular sessions in the laboratory viewing the videos of their performances, discussing the computerised analyses and planning practices for the following week. Finally, a second series of competitive matches (N=4 for each player) was recorded and analysed (T2). By comparing the results of T1 and T2 differences in performance could be recorded. Training diaries were kept and psychological (S.P.S.Q.) questionnaires were administered at the beginning of T1 and T2. A Chi-square test was employed to compare the results of T1 and T2 to test for significant changes.

3 Results and Discussion

Table 1. Chi-square values representing changes in specific shots between T1 and T2 for elite and sub-elite performers. The shaded areas refer to shot types showing significant change (P<0.05), all changes were improvements, i.e. more winners, fewer errors.

	ELITE		SUB-ELITE	
SHOT TYPE	**WINNERS**	**ERRORS**	**WINNERS**	**ERRORS**
Drive	*5.52*	*0.89*	*0.03*	*4.38*
Drop	*0.91*	*0.41*	*3.14*	*3.21*
Boast	*1.23*	*0.43*	*2.96*	*3.76*
Lob	*0.04*	*0.04*	*2.83*	*0.03*
Volley short	*0.03*	*0.76*	*3.31*	*1.91*
Volley long	*0.47*	*0.51*	*1.23*	*0.15*

It is evident from the above results that the sub-elite performers showed a greater improvement in the specific shot types. The most significant changes of all the shots in both groups were decreases in sub-elite errors in their drives, drops, and boasts (P<0.05). Although the elite performers only displayed a slight increase in performance, this would still have affected performance, as small changes in performance at an elite level can change the outcome of a match (Thomas and Thomas, 1994).

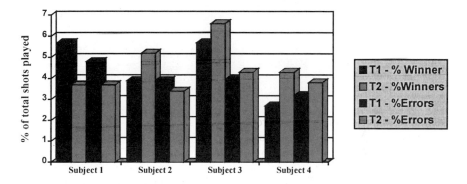

Figure 1. Changes in performance between T1 and T2 for elite performers.

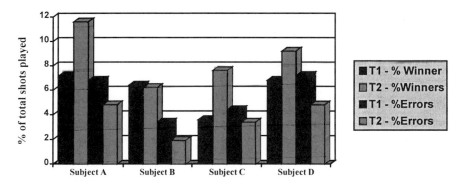

Figure 2. Changes in performance between T1 and T2 for sub-elite performers

Figures 1 and 2 show the subjects' change in winners and errors over the period of feedback provision. It is clear that the sub-elite performers produced greater changes than the elite. Elite subjects 2 and 3 displayed a marginal increase in winners, but these results were not significant (P>0.05). Elite subject 4 showed an increase in winners (P<0.01) suggesting a more positive approach to the game in T2. Sub-elite performers A, C and D all showed significant (P<0.05) increases in winners, with subject B showing a slight, although not significant (P>0.05) decrease.

The elite subjects showed mixed results with respect to errors (see Figure 1). Subjects 1 and 2 displayed a slight decrease in errors, while subjects 3 and 4 showed a slight increase, none of these results were significant (P>0.05). The sub-elite performers as a group (see Fig. 2) all displayed a significant decrease (P<0.05) in the number of errors played between T1 and T2.

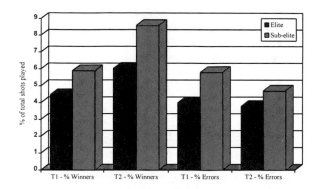

Figure 3. Elite and Sub-elite differences between T1 and T2.

It is evident from Figure 3 that the sub-elite group as a whole performed better at T2 than T1 and this may be because they reacted more positively to provision of the feedback. The elite performers displayed the same trends, although the differences were not significant (P<0.05).

Table 2. S.P.S.Q. results for elite performers. Figures in brackets refer to Male Elite S.P.S.Q. mean scores (calculated by C. Whiteaway, 1997, personal communication).

S.P.S.Q. Construct	Subject 1		Subject 2		Subject 3		Subject 4	
	T1	T2	T1	T2	T1	T2	T1	T2
Imagery (35.7)	18	19	34	43	30	26	19	24
Mental Preparation (35.3)	31	33	35	39	24	21	16	32
Self Confidence (35.4)	45	44	37	45	37	15	26	35
Anxiety Management (32.6)	22	28	35	44	35	14	33	38
Concentration (37.6)	29	32	35	39	28	17	2	40
Relaxation (30.6)	36	30	34	40	35	20	31	31
Motivation (41.4)	48	48	42	47	41	35	39	38

The sub-elite performers showed no change in psychological states between T1 and T2. Due to interpersonal nature of group of elite performers the performance of any given subject could have a direct effect upon another member of the group. The four elite subjects were all competing for a place in the Welsh national first team. With this additional pressure and motivation for places, the four elite players were playing against each other on a regular basis. The inter-personal relationship of the group clearly had an impact on subject 3 who, because of tournament results against the other subjects, dropped from number 5 to number 9 in the national rankings during the study period. Subjects 1 and 2 had a very good season and had their best results throughout the period of the study. This affected the motivation of subject 3 to train and play and also his playing patterns. It may be argued that it also affected his psychological state (see Table 2). Having received the initial feedback at the end of T1, subject 4 initiated himself on a psychological skills training programme, and although there was no evidence that this affected his match-play, it appeared to put him in better state of mind at T2 (see Table 2). Normally squash is regarded as an individual sport, and these inter-personal effects are not usually considered by coaches, but they are very important where squad players are brought together to play and train - particularly when there are prestigious places in a representative team at stake.

Table 3. Mean hours training per week for elite and sub-elite players

Elite subject	Hours training per week	Sub-elite subject	Hours training per week
1	19.5	A	3.6
2	13.4	B	6.1
3	11	C	3.1
4	10.2	D	5.8

The elite players spent considerably more time training than the sub-elite (see Table 3). This reflected their dedication and motivation towards the game. Elite subject 1 spent the most hours training, had the best outcome results, and a strong psychological state. In contrast elite subjects 3 and 4 trained the least of the elite, showed the most unstable mental states over the study period and produced the worst performances. Sub-elite subjects A and C spent the least amount of time training, nevertheless, they showed the greatest improvement in performance. Although no conclusions are drawn from these questionnaire data, they do highlight the need for more detailed research.

Both groups in this study reacted positively to the feedback provided. The sub-elite group showed a greater change in performance, but the small change in the performance of the elite players could have had as great an effect on match results.

The sub-elite performers displayed significant improvements ($P<0.05$) in specific shot types. Arguably, this is representative of the relatively easy task of improving performance when at a lower level of competence (Thomas and Thomas, 1994). It is clear that the intra-personal nature of the elite group had an impact on the study. This should be noted by coaches working with such groups in the future. The psychological states of the subjects are also likely to affect their performance, be it positive or negative, and evidently further research into this area would improve the status and understanding of the competitive squash coach.

4 Conclusions

In this study quantitative feedback was provided to elite and sub-elite players, and a temporal transition in performance levels of both groups was noted. It may be that the feedback influenced the performance, which would be consistent with earlier research on the effect of quantitative feedback (Schmidt, 1982; Salmoni et al., 1984; Franks, 1997). If this is the case then it would suggest that a more detailed experimental study would be worthwhile.

5 References

Brown, D and Hughes, M.D. (1995) The effectiveness of quantitative and qualitative feedback on performance in squash, in **Science and Racket Sports** (eds T. Reilly, M. Hughes and A. Lees), E. and F.N. Spon, London. pp. 232-236.

Butler, R.J., Smith, M. and Irwin, I. (1993) The performance profile in practise, **Journal of Applied Psychology**, 5, 48-63.

Franks, I.M. (1997) The use of feedback by coaches and players, in **Science and Football III** (eds T. Reilly, J. Bangsbo and M. Hughes), E. and F.N. Spon, London, pp. 267-278.

Hughes, M.D. (1985) A comparison of patterns of play in squash. in **International Ergonomics** (eds I.D. Brown, R. Goldsmith, K. Coombes and M.A. Sinclair), Taylor and Francis, London, pp. 139-141.

Hughes, M.D. (1986) A review of patterns of play in squash at different competitive levels, in **Sport Science** (eds J. Watkins, T. Reilly and L. Burwitz), E. and F.N. Spon, London, pp. 363-368.

Kazmier, L.J. (1988) **Business statistics (2nd edition)**, McGraw-Hill Publishing Co., NewYork.

Knight, P. and Hughes, M.D. (1995) A comparison of playing patterns of elite squash players, using English scoring to point-per-rally scoring, in **Science and Racket Sports** (eds T. Reilly, M. Hughes and A. Lees), E. and F. N. Spon, London, pp.257-259.

McGarry, T. and Franks, I.M. (1996) In search of invariant athletic behaviour in sport: An example from championship squash match-play, **Journal of Sports Sciences**, 14, 445-456.

Salmoni, A.W., Schmidt, R.A. and Walter, C.B. (1984) Knowledge of Results and Motor Learning: A review and reappraisal, **Psychological Bulletin**, 95, 355-386.

Schmidt, R.A. (1975) A schema theory of discrete motor skill learning theory, **Psychological Review**, 82, 225-260.

Schmidt, R. A. (1982) **Motor Control and Learning: A Behavioural Emphasis**, Human Kinetics, Champaign, IL.

Thomas, K.T. and Thomas, J.R. (1994) Developing expertise in sport: the relation of knowledge and performance. **International Journal of Sports Psychology**, 25, 295-312.

34 A notational analysis of time factors of elite men's and ladies' singles tennis on clay and grass surfaces

P. O'Donoghue[1] and D. Liddle[2]

[1]*Faculty of Informatics, University of Ulster, County Antrim, Northern Ireland and* [2]*Causeway Institute of Higher and Further Education, County Londonderry, Northern Ireland*

1 Introduction

The serve and volley style associated with grass court tennis has produced shorter rallies than the baseline rally style associated with clay court tennis. Richers (1995) used time-motion analysis to report average rally times of 4.3±2.7 s on grass and 7.6±6.7 s on clay for elite competitive tennis players, although the gender of the subjects of this study were not reported. As part of a study of elite tennis strategy, Hughes and Clarke (1995) analysed time factors of elite male players on grass and synthetic surfaces. They reported a mean rally time of 2.52 s on grass and 4.87 s on clay. Time factors can provide an indication of work rate through rally lengths as well as an insight into some aspects of elite tennis strategy. For example, Hughes and Clarke (1995) reported that longer inter-service times on grass may be a result of players attempting to follow up the first serve by attacking the net. Time-motion analysis is the systematic gathering and analysis of detailed information relating to human movement in competitive sport. The introduction of computerised notational analysis systems has greatly improved the efficiency of data gathering and analysis (Hughes, 1995). Therefore, the tool of computerised time-motion analysis was incorporated into this study.

 Clay courts are considered to be slower than grass as when the ball strikes the surface it bounces higher and loses pace. This results in a greater frequency of baseline rallies than on grass where the ball bounces lower and faster (Richers, 1995). On the other hand, serve and volley tactics are adopted on grass surfaces. The reason for the study stems from the introduction of a slower ball at Wimbledon and a faster ball at Roland Garros in the 1996 season. In 1996, Michael Stich (who is not considered to be a clay court specialist) was the runner-up in the men's singles at Roland Garros, beating Thomas Muster (the 1995 champion) en route to the final. At Wimbledon, in 1996, the men's singles final was contested by two non-seeded players. The ladies' singles finals of the two tournaments were contested by the same two players, Steffi Graf and Aranxa Sanchez-Vicario. Therefore, the aim of this study was to determine whether the introduction of the new balls had resulted in similar games for men's and ladies' singles at the two tournaments.

Science and Racket Sports II, edited by A. Lees, I. Maynard, M. Hughes and T. Reilly. Published in 1998 by E & FN Spon, 11 New Fetter Lane, London EC4P 4EE, UK.   ISBN: 0 419 23030 0

2 Methods

A computerised timing system was developed to allow the timing distributions of rally, inter-service, inter-point and inter-game times to be entered and stored for subsequent analysis. The system was implemented on a Seimens Nixdorf notepad computer with a 486 processor. The function keys were used to enter services as well as end of points as shown in Figure 1. The regulations of lawn tennis relating to when a point ends were applied during observation so that the data could be entered in an objective manner.

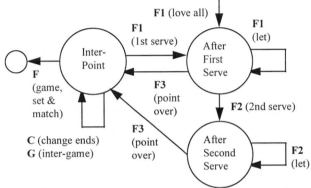

Figure 1. State transition diagram of system execution.

This system did not use computer interactive video and the accuracy of the timing information entered was limited. It was therefore necessary to train the system users and undertake a reliability study to assess the accuracy of the methodology. An inter-observer reliability study was conducted on the first set of the ladies' final of the French Open using Method Errors (ME) (Sale and Norman, 1991). These were 1.71% for rallies, 0.83% for inter-service periods and 0.46% for inter-point periods.

Matches from the 1996 French Open and the 1996 Wimbledon Championships were recorded from broadcast coverage. These matches from the third round to the final were analysed on the basis of the guidelines set by Hughes and Clarke (1995) which classified players as being of elite status on a particular surface following victory over two other professional players. In total over 55 hours of tennis were (Table 1).

Table 1. Summary of match analysis data

	French Ladies'	Wimbledon Ladies'	French Men's	Wimbledon Men's
Matches Analysed	10	11	9	14
Players Involved	13	15	11	15
Hours of Play Analysed (hours)	10:33:33	9:17:44	19:25:45	15:44:08
Number of Rallies Analysed	1006	939	1859	1768

3 Results

The results of the time analysis are presented in Table 2. Despite the introduction of different balls at the two tournaments, rallies were significantly longer on clay for both men's (P<0.001) and ladies' (P<0.01) singles. The proportion of the match spent rallying was also longer on clay than grass. This is further illustrated in Figure 2. Rallies in ladies' singles were significantly longer than in men's singles on both clay (P<0.001) and grass (P<0.001). Inter-serve, inter-point and inter-game times were similar in all games except when players changed ends.

Table 2. Summary of analysis of ladies' and men's singles at the two tournaments

	French Ladies'	Wimbledon Ladies'	French Men's	Wimbledon Men's
Rally Time (s)	8.05+6.14	5.99+4.33	5.64+ 4.69	3.69+2.54
Inter Serve Time (s)	10.38+2.76	10.60+3.26	10.13+3.63	10.53+2.49
Inter Point Time (s)	19.53+6.30	19.17+5.36	19.96+5.44	18.42+5.33
Inter Game-same ends (s)	28.12+5.96	27.43+6.02	28.11+5.61	27.15+5.47
Inter Game-change ends (s)	100.08+18.30	94.14+32.91	102.91+10.74	84.12+9.32
%Match playing rallies	21.30%	16.81%	14.99%	11.52%

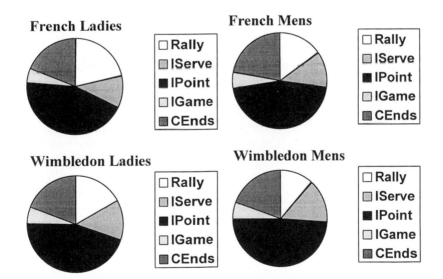

Figure 2. Distribution of match time the four games.

Figures 3 and 4 illustrate the distribution of rally lengths at Roland Garros and Wimbledon for ladies' and men's singles respectively. In the ladies' singles there are fewer rallies of under 6.5 s on both surfaces than in the men's singles.

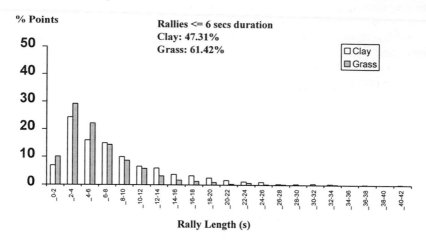

Figure 3. Distribution of rally lengths in ladies' singles.

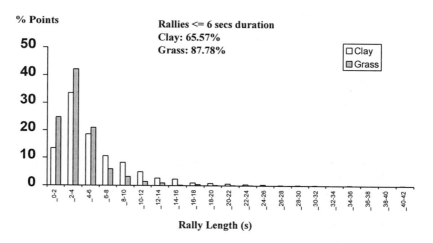

Figure 4. Distribution of rally lengths in men's singles.

4 Discussion

The results suggest that a normalised men's singles match of 6-4, 6-4, 6-4 (Hughes and Clarke, 1995) will take 1 hour 52 min on clay and 1 hour 38 min on grass. The results of Hughes and Clarke for the 1992 season shows that times for men's singles of 1 hour 54 min at Wimbledon and 2 hours 1 min on the synthetic surface of the Australian Open. A comparison between the normalised match length results of Hughes and Clarke's (1995) study and the current study are illustrated in Figure 5. The men's rally length at Wimbledon of 3.69 s is now longer than the 1992 mean of 2.52 s. The men's rally length at Roland Garros is also longer than the 1992 mean for the Australian Open of 4.87 s. However, match length for men's singles at Wimbledon has reduced as a result of players taking shorter breaks between points and games in the 1996 tournament.

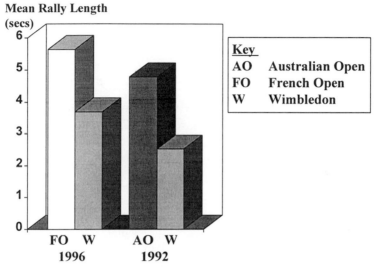

Figure 5. Comparison of mean rally lengths for men's singles reported by Hughes and Clarke (1995) with those of the current study.

The mean inter-serve time reported by Hughes and Clarke (1995) of 11.06 s at Wimbledon and 9.61 s at the Australian Open suggests that players may often attempt to follow up their first service on grass resulting in an observably longer inter-serve time. The results of the current study do not appear to support this finding which is surprising as clay is considered to be slower than the synthetic surface used in the Australian Open. This suggests that the ball changes at the French Open in 1996 may have resulted in an increase in serve-and-volley style. A further explanation may be that male players not noted as clay court specialists did particularly well at Roland Garros in 1996 which accounted for an unusually large proportion of the data gathered and used. Unlike the study of Hughes and Clarke (1995), the longer time taken for changing ends at the French Open is explained by some players taking injury breaks of up to three minutes.

There is little available research relating to timing factors within Grand Slam tournaments for the ladies' singles game. However, the results may still be discussed in relation to the original aim of the study which was to investigate whether the introduction of new balls at the two tournaments had resulted in similar games. The same two players, Steffi Graf and Aranxa Sanchez-Vicario, contested the finals of the French and Wimbledon Opens. Although the same two players were involved, the two matches produced different timing results. There was a 7% greater amount of match time spent rallying on clay.

The methodology is limited in that it does not address the intensity of play on the two surfaces. However, there was a longer amount of rally time on clay with similar resting times in both men's and ladies' singles. A further investigation could integrate heart rate data with time-motion results. Reilly and Palmer (1995) have found that server's heart rates were significantly higher than those of the receiver in during men's singles. Hughes and Clarke (1995) were able to combine rally lengths with the number of shots per rally. A further technique adopted by Richers (1995) was to combine rally lengths with sets of continuous foot steps within rallies and the number of steps taken within each set. Richers (1995) reported that similar numbers of footsteps were made within a set of continuous footsteps on clay, grass and hard court surfaces. The major differences were in the rally lengths and the number of sets of continuous footsteps per rally. Such results give a greater insight into the intensity of elite tennis. The computerised notational analysis system used within the current study should be extended to record shots and sets of continuous footsteps as well as timing information. This would require two separate observations of the data but would also provide valuable objective information for use within the coaching process.

5 Conclusions

The introduction of new balls at Roland Garros and Wimbledon in 1996, created significant differences in rally lengths at the two tournaments for both men's and ladies' singles. The mean rally length within men's singles were significantly shorter than in ladies' singles at both tournaments. Therefore, elite players should tailor their preparation for the singles championships at these two tournaments to reflect the differing rally lengths involved.

6 References

Hughes, M. (1995) Computerised notation of racket sports, in **Science and Racket Sports** (eds T. Reilly, M. Hughes and A. Lees), E. & F.N. Spon, London, pp. 249-256.

Hughes, M. and Clarke, S. (1995) Surface effect on elite tennis strategy, in **Science and Racket Sports** (eds. T. Reilly, M. Hughes and A. Lees), E. & F.N. Spon, London, pp. 272-277.

Reilly, T. and Palmer, J. (1995) Investigation of exercise intensity in male singles lawn tennis, in **Science and Racket Sports** (eds T. Reilly, M. Hughes and A. Lees), E. & F.N. Spon, London, pp. 10-13.

Richers, T.A. (1995) Time motion analysis of the energy systems in elite competitive singles tennis. **Journal of Human Movement Studies**, 28, 73-86.

Sale, D.G. and Norman, R.W. (1991) Testing strength and power, in **Physiological Testing of the High Performance Athlete**, 2nd Edition (eds J.D. MacDougal, H.A. Wenger and H.J. Green), Human Kinetics Publishers, Leeds, pp. 7-37.

35 A match analysis of elite tennis strategy for ladies' singles on clay and grass surfaces

P. O'Donoghue[1] and D. Liddle[2]
[1]Faculty of Informatics, University of Ulster, County Antrim, Northern Ireland and [2]Causeway Institute of Higher and Further Education, County Londonderry, Northern Ireland

1 Introduction

An understanding of elite tennis strategy on different surfaces provides important feedback within the coaching process. Limited detail can be recalled from the match from direct subjective observation of elite player performance. Video and television equipment support the extraction of detailed objective information from tennis matches (Underwood and McHeath, 1977). Further advances in observation and evaluation of sports performance involve notational analysis which provides systematic objective support for coaching. Hand notation has been applied to tennis (Downey, 1992). More recently, computerised notational analysis has been applied to racket sports (Hughes, 1995) with the advantages of historical databases, automated data analysis and flexible querying.

All four 'grand slam' tournaments are now played on different surfaces. The strategy adopted by elite male players on synthetic surfaces and grass surfaces has been investigated, concentrating on time factors, serve, return of serve, error and winner distributions as well as player positioning (Hughes and Clarke, 1995). However, Hughes and Clarke (1995) also found that there is a lack of information relating to elite tennis strategy with few studies addressing patterns of play adopted on different surfaces. The purpose of this study was to investigate whether elite female players win a greater proportion of points on serve and at the net on grass than clay surfaces. This would provide further objective information by relating to the strategies adopted by the players on both surfaces within the singles game.

2 Methods

The classification of points shown in Figure 1 identifies the various winning and losing outcomes. These include points being won on serve, at the net and from the baseline. With players attacking the net on both surfaces, the point classification scheme also addresses the **cause** and **effect** of players approaching the net.

Science and Racket Sports II, edited by A. Lees, I. Maynard, M. Hughes and T. Reilly. Published in 1998 by E & FN Spon, 11 New Fetter Lane, London EC4P 4EE, UK. ISBN: 0 419 23030 0

The **causes** of players approaching the net were classified into two types. The first of these is where that player attacks the net to **pressurise** the opponent. This includes attacking the opponent's serve, following up a good service or a good approach shot. The second cause of approaching the net is where the player is **drawn** to the net by an opponent's drop shot or short length shot.

The **effects** of attacking the net were classified as follows -

(1) points won immediately at the net using volley, overhead, drive winner, drop shot and opponent error;
(2) points lost immediately at the net by being lobbed, passed or making a net error;
(3) retreating from the net.

Once the initial investigation had provided an insight into elite tennis strategy and the important aspects of the game had been identified, a special purpose computerised notational analysis system was developed to record and analyse detailed information relating to competitive tennis. An initial registration screen allowed match and player details to be entered as well as the score and serving player at the start of the analysis. The menu structure within the match data entry screen reflected the point classification, shown in figure 1, with an additional menu to capture the **cause** of players attacking the net. As successive points were entered, the system automatically updated the score and, where necessary, the serving player. The system also allowed non-scoring points, such as "lets" to be identified. The data were entered and the following details were stored for each point:-

(1) score (sets, games and points) at start of point;
(2) serving player;
(3) whether point emanated from first or second service;
(4) the type of point (ace, double fault, serve winner, serve return winner, server attacks net first, receiver attacks net first or baseline rally);
(5) outcome of point (winning player as well as whether point was won with a winner or an opponent error). This included the **effect** of attacking the net;
(6) the **cause** of player attacking the net.

The 1996 French Open Championships and the 1996 Wimbledon Championships were recorded from broadcast coverage. The matches used within this study were from the third round to the final, using the criteria of Hughes and Clarke (1995), for classifying elite players. The data entered included 1006 points from 10 matches involving 13 different players from the 1996 French Open and 939 points from 11 matches involving 15 players from the 1996 Wimbledon Open. The data were entered using the computerised match analysis system. This allowed the effect of various aspects such as surface, the current scoreline, timing factors and whether points emanated from first or second services could be explored.

3 Results

The data shown in Figure 1 are the percentage of all points that fall within the given class of point at Roland Garros (RG) and Wimbledon (WD). These data can be further summarised to provide results relating to various aspects of elite tennis strategy. Figure 2 reduces the results to 7 classes of point, distinguishing between those won and lost by the serving player. Figure 2 also separates the points that emanated from first and second services.

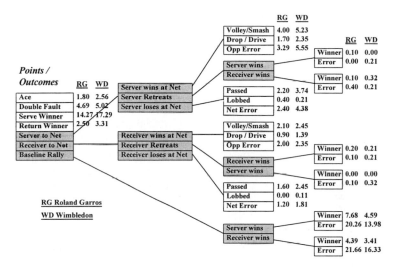

Figure 1. Classification of point types.

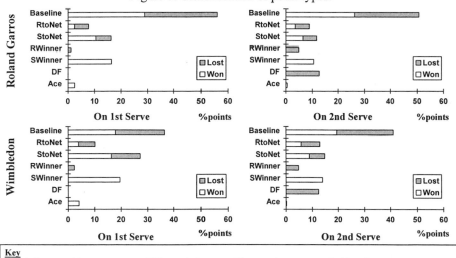

Figure 2. Summary of analysis for first and second services at the two tournaments.

At Roland Garros, 63.2% of points emanated from a first serve compared with 59.5% of points at Wimbledon. Similar percentages of points were won by the server on first and second serves on each surface; 61.0% on first service and 47.4% on second service at Roland Garros compared with 61.9% on first service and 48.4% on second service at Wimbledon.

Table 1 further reduces the data of Figures 1 and 2. It shows that on clay, there are more baseline rallies and fewer points won on serve and at the net than on grass. Points won on serve by receiving players are double faults by the server and serve return winners by the receiver. Points won from the baseline can be classified as winners (including passing or lobbing a player at the net) or opponent errors (forced and unforced). The ratio of winners to errors, when points are won from the baseline was 1 : 2.9 at Roland Garros and 1 : 2.6 at Wimbledon. Both serving and receiving players attacked the net more on grass. At Roland Garros, the winning and losing players won similar proportions of their points from the baseline. However, during their service games, the winning player won marginally more points on serve and marginally fewer points at the net than the losing player. At Wimbledon, the proportions of points won on serve, at the net and from the baseline were similar for winning and losing players.

Table 1. Percentage of points won on serve, at net and from baseline at both tournaments

	Roland Garros Server	Roland Garros Receiver	Wimbledon Server	Wimbledon Receiver
On Serve	28.7%	16.3%	35.3%	19.1%
At Net	16.1%	11.4%	23.3%	14.2%
From Baseline	55.3%	72.3%	41.7%	66.7%

The distribution of **effects** (outcomes) of approaching the net is similar on both surfaces when the server or receiver attacks the net as shown in table 2. These results are derived from figure 1 by expressing the percentage of those points where the server or receiver approached the net.

Table 2. Summary of analysis of the **effect** of attacking the net

	Roland Garros Server to Net 1st	Roland Garros Receiver to Net 1st	Wimbledon Server to Net 1st	Wimbledon Receiver to Net 1st
Volley, Smash or Overhead	27.4%	25.6%	23.6%	21.7%
Drop Shot or Drive Winner	11.6%	11.0%	10.6%	12.3%
Opponent Error	22.6%	24.4%	25.0%	20.8%
Retreat and Win Point	0.7%	3.7%	1.0%	3.8%
Retreat and Lose Point	3.4%	1.2%	2.4%	2.8%
Passed	15.1%	19.5%	16.8%	21.7%
Lobbed	2.7%	0.0%	1.0%	0.9%
Net Error	16.4%	14.6%	19.7%	16.0%

The **cause** of elite ladies attacking the net differed between the two surfaces. There appeared to be two main reasons for attacking the net. The first of these was that the player wishes to **pressurise** the opponent by following up a good serve, following up a good approach shot or by attacking the opponent's serve. The second of these was being **drawn** to the net (by an opponents short ball or drop shot). On clay, elite ladies were **drawn** to the net on 49.1% of occasions, winning 58.9% of such points. On grass, they are **drawn** to the net on 14.7% of occasions, winning 71.7% of such points. Of the 41.1% of such points lost on clay, the breakdown of effects is as follows: 17.9% passed, 2.7% lobbed, 18.8% net errors and 1.8% retreating from net and losing point.

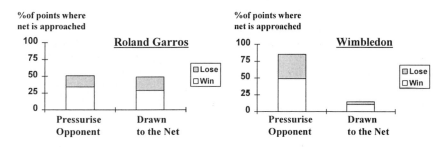

Figure 3. Summary of analysis of the **cause** of attacking the net.

Results were also produced to assess the effect of the current scoreline on elite tennis performance. Serving players on both surfaces won more points, particularly on serve, when they were ahead on service breaks than when level or behind on service breaks. This finding reflects the fact that on 79.0% of these points on clay and 79.0% of these points on grass, the eventual match winner was serving. When the server was ahead on points in the current game, there were marginally more serve winners and points won and lost at the net than usual on both surfaces. When the server was behind on points, there were marginally more double faults and baseline rallies than usual on both surfaces. Figure 4 shows the effect of the current scoreline on performance.

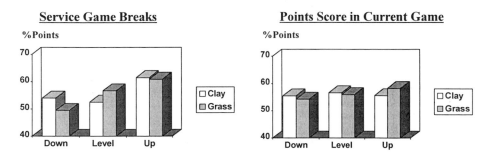

Figure 4. Summary of analysis of current scoreline on elite tennis performance.

4 Discussion

The results confirm that elite ladies tennis involves more points being won on serve and at the net on grass than on clay and that there are more baseline rallies in clay court competition. However, the most interesting findings of the study relate to the **causes** of players attacking the net. The result of **drawing** a player into the net on grass is that the opponent has a greater chance of winning the point than at Roland Garros. Therefore, players did not draw their opponents into the net as much at Wimbledon as they did at Roland Garros.

Although a player loses less points at Roland Garros (58.9%) by **drawing** the opponent to the net than at Wimbledon (71.7%), she still loses the majority of such points. It would appear that a decision to adopt such a strategy would depend on current baseline and net capabilities. In the singles game, elite ladies tennis players should introduce specific technical and tactical preparation into their training to support the necessary strategy to be adopted on the particular surface for which they are preparing. The strategy of **drawing** a player into the net on clay has the purpose of producing a winning passing shot or lob. However, playing a shot too short will risk losing the point to an opponent's drop shot or an angled shot to the side line. It is, therefore, essential for elite players, wishing to adopt such a strategy on clay, to introduce specific on-court technical preparation, concentrating on short length shots to improve this skill while minimising the inherent risks involved when playing elite opponents.

5 Conclusions

This study was limited to ladies singles in the 1996 French and Wimbledon Open Championships. The computerised notational analysis system used within this study can be applied to men's as well as ladies matches. It is necessary to identify whether or not the current match being analysed is a mens or a ladies match so as the automatic updating of the match score will recognise where tie breaks are being played and when the match is in the final set. Therefore, further work should be undertaken to provide more objective information relating to elite strategy. This will enable analyses to be expanded to cover male players, the doubles games and other surfaces such as hard court and synthetic surfaces.

6 References

Downey, J. (1992) Tennis notation, **Proceedings First World Congress of Notational Analysis of Sport**, November, Burton Manor.

Hughes, M. (1995) Computerised notation of racket sports, in **Science and Racket Sports** (eds T. Reilly, M. Hughes and A. Lees), E. & F.N. Spon, London, pp. 249-256.

Hughes, M. and Clarke, S. (1995) Surface effect on elite tennis strategy, in **Science and Racket Sports** (eds T. Reilly, M. Hughes and A. Lees), E. & F.N. Spon, London, pp. 272-277.

Underwood, G. and McHeath, J. (1977) Video analysis in tennis coaching, **British Journal of Physical Education**, 8, 136-138.

36 Movement analysis of elite level male 'serve and volley' tennis players

M. Hughes and P. Moore
Centre for Notational Analysis, UWIC, Cardiff, UK

1 Introduction

In tennis, players will often 'run round' a shot to change the ball to their favoured side. This is never done at elite level in squash or badminton because of the speed of the game at this level. This inefficient movement will have a deleterious effect upon the recovery of the player back to a central position on the court. Previous notational analysis research in racket sports has mainly concentrated on playing patterns. Time motion analysis has been applied to squash and badminton (Hughes, 1995), but none has been applied to tennis. The aim of this study is to investigate whether these inefficient movements have an effect on the ends of rally results. It is also intended that the study will broaden the existing research in movement analysis by providing a framework of the basic footwork movements of the tennis player, in preparation for the shot, at impact and during recovery.

2 Methods

This study was limited to analysing the movement of elite level male 'serve and volley' players, in an attempt to eliminate subjects' fundamental playing differences as a dependent variable affecting the conclusions. The purpose of the hand notation system was to define successful footwork patterns in 'serve and volleys', pre-shot (skipchecks, ready positions), during impact (ground contact) and in recovery (speed of change of direction). 'Skipcheck' was defined as a two footed split step for balance and the 'ready position' as the best position on court to wait for the return

A hand notation system was designed to record the relevant aspects of movement and footwork patterns to satisfy the aims of the study. The system enabled the user to record background information about the match:- the players, the tournament, the scores at the start and finish of the section of notation, the video cassette and counter number on which the match is stored to facilitate retrieval of the game if necessary. A simple box and column system was used to record the server, and the score at the start of every point. The column adjacent was then used to record the movement patterns

Science and Racket Sports II, edited by A. Lees, I. Maynard, M. Hughes and T. Reilly. Published in 1998 by E & FN Spon, 11 New Fetter Lane, London EC4P 4EE, UK.   ISBN: 0 419 23030 0

by letters and symbols. These notate the skipcheck, ready position on court, the use of ground contact or jumping just prior to impact with the ball, the shot played, the number of steps taken in a disadvantageous direction (i.e. away from the centre of the court) before changing direction, and the effectiveness of the shot. A validation study, notating the same set of play, at the same time of day, with one week's intervening rest period gave an intra-observer reliability of 99.05%.

Seven matches in total were notated, providing 14 movement performances as data for analysis, as each match was notated for both players. Concentrating on the eight players in the quarter-finals of Wimbledon, and beyond, ensured the very highest standard of players was available for the sample population.

3 Results

The average number of shots per rally was 2.97 (2255 shots in 759 rallies), which is close to the figure of 3.09 obtained by Hughes and Clark (1995). Within the 131 games notated, 121 serves were either aces or double faults, leaving 2134 shots influenced by footwork patterns and the opposition's play. Of these, 1527 were shots that were successfully returned into the court, but were not winners. Winners were defined as shots that could not have been reasonably returned by the players and there were 244 in total. Errors numbered 363 in total, this was 14.9% of the total number of shots. When broken down into shots played by winning and losing players, the numbers were very similar, with the total shots in each category divided almost equally in half. Losing players exhibited slightly more errors than winning players, and similarly winning players exhibited slightly higher numbers of winning shots than did losing players. The data collected for winning and losing players were similar, with the greatest difference being only 1.6%, between the errors of winning and losing players.

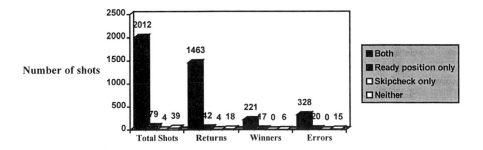

Figure 1. An analysis of the number of shots played with each of the different footwork preparations.

When the data were divided into pre-shot footwork groups, patterns could be more clearly seen, as shown in Fig. 1. The largest group of shots were those preceded by a skipcheck in the ready position, with over 94% of all shots falling into this category. Interestingly, if the player skipchecked, but failed to make it to the ready position, or neither skipchecked nor made it to the ready position, more errors were made than winning shots. Few shots were played straight from the ready position without skipchecking - these totalled four returns. There were over four times as many returns, after reaching the ready position and skipchecking, as errors in the same category, and over six times as many returns after reaching the ready position and skipchecking, as winners in the same category. A chi-square test indicated that there was no significant difference between the variables (P<0.05).

Winning games showed a much higher percentage of winning shots than errors. The reverse effect can be seen, more markedly, in losing games, where over two thirds of shots that ended the rallies were errors. Chi-square tests were carried out, comparing the types of winners and errors played in successful and unsuccessful games. The results were as follows:

*There was a significant difference (P<0.05) between the types of winning shots and the types of errors in successful games.
*There was no significant difference (P<0.05) between the types of winning shots and the types of errors in unsuccessful games.
*There was a significant difference (P<0.05) between the types of winning shots in successful games and the types of winning shots in unsuccessful games.
*There was a significant difference (P<0.05) between the types of errors in successful games and the types of errors in unsuccessful games.

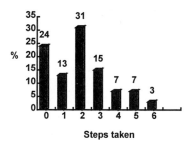

Figure 2. The percentage of outright opposition winners plotted against the number of steps taken in playing the preceding shot.

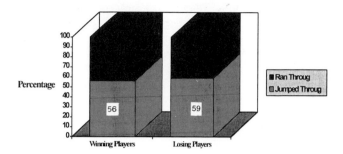

Figure 3. The percentage of post-impact movement by winning and losing
players.

The players returned 45 shots that were then outright (untouchable) opposition
winners. Interestingly, 17 of these 45 were preceded by an opposition return of service
- indicating a three-shot rally of service, return (the player's shot) and outright winner.
Twenty eight of these were at a later stage in the rally, as they were not preceded by an
opponent return of service. Of these shots, 73.4% were made after a skipcheck in the
ready position. The remaining shots that led to outright winners were divided evenly
between skipcheck only as preparation (i.e. not made in the ready position) and neither
skipcheck nor ready position. Moreover, a large proportion of these player shots that
led directly to an outright winning shot were followed by steps away from the centre of
the court post-impact (see Fig. 2); 31.1% of such shots were followed by two steps
away from the centre of the court, decreasing progressively through to 2.2% of shots
followed by six steps away from the court centre line.

Incorporating the total number of post-impact steps away from the centre line with
the total shots played, allows the mean steps taken away from the centre of the court to
be calculated. Fig. 3 shows clearly that losing players exhibited a higher mean than
did winning players. The distribution of jumps on the forehand and backhand sides is
similar. Forehand shots played with a jump totalled 234 shots in both winning and
losing players, whilst 232 and 244 shots were played with a jump on the backhand side
in winning and losing players respectively. Winning and losing players also showed
similar percentage values when examining whether post-impact steps away from the
centre were preceded by a jump on impact or purely running through a shot. Winning
players exhibited a slightly higher 'jump through' value than 'ran through', whilst the
situation was reversed for losing players (see Fig. 3). There was no significant
difference when a chi-square analysis was performed on the numbers of 'jump through'
and 'run through' shots with varying numbers of post-impact paces. There was no
significant difference (P>0.05) between successful and unsuccessful players.

Finally, the disadvantage of increased distance from the ready position, created by
post-impact paces, is demonstrated by the data in Figs. 4 and 5. These show a strong
negative relationship - a higher mean value for steps per shot away from the centre of
the court correlated strongly with a lower percentage of games won by the player.
Similarly, the higher the percentage games won, the lower the mean post-impact steps
away from the centre of the court per shot.

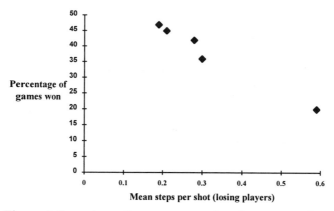

Figure 4. Percentage of games won against the mean number of steps per shot for losing players.

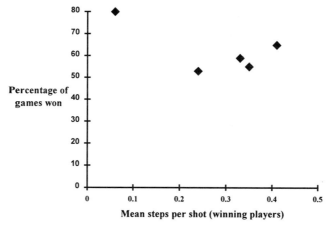

Figure 5. Percentage of games won against the mean number of steps per shot for winning players.

There were a small percentage (3.7%) of occasions when the player did not regain the 'ready' position, which was operationally defined as not being fixed relative to the court but varying with respect to the angle of the impending shot due to ball position. Taking paces through the shot and moving away from the centre of the court was more common (8.4%), as was jumping through the shot (7.2%). These 'inefficient' aspects of movements, the mean number of steps taken per shot correlated highly with losing the rally ($r = -0.88$). Winning players averaged 0.348 steps per shot away from the centre of the court, whereas losing players averaged 0.384 steps per shot, although this was not significantly different ($P>0.05$). In addition there were no significant differences when comparison was made between winning and losing players for frequencies of 'skipcheck' and 'jump through'.

4 Conclusions

The efficiency of movement in tennis was far higher than expected, but when players did run or jump through their shots, the data suggested that this placed pressure on them which often resulted in losing the rally. It is suggested that this study be extended to match-play by women and also that the analysis itself be extended to include sequences of these movements, a sufficiently large database would have to be gathered and analysed to enable statistical analysis.

5 References

Hughes, M. (1995) Computerised Notation of Racket Sports, in **Science and Racket Sports** (eds T. Reilly, M. Hughes & A. Lees), E. & F. N. Spon, London, pp. 249-256.

Hughes, M. and Clark, S. (1995) Surface effect on elite tennis strategy, in **Science and Racket Sports** (eds T. Reilly, M. Hughes & A. Lees), E. & F. N. Spon, London, pp. 272-277).

37 A comparison of patterns of play between the top under 18 junior tennis players in Britain and in the rest of the world

M. Taylor and M. Hughes
Centre for Notational Analysis, UWIC, Cardiff, UK

1 Introduction

Recent successes within British junior tennis have included James Baily who won the Junior Australian Open title in 1994, Martin Lee and James Trotman who won the Wimbledon Junior Doubles title in 1995 and Martin Lee who became number one in the junior World Rankings during 1996. Despite success at this level there is still no evidence of British senior players making the same impact on the elite levels of tennis. With the emergence of new nations on the tennis scene, such as Croatia, Ukraine, Czech Republic and Slovakia, a set of stronger junior players has been created who are capable of performing on any of the courts used on the international circuit.

Although the first published notation system for sport was for tennis (Downey, 1973), it has not received as much attention from researchers in notational analysis as sports such as soccer, squash and rugby (Hughes and Franks, 1997). Recent research reports include Sailes (1989), who investigated the differences between three different methods of target-orientated hitting of groundstrokes from the back of the court, Furlong (1995), who analysed the effectiveness of serves on different surfaces and Hughes and Clarke (1995), who compared the patterns of play on different surfaces. No attempt has been made to model performance in tennis and offer templates for aspiring coaches and athletes to emulate. The aim of this research was to analyse how the top U.18 juniors from Britain play in terms of winning and losing major international matches, both against British opposition and players from other countries. It was hypothesised that British elite junior tennis players have different patterns of play to elite tennis players from the rest of the world.

2 Methods

2.1 Data collection system
It was decided to design a hand notation system, for this study, which could analyse all aspects of tennis. The following symbols were used to define a battery of actions:-

Science and Racket Sports II, edited by A. Lees, I. Maynard, M. Hughes and T. Reilly. Published in 1998 by E & FN Spon, 11 New Fetter Lane, London EC4P 4EE, UK. ISBN: 0 419 23030 0

F   = Forehand.
B   = Backhand.
V   = Volley.
S   = Slice.
T   = Topspin.
1st   = 1st Serve.
2nd   = 2nd Serve.
DS   = Drop Shot.
SM   = Smash.
HV   = High Volley.
c   = Cross court.
L   = Down the Line.
w   = Winner.
e   = Miss / Out / Net.

Analysis of elite players was based upon four zones of the court (see Figure 1). Within each of these zones, players adopt different tactics depending upon their perceptions of their own, and their opponents', strengths and weaknesses.

2.2 Data collection

Data were collected from two different tournaments; both were just before the 1996 Wimbledon Championships, and they attracted top players from all over the world. These tournaments were the I.T.F. Group 2 Tournament held at Imber Court, London and the I.T.F. Group 1 Tournament held in Roehampton, London. Eight matches were video-taped. The data included matches for British (N=6), Europeans (N=6) and Americans/ Canadian (N=3). The position of the players were specified using the sections defined in Fig.1. The matches were analysed using slow motion and replay when necessary to ensure accuracy. To validate the system, six games were analysed from a randomly selected match, after several weeks they were renotated. Using an ANOVA to measure reliability (Safrit and Wood, 1989) an R value of 0.94 was obtained. Chi-square was used to compare the frequency distributions of shots, winners and errors across the four positions of the court, a probability level of $P<0.05$ was deemed significant.

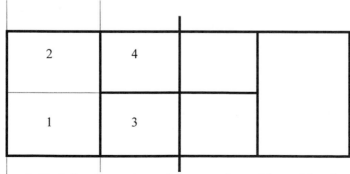

Figure 1. To define the sections of the court for positions of the players.

3.2 Description of hardware

When collecting this data a JVC, HR-J429 video recorder was used, which had a jog-shuttle system. This enabled both replay and slow motion editing of the action so that the position and bounce of the ball, as well as the type of shot used during each rally, could be accurately recorded. A data collection sheet was designed which included a vertical court outline, player's names, score between points, the number of games won, and number of sets won. Once the data was collected the results were processed using Windows Excel (4.0). A normal spreadsheet layout was used which incorporated all the shots notated and whether the shot was hit in or out.

3 Results and Discussion

Results from the eight matches were split into three groups of data, these were British, European and American players and are summarised in Table 1. Individual player analyses were also completed.

British players hit more groundstrokes from the back of the court than either of the other two groups. However, within both sections 1 and 2 of the court the British players only managed between 81% - 82% of all their shots in. When analysing shots in section 1 it was found that the British players were successful with the forehand, with a high percentage of winners down the line and cross court. In section 2, the backhand cross-court was the shot with the highest frequency, it had an 83% success rate compared to the second highest frequency shot, the forehand cross-court, which was successful for 85% of the shots. On analysing the volleys, it was found that the British hit nearly double the amount of volleys either of the other groups hit. From 159 attempts only 79% went in, which is only one percent behind the American players who hit 80% of all volleys in, whereas the Europeans hit only 77% of volleys in.

In a large number of situations the British players use inside-out forehands rather than backhands in the backhand court. This could demonstrate a lack of confidence in their backhands, and in some instances it was found that these British players, who hit more inside out forehands on the backhand side, were also hitting more errors on their backhands. The British players hit more volleys, which might explain why they made more errors. By trying to pressure their opponent through forcing the pace of the play - a higher risk strategy - they become more prone to making mistakes. It can be seen that the British players hit approximately 40 volleys per game, with almost 70% accuracy.

When analysing the errors of the British players, it was found that they made more on the backhand side, with only 70% - 87% of shots going in, compared to between 76% - 90% on the forehand side. British players have weaker groundshot profiles than their opponents from the other countries; this may be due to the types of surfaces on courts in this country. These courts have mainly fast surfaces which encourage the player to play at the net, whereas in Europe most courts are clay, which encourage the player to play a more rallying tactic from the baseline.

Comparison of the baseline figures of the American players to the British showed that the Americans were more consistent, between 82% - 84% of all their shots went in. Their groundstrokes were even more accurate, between 84% - 88% going in. The 'forehand down the line' was found to be less accurate than that of the British players, in that only 76% went in, compared to the British who got 81% in. When evaluating their volleys it was seen that they hit only 75 attempts at the net with an 80% accuracy rate.

The American players hit around the same number of shots from the back of the court as the British players but they hit between five and six errors less than the British players. Unlike the British players, the American players did not use the inside-out forehand as much, instead they hit more backhands with both topspin and slice. They also hit, on average, twenty volleys in a match, with only three or four misses, compared to the British who hit between 8 and 9 out. Like the British, the Americans and the Europeans hit one in six shots out, with the down the line shots creating the most errors. The most errors within the American players' games were within section 2 (on the backhand side) with between 77% - 86% of shots within this section going in, compared to 83% - 85% going in within section 1 (or forehand side). In this section the Americans were stronger on the forehand side compared to the Europeans, but were slightly weaker on the backhand side.

The Americans used both the drive backhand and the slice backhand during the rallies, compared to the Europeans who generally hit mostly drive backhands. The difference between the two is that the drive backhands are hit with topspin which allows the shot to travel high over the net, whereas the slice backhand is hit low over the net and skids through, when making impact with the ground. In using the slice backhand the Americans are more likely to make mistakes because the ball is travelling low over the net. Like the Europeans, the Americans used a variety of different shots in which to break up the rhythm of the opponent; instead of simply playing a back court or baseline game they chose to attack more. They hit between 5 to 25 volleys during a match compared to between 4 and 17 volleys hit by the Europeans.

One other point which was noticed when evaluating the results was that compared to the other two groups the Americans hit significantly ($P<0.01$) fewer errors within each of the sections. A reason for this could be that they play more competitive matches than the other players or that they train more on certain playing patterns.

The European players showed a significant difference between section 1 and section 2 ($P<0.01$), within section 1 only 78% of the shots went in, compared to 82% within section 2. The European players hit more errors on the forehand side, whereas on the backhand side it was found that 86% of all backhand attempts went in. Again when analysing the volleys it was also found that only 77% of volleys went in. Which is quite low compared to the British and Americans who managed respectively 79% and 80% of volleys in.

The European players generally played their games from the baseline and rarely played more than ten volleys during the match. A reason for this may be that nearly all the European players play their tournaments and practices on clay and hard courts, and rarely play on fast courts like grass and synthetic grass. Another difference between the British and Americans was that they hit significantly more ($P<0.01$) of their shots cross court rather than down the line. This is good practice as the net is lower in the middle, making the shot easier, compared to down the line which is where the net is at its highest. The European players struck one in four shots out during a rally, which is a high error rate compared to the British, which was one in six. A reason for this might be that the Europeans are playing a more 'open', i.e. all-court, game in which they are forcing the opponent around the court; in turn this means that they hit to a small margins of error. The European players were weaker on their forehand side with between 69% - 84% of all shots played in section 1 going in during a rally, compared to between 79% - 88% of shots played in the section 2 (or the backhand side) going in.

4 Conclusions

There were significant differences (P<0.01) in the patterns of play of the British under-18 players and those from Europe and North America in as much that:-

1. British players made more unforced errors from the back of the court.
2. European players hit more attacking from the back of the court.
3. British players played more defensive shots from the back.
4. British players won most points from the net, whereas continental players won more points from the back of the court.
5. British players had lower a percentage of passing shots than players from other continent.

Further research is suggested in analysing, at all levels, individual countries within Europe and comparing these with British players, and perhaps linking this with coaching styles in the respective countries. Analysis of particular areas of the courts and comparing from where the winners and errors are most likely to be hit would be informative about the different ways players are developing in different countries.

5 References

Downey, J.C. (1973) **The Singles Game**. London: E.P. Publications, London.
Furlong, J.D.G. (1995) The service in lawn tennis: how important is it? in **Science and Racket Sports** (eds T.Reilly, M.Hughes and A. Lees), E. & F.N.Spon, London, pp. 266-271.
Hughes, M. and Clarke, S. (1995) Surface effect on elite tennis strategy, in **Science and Racket Sports** (eds T.Reilly, M.Hughes and A. Lees), E. & F.N.Spon, London, pp. 272-277.
Safrit, M.J. and Wood, T.M. (1989) **Measurement Concepts in Physical Education and Exercise Science**. Human Kinetics, Champaign, Il.
Sailes, G. (1989) A comparison of three methods of target-orientated hitting on baseline groundstroke accuracy in tennis. **Journal of Applied Research in Coaching and Athletics,** 4 (1), 25-34.

38 Reliability and validity of a computer based notational analysis system for competitive table tennis

K. Wilson and C.A. Barnes

School of Social Sciences, University of Teesside, Middlesbrough, UK

1 Introduction

Despite the fact that the use of notation in the expressive arts to define and describe movement dates back thousands of years, its usefulness as an aid to understanding sports performance has only recently been recognised. The first notational analysis system to be produced for racket sports was that developed by Downey (1973) specifically for use in tennis. This and other early systems notated actions and activities by hand, with significant experience being needed to record data in 'real time'.

Advances in information technology over the past 20 years have led to the development of more efficient computer based notation systems. These have been shown to be effective tools in providing feedback on performance for coaches and athletes, and in gaining a greater understanding of the nature of specific sports. In racket sports, computer based systems have been developed and utilised for squash (Hughes, 1995; Hughes and Knight, 1995; Brown and Hughes, 1995) and tennis (Hughes and Clarke, 1994). To date no computer based notational analysis system has been developed for use in table tennis.

The physical and technical demands of table tennis at the highest level are comparable with other racket sports. Rallies are rapid, and often feature a wide range of shots and movement patterns, with matches often lasting over 2 hours. Given this fact, post-match analysis based on individual recollection is not likely to produce a truly objective account. A notational analysis system, either carried out in real time or post-match from video recordings, would offer the same benefits to table tennis as established systems provide for other sports.

One potential limitation with any notational analysis system concerns the reliability of data input. Inconsistent interpretation of performer actions or movement patterns, particularly in table tennis where differences may be very subtle is a threat to overall system reliability, and the validity of subsequent analysis.

Whilst previous studies justify the reliability of notational analysis systems on the basis of a set period of system familiarisation time(e.g. Brown and Hughes, 1994), few then quantify reliability of inputted data in statistical terms. The aim of this study was

Science and Racket Sports II, edited by A. Lees, I. Maynard, M. Hughes and T. Reilly. Published in 1998 by E & FN Spon, 11 New Fetter Lane, London EC4P 4EE, UK. ISBN: 0 419 23030 0

to evaluate the reliability and concurrent validity of data inputted into a computer based notational analysis system designed and developed for use in table tennis.

2 Methods

2.1 Development of the notational analysis system
Prior to developing the notation system, a comprehensive glossary of descriptors for table tennis shots and player movements was assimilated. This followed detailed discussions with national league players and coaches, analysis of video footage and examination of existing programs written for the notation of other racket sports.

The final system was Windows© based with data being entered using the 'Mouse' via a graphical representation of a table tennis table and criteria icons. The system enables data input relating to the following parameters:- serve (type and ball end destination); return of serve(type and ball end destination); mid-rally details including nature of shot (positive or negative), movement of player (advance, retreat, stood ground), position of ball when taken (rising ball, top of bounce, dropping ball), type of shot (top spin, push, flick, back spin, wiggly); where the ball bounced on the table, and end of rally details.

The analysis component of the system provides details ranging from basic outcomes (e.g. number of points won and lost on own/opponents serve) to more complex permutations drawing from multiple inputs (e.g. the distribution of serves from which points were won).

2.2 Procedure
Six national league men's singles matches were video recorded, with six games being randomly sampled for subsequent analysis. The video camera was set up along the net line of the table, the camera view allowing for film to be collected to a minimum of 3 m behind the end lines of the table.

Two observers were trained in the operation of the system through practice sessions in the presence of an experienced table tennis coach (to verify shot selection) and a second individual who was involved with the design of the system. Of the observers who were testing the reliability of the system, one had over 10 years playing experience at a high standard, the other was not a table tennis player but had experience in the operation of similar notational analysis systems. Training sessions were conducted until the observers, the experienced coach and the system designer were confident with the operation of the system and input of data. Due to the speed of table tennis, data input was conducted post-event in slow motion from video using a jog/shuttle facility enabling play to be notated frame by frame.

2.3 System reliability and concurrent validity
Inter-tester reliability for the system was determined for the 2 observers notating the 6 games. Intra-tester reliability was evaluated by one of the observers (the experienced player) re-notating the same 6 games, with the second notation session occurring 7 days after the first. Inter- and intra-tester reliability measures were calculated for all observed sections of the game using Cronbach's alpha coefficient. An alpha value of 0.6 was set as the criterion level for acceptable reliability (Weiss et al., 1985).

Concurrent validity of the system was determined by comparing results from the 6 computer notated games by the experienced player with the same 6 games notated manually by an experienced international table tennis coach. The 'hand notation' system was based on the same parameters used for the computer software to facilitate subsequent comparative analysis. The validity of the computerised system was quantified using a measure of overall percentage agreement - the ratio of observed agreement to total number of observations from which the agreements were taken. The acceptable limit for this method proposed by Rushall (1977) being 80%.

3 Results and Discussion

Table 1 highlights inter- and intra-observer reliability coefficients for each of the notated components of the game. Intra tester reliability, based on the data inputted by the experienced player, was high on all areas, ranging from 0.86 (rally shot movements) to 0.98 (rally shot details and end of rally details). These results suggest that individuals with substantial experience of table tennis identify player actions and movements consistently.

Inter-tester reliability, as determined by comparison between the data inputted by the experienced player and that of the non-experienced player raises questions over the consistency with which actions and movements were identified and subsequently notated. Alpha coefficients ranged from 0.40 (service type) to 0.91 (rally shot details), indicating obvious differences in interpretation of the video footage.

Table 1. Reliability coefficients (Cronbach's alpha) for inter- and intra-tester reliability

	Reliability coefficient	
Parameter	Intra observer	Inter observer
Service type	0.97	0.40
Service return type	0.97	0.46
Rally shot details	0.98	0.91
Rally shot movements	0.86	0.75
End of rally details	0.98	0.88

Concurrent validity as determined by overall percentage agreement between the computer notated data of the experienced player and the hand notated data of the experienced coach was 95.2%, in excess of the criterion level. This would suggest that the data inputted by the experienced player was both valid and reliable. However, discrepancies between data input by the experienced player and the inexperienced player raise questions over the validity of interpretations of the latter.

The results of this study highlight a number of issues concerning the design and operation of computer-based notational analysis 'packages'. Firstly, the table tennis system in question requires that observers make a number of subjective decisions regarding shot selection, for example whether the shot made was 'positive' or 'negative' or whether errors were 'forced' or not. This, coupled with the subtlety with which players disguise spin, makes accurate assessment of shots (even post-event using frame by frame video footage) a difficult task. Secondly, the assumption that a reasonable period of system familiarisation is sufficient to guarantee reliable data would, on the basis of the results of this study, appear to be invalid. Indeed, the data would suggest that this system should only be used by persons who satisfy the criteria of substantial table tennis experience and system familiarisation. Thirdly, it is suggested that in the design of computer based notation systems, care should be taken to minimise subjective interpretation on the part of the observer. Finally, prior to reporting results from the output component of notational analysis systems, input reliability and validity should be quantified in future studies.

4 Conclusions

This results of this study have highlighted specific methodological considerations which must be addressed with regards to inputted data in computer based notation systems. Without adequate quality control over inputted data the reliability and validity of subsequent outputs and analysis will remain questionable.

5 References

Brown, D. and Hughes, M. (1994) The effectiveness of qualitative and quantitative feedback on performance in squash, in **Science and Racket Sports** (eds T. Reilly, M. Hughes and A. Lees), E. and F. N. Spon, London, pp. 232-237.

Downey, J.C. (1973) **The Singles Game**. E.P. Publications, London.

Hughes, M. (1995) Using notational analysis to create a more exciting scoring system for squash, in **Sport, Leisure and Ergonomics** (eds G. Atkinson and T. Reilly), E. and F.N. Spon, London, pp 243 - 247.

Hughes, M. and Clarke, S. (1994) Surface effect on elite tennis strategy, in **Science and Racket Sports** (eds T. Reilly, M. Hughes, A. Lees), E. and F. N. Spon, London, pp. 272-277.

Hughes, M. and Knight, P. (1994) Playing patterns of elite squash players, using English and point-per-rally scoring, in **Science and Racket Sports** (eds T. Reilly, M. Hughes, A. Lees), E. and F. N. Spon, London, pp 257-259.

Rushall, B.S. (1977) Two observation schedules for sporting and physical education environments. **Canadian Journal of Applied Sports Science**, 2, 15-21.

Weiss, M.R., Bredemeier, B.J. and Shewchuck, R.M. (1985) An intrinsic/extrinsic motivation scale for the youth sport setting: A confirmatory factor analysis. **Journal of Sports Psychology**, 7, 75-91.

39 Game performance and game understanding in badminton of Finnish primary school children

M. Blomqvist, P. Luhtanen and L. Laakso
*Research Institute for Olympic Sports, Jyväskylä, Finland,
Department of Physical Education, University of Jyväskylä,
Jyväskylä, Finland*

1 Introduction

Game performance can be divided into cognitive and skill components. In sports the cognitive component includes decision making and knowledge, whereas the skill component includes motor execution. Quality of decision making in a game situation is often as important as execution of the motor skills, and both of these determine successful performance in sport (Thomas, 1994).

The relationship between cognition and motor skill is important in the development of skilled sport performance in young children. However, it has been shown that the development of cognitive skills progress at a faster rate than the development of motor skills (Thomas et al., 1988).

In the case of developing good decision makers in games, a model presented by Bunker and Thorpe (1982) can be used. This "teaching for understanding" approach provides learning tasks that give learners the opportunity to make tactical decisions in the context of the game.

The purpose of this study was to compare subjects' game understanding and game performance in badminton between two age groups and gender.

2 Methods

2.1 Subjects
Primary school children in two different age groups 9-10 years (girls N=5 and boys N=5) and 12-13 years (girls N=5 and boys N=5) served as subjects.

2.2 Procedure
First, the subjects played modified singles badminton 2 x 5 min against different opponents in a standard badminton court. No strategic or tactical advice was given during the matches and all matches were video recorded for further analysis.

Science and Racket Sports II, edited by A. Lees, I. Maynard, M. Hughes and T. Reilly. Published in 1998 by E & FN Spon, 11 New Fetter Lane, London EC4P 4EE, UK.   ISBN: 0 419 23030 0

Afterwards, the subjects took part in a video test, which was produced in order to measure their game understanding in badminton. In the same test situation subjects also filled a questionnaire which measured their involvement in sport activities.

2.3 The notation system

A computerised notation system (SAGE Game Manager™ for badminton software) was used to analyse all matches. For every shot, the player's position, time, and action were recorded. The differences in the patterns of play between the age groups were compared in eight different variables:- amount of shots, amount of rallies, effective playing time, distance travelled by player, length of the shots and percentages of different shots, successful shots and unforced errors.

2.4 The video test

The game understanding video test consisted of 19 different sequences which were simulations (video) of actual offensive and defensive match situations. The two badminton players in the test video were asked to play using given patterns of play. All the events were recorded by JVC GY-X2 video camera. With a coach's assistance, 19 different situations were selected for editing on to the video test tape. The editing system used included two computer driven JVC BR-S500E video cassette players and a Movie Studio editing program. In the test situation the video sequences were shown on a large screen by Sharp Vision XV-330H videoprojector.

Each video sequence contained three stages. First, each sequence started with a serve followed by play for 4-7 s. Second, a still frame of the situation in which the other player was getting ready to play his shot was shown for 10 s. Finally, a diagram from which the subject could choose his/her response from arrows representing three optional player's shot responses was shown for 10 s. The sequences were separated by 30 s of blank tape, during which time the subjects had to select the correct shot option out of three alternatives on a separate sheet of paper. In addition, the subjects had to choose two arguments, the best argument and second best argument, from a set of ten arguments stating why they operated in the chosen way.

A weighting scheme was used to score the subject's responses to the sequences. From the video test, each player received a combined score in the video test (CSV). It was a sum of the points obtained from correctly selected shot options, the best argument options and second best argument options (maximum 114 points).

2.5 Statistical analysis

The means and standard deviations of the game understanding scores and the descriptive variables in game analysis by age and gender were calculated. A t-test was applied to evaluate the differences between age groups and gender. In the game analysis, percentage calculations and a Chi-square test were used to evaluate the statistical differences between the age groups and gender. A value of $P < 0.05$ was required for significance.

3 Results and Discussion

The results of the questionnaire in sport activities showed that the subjects had almost no previous experience in badminton.

Table 1 shows that the combined scores of the video test were between 46-54% of the maximum (114 points) and almost the same between the age and gender groups. This implies that the basic tactical ideas in badminton could partly be understood even though the subjects had only little experience in badminton.

Table 1. Selected mean and S.D. scores for the different age and gender groups
(CSV=combined score in the video test, AR=number of rallies, AS=number of shots, ET=effective playing time and DT=distance travelled)

	CSV	AR	AS	ET (s)	DT (m)
G: 9-10	52±15	22±8	69±21	169±58	126±38
B: 9-10	56±19 ⌐ ns	22±9 ⌐ ns	59±14 ⌐***	137±41 ⌐ ***	79±26 ⌐ ***
G: 12-13	62±9 _	20±8 _	97±6 _	274±29 _	174±20_
B: 12-13	56±10	24±12	118±19	298±78	204±35

P<0.05 *, P<0.01 ** and P<0.001 ***

Comparison of the game performance in the age groups and gender revealed that the significant differences were mostly found between the age groups. There was a significant difference between the age groups in AS, ET and DT (P<0.001). These results indicated that the effective playing time was shorter and due to this, the number of shots and the distance travelled were lower in the younger subjects compared to the older ones. Based on the number of rallies it can be concluded that the younger subjects played shorter rallies than the older ones. This may be due to their lower skill level in badminton.

The shots were divided into three different categories: successful shots, unforced errors and forced errors. The percentage of successful shots was better in the age group 12-13 years (91%) than in the age group 9-10 years (80%). The percentage of unforced errors was 17% in the age group 9-10 years and 8% in the age group 12-13 years. In both cases the difference was significant (P< 0.001). The lower percentage of unforced errors supports the idea of better racket handling skills in the older subjects.

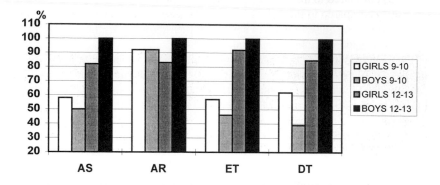

Figure 1. Descriptive game analysis variables in the different age and gender groups
(AS=number of shots, AR=number of rallies, ET=effective playing time and
DT= distance travelled).

When comparing the relative distributions of the game analysis variables; AS, AR,
ET and DT (Figure 1), one finding was noteworthy. In the age group 12-13 years the
boys were better than the girls while in the younger age group the reverse applied. It
seems that in the younger age group the girls were more skillful than the boys and thus
also played longer rallies.

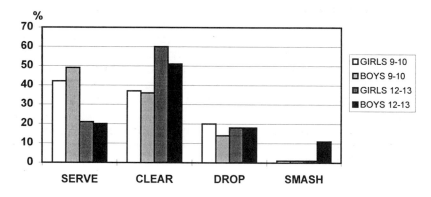

Figure 2. A comparison of shots used in the different age and gender groups.

The overall average number of serves, clears, drops and smashes were 128, 206, 76
and 20, respectively. The relative distributions of the respective shots can be seen in
Figure 2. Chi-square analysis of the distribution of all the shots revealed that there was
a significant difference (P<0.001) between the age groups in the shots used. The
serves played greater importance in the game of the younger subjects whereas the older
subjects played more clears and smashes (Figure 2) compared to the younger ones. In
addition, the younger subjects played more underarm (P<0.01) and lower shots

(P<0.05) compared to the older ones. The boys played significantly more smashes (P<0.001) compared to the girls and thus were more attacking in their playing pattern.

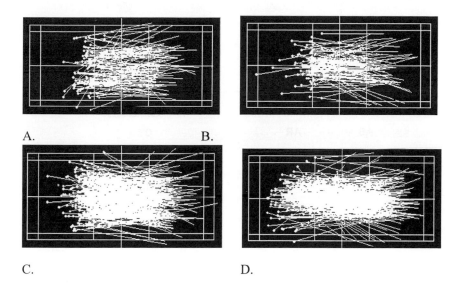

Figure 3. Graphical analysis of clears (A. girls 9-10 years, B. boys 9-10 years, C. girls 12-13 years and D. boys 12-13 years).

The graphical analysis of clears (Figure 3) indicated that the older subjects utilised the length of the courts more in their game than the younger ones. The average length of the shots in different age and gender groups: G:9-10, B:9-10, G:12-13 and B:12-13 was 479±32 cm, 429±33 cm, 501±30 cm and 591±51 cm, respectively. The difference between age groups was significant (P<0.01). In the older subjects a significant difference (P<0.05) was also found between the girls and the boys. It seems, that the boys kept the shuttle even deeper than the girls, who moved their opponents more from side to side. The ability to hit the shuttle harder could be based on better technical skills and strength level of the boys.

4 Conclusions

The scores of the game understanding test implied that the younger subjects had already developed their game understanding almost to the level of the older subjects even though their technical skills were not as good as the skills of the older subjects. This reinforces the idea (Thomas et al., 1988) that the development of the cognitive component, which includes decision making and knowledge, progressed at a faster rate than the development of the motor skills.

Although it seems that the basic tactical ideas in badminton are quite easy to understand, it is difficult at least for the younger children, to keep the shuttle alive and thus carry out their tactical decisions in actual game play. Therefore, it would be crucial from the tactical perspective to use modified games (Doolittle and Girard, 1991), in which players can either play a simple tactical game or even employ more complex tactics in a situation were their skill level does not restrict the use of their tactical knowledge.

5 References

Bunker, D. and Thorpe, R. (1982) A model for teaching of games in secondary schools. **Bulletin of Physical Education**, 19 (1), 5-8.

Doolittle, S. A. and Girard, K.T. (1991). A dynamic approach to teaching games in elementary PE. **Journal of Physical Education**, Recreation and Dance, 62(7), 57-62.

Thomas, K.T. (1994). The development of sport expertise: From Leds to MVP Legend. **Quest**, 46, 199-210.

Thomas, J.R. French, K.E., Thomas, K.T. and Gallagher, J.D. (1988). Children's Knowledge Development and Sport Performance, in **Children in Sport** (3rd Edition). (eds F.L.Smoll, R.A. Magill, and M.J. Ash), Human Kinetics, Champaign, IL.

40 Notational analysis of rallies in European circuit badminton

D. Liddle[1] and P. O'Donoghue[2]
[1]Causeway Institute of Higher and Further Education, County Londonderry, Northern Ireland and [2]Faculty of Informatics, University of Ulster, County Antrim, Northern Ireland

1 Introduction

Badminton is a racket sport played on a relatively small court using a shuttlecock rather than a ball. It is both psychologically (Jones, 1995) and physiologically demanding and typically involves more severe injuries than most other sports (Hoy et al., 1995). The most frequent shots tend to be fast stretching movements called lunges (Smith and Lees, 1995) that involve forces applied to the ground which can lead to high forces in the lower limb musculature (Lees and Hurley, 1995).

Compared with tennis, badminton appears to be more intense and lies close to squash in terms of heart rate response, lactate build up and energy expenditure. A badminton match at elite level can have a duration of 45-60 min with the shuttlecock in play between 60% and 70% of the match (Turnbull, 1992). Liddle et al. (1996b) found average rally lengths in elite male singles play to be greater than 6 s, significantly longer than average rally lengths in doubles.

The physiological demands of elite badminton combine speed, power and endurance. Training for badminton must be specific to the demands of the game. Therefore, specialised drills have been devised. Training can be categorised into on- and off-court preparation, game specific adaptation and technical development (Hughes, M.G., 1995). Training for elite players is predominantly aerobic, placing considerable stress on the cardiovascular system, although specific preparation and actual competition are sufficiently intense to cause blood lactate accumulation (Hughes, M.G., 1995). A primary objective of any badminton training programme is to increase $\dot{V}O_2$ max. Dias and Ghosh (1995) have reported a significant improvement in $\dot{V}O_2$ max. at training intensities of 78% and 90% of maximum heart rate in accordance with the recommendations of Pollock (1977) but indicate the importance of intermittent training to increase maximal exercise capacity. Such training is valuable for physically demanding matches. Liddle et al. (1996b) found that for elite male badminton, the singles game has a significantly greater mean %maximum heart rate than doubles with a greater proportion of the match where the player's heart rate is over 90% HR max. The higher heart rates of the singles game may be partly explained by the braking action used to recover to base after each stroke (Astrand and Rodahl, 1986).

Science and Racket Sports II, edited by A. Lees, I. Maynard, M. Hughes and T. Reilly. Published in 1998 by E & FN Spon, 11 New Fetter Lane, London EC4P 4EE, UK.   ISBN: 0 419 23030 0

Notational analysis is the systematic gathering, analysis and communication of detailed information relating to competitive sport. Notational analysis of badminton has also been used in conjunction with force plate study in order to evaluate shoe surface interaction (Smith and Lees, 1995). Liddle and Murphy (1996) performed a single subject notational analysis study to provide a qualitative explanation of the physiological demands of the singles and doubles games in elite male badminton. Video and manual analysis methods were used. The subject covered an average of 18.6 m per rally in the singles game and 9.5 m per rally in the doubles game. In total 3.12 strokes were played per rally in the singles match compared with 1.46 shots per rally in the doubles match and a greater proportion of the singles game was spent performing medium and high intensity activity. Another important observation was that 54% of shots in the singles match were overhead compared with 33% in the doubles match. The major limitation of this was that it used manual methods, restricting the study to a single subject. The need to apply computerised techniques to the study of badminton has been recognised (Liddle et al., 1996a). The development of computerised systems for racket sports (Hughes, 1995) followed advances in portability, memory capacity and human computer interaction. Computerised systems introduce the benefits of historical databases, efficient querying and automatic control of video feedback (Franks et al., 1983). Hughes et al. (1989) recommended that advances in methodology should be validated and system users should be sufficiently trained. The development process for time and motion analysis applications should address end-user training requirements as well as reliability assessment (O'Donoghue et al., 1996). The purpose of this study was to investigate differences in shot rates between singles and doubles in the men's and ladies' games using a computerised shot and rally analysis system.

2 Methods

2.1 System development, end-user training and reliability evaluation

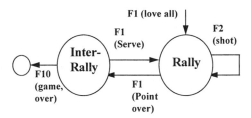

Figure 1. State transition representation of system execution.

A computerised system was developed for IBM compatible PCs to record rallies in racket sports. The system contains capture, analysis and merge facilities and uses function keys for data entry. The system records a full match history and accumulated totals. Two observers were trained to operate it before simultaneously using the system on two separate notepad computers over a four match reliability study (using

Ulster League Division One matches). This was live rather than post-match video-analysis and inter-observer variation did not exceed 1.5% for the time recorded for rallies. During the reliability study, qualitative observation suggested that there were differences in shot tallies within the men's and ladies' games. Therefore, the system was amended in order to capture shots as well as rallies. A further reliability study assessed inter-observer variation in shots per rally for a men's doubles game of 157 rallies. The number of shots entered by the two observers for 5.1% of the rallies differed by one shot. The observers recorded the same number of shots for the remainder of the rallies.

2.2 Subjects
The activity of elite players participating in 17 matches of the European Badminton Circuit tournament at Lisburn, Northern Ireland (5th-7th December 1996) was analysed using the system. Four of the matches were men's singles (MS), four were ladies' singles (LS), five were men's doubles (MD) and four were ladies' doubles (LD). As in the reliability studies, match data were entered into the system during competition.

3 Results

The mean rally lengths (MS 9.15 $\pm$0.43 s, LS 6.73 $\pm$1.25 s, MD 6.35 $\pm$1.39 s, LD 7.61 $\pm$1.81 s) and rest times (MS 13.84 $\pm$1.16 s, LS 11.03 $\pm$2.09 s, MD 15.01 $\pm$1.63 s, LD 11.72 $\pm$0.87 s) are shown in Figure 2. Men's singles rallies were significantly longer than those of ladies' singles ($P<0.01$) and men's doubles ($P<0.01$). Male players took longer rest times than ladies' in both singles ($P<0.05$) and doubles ($P<0.01$).

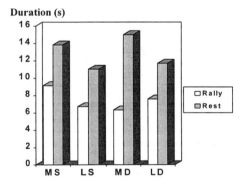

Figure 2. Mean rally and rest durations.

There was little variation in inter-shot times for the matches analysed within individual disciplines. There were 1.004 $\pm$0.046 shot.s^{-1} in MS, 0.862 $\pm$0.034 shot.s^{-1} in LS, 1.349 $\pm$0.052 shot.s^{-1} in MD and 1.183 $\pm$0.029 shot.s^{-1} in LD as illustrated in figure 3. The shots per second results are significantly greater for men's badminton than ladies' for both singles ($P<0.01$) and doubles ($P<0.001$) play. Although the doubles games involved two people on each side of the net, shots did not alternate between them. Therefore, the greater shot rate for doubles requires greater reactions from the doubles player.

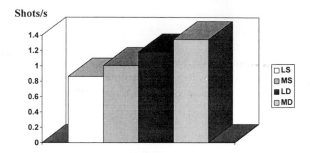

Figure 3. Mean number of shots per second in the four disciplines

In addition to the mean rally length in each discipline, the distribution of rally lengths was also considered. The results of this analysis are presented in table 1. Ladies' singles involved significantly fewer rallies over 16 seconds than men's singles ($P<0.01$). The rallies in men's singles were significantly longer than in ladies' singles ($P<0.01$) and men's doubles ($P<0.01$). There were significantly more rallies of less than two seconds in doubles than singles in both the men's and the ladies' games ($P<0.001$).

Table 1. Summary rally analyses for each discipline (mean ± S.D.)

Rallies	Men's Singles	Ladies' Singles	Men's Doubles	Ladies' Doubles
% 0 to <2 s	4.29+2.69	1.88+3.25	27.65+3.49	16.42+3.44
% 2 to <4 s	20.87+3.70	29.37+10.53	26.42+6.02	22.57+4.34
% 4 to <8 s	30.83+3.32	39.75+4.47	21.28+3.64	28.73+8.28
% 8 to <16s	30.62+4.00	25.47+8.15	15.46+4.07	22.28+5.11
% >=16 s	13.17+2.18	3.79+3.87	9.20+4.72	10.11+5.48

During data entry, qualitative observation suggested that those rallies immediately following long rallies were often of short duration primarily as a result of unforced errors. With complete rally histories being available for each match, the issue of long rallies could be analysed. Seventeen of all rallies recorded were over 30 s duration. These occurred in 9 of the 17 matches analysed. The mean duration of the three rallies that followed each of these (6.77, 6.15 and 6.76 s) was observably shorter than the mean rally length within these matches (8.52 s). Figure 4 identifies this trend.

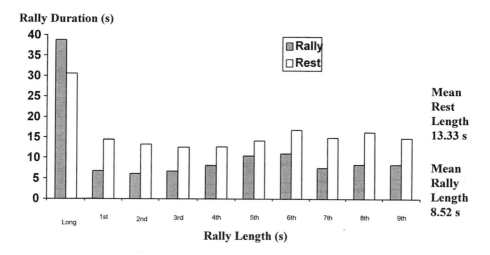

Figure 4. Duration of rallies and rests that follow long rallies.

4 Discussion

The differences recorded for the male and female disciplines indicated that badminton training should be game specific. Timing information analysis can be incorporated into practice situations to highlight lapses of concentration, particularly after long rallies. Players can identify areas of the game where fatigue is leading to a detriment in performance.

This study highlights shorter inter-rally recovery times throughout the ladies' game compared to the men's game. This may be due to the greater intensity, speed of play and the longer rally lengths in men's singles. A further explanation may be that ladies' do not incorporate tactical manoeuvres between rallies. It is difficult to make such a conclusion from the current study, even though the results were statistically significant.

5 Conclusions

This study provides evidence that elite ladies' and men's singles and doubles badminton matches are characterised by different distributions of rally lengths, rest times and shot rates. Therefore, coaches should devise training sessions that are specific to the disciplines for which their players are preparing. All players should consider how to best utilise inter-rally time, particularly in the doubles games, where the strategy to be adopted must be understood by both players.

6 Acknowledgements

The authors wish to thank Raymond Stevens (Irish National Badminton Coach) and members of the Danish squad for their interest in this study and the discussion of how such results can be applied in practice by coaches and players.

7 References

Astrand, P.O. and Rodahl, K. (1986) **Textbook of Work Physiology**, (3rd Edition). New York, McGraw-Hill.

Dias, R. and Ghosh, A.K. (1995) Physiological evaluation of specific training in badminton, in **Science and Racket Sports**, (eds T. Reilly, M. Hughes and A. Lees), E. & F.N. Spon, London, pp. 38-43.

Franks, I.M., Goodman, D. and Miller, G. (1983) Analysis of performance: qualitative or quantitative, **Scientific Periodical on Research and Technology in Sport**, Coaching Association of Canada, Ottawa, March.

Hoy, K., Terkelson, C.J., Lindblad, B.E., Helleland, H.E. and Terkelsen, C.J. (1995) Badminton Injuries, in **Science and Racket Sports** (eds T. Reilly, M. Hughes and A. Lees), E. & F.N. Spon, London, pp. 184-185.

Hughes, M. (1995), Computerised Notation of Racket Sports, in **Science and Racket Sports** (edsT. Reilly, M. Hughes and A. Lees), E. & F.N. Spon, London, pp. 249-256.

Hughes, M.G. (1995) Physiological demands of training in elite badminton players, in **Science and Racket Sports** (eds T. Reilly, M. Hughes and A. Lees), E. & F.N. Spon, London, pp. 32-37.

Hughes, M., Franks, I.M. and Nagelkerke, P. (1989) A video system for quantitative motion analysis of athletes in competitive sport. **Journal of Human Movement Studies**, 17, 212-227.

Jones, G. (1995) Psychological preparation in Racket Sports, in **Science and Racket Sports** (eds T. Reilly, M. Hughes and A. Lees), E. & F.N. Spon, London, pp. 203-211.

Lees, A. and Hurley, C. (1995) Forces in a badminton lunge movement, in **Science and Racket Sports** (eds T. Reilly, M. Hughes and A. Lees), E. & F.N. Spon, London, pp. 186-189.

Liddle, S.D. and Murphy, M.H. (1996) A comparison of the demands of singles and doubles badminton among elite male players. **World Congress of Notational Analysis of Sport**, Antalya, Turkey, 18th-20th September 1996.

Liddle, S.D., Murphy, M.H. and Bleakley, E.W. (1996a) A comparison of the demands of singles and doubles badminton among elite male players: a heart rate and time/motion analysis. **Journal of Human Movement Studies**, 29, 159-176.

Liddle, S.D., Murphy, M.H. and Bleakley, E.W. (1996b) A comparison of the physiological demands of singles and doubles badminton among elite male players. **BASES**, Lilleshall, 7-9th September 1996.

Pollock, M.L. (1977) Submaximal and maximal working capacity of elite distance runners, Part 1: Cardio-respiratory aspects. **Annals of the New York Academy of Science**, 301, 310-322.

O'Donoghue, P.G., Martin, G.D. and Murphy, M.H. (1996) Systematic development of time and motion analysis applications. **Proceedings of the 2nd International Conference of Technical Informatics**, Timisoara, Romania, pp. 123-130.

Smith, N. and Lees, A. (1995) An ergonomic evaluation of the shoe-surface interface in badminton, in **Science and Racket Sports** (eds T. Reilly, M. Hughes and A. Lees), E. & F.N. Spon, London, pp. 121-124.

Turnbull, A. (1992) Health and Fitness : Strung out, in **Rackets; The Official Magazine of the Racket Sports Association**, 9-10.

Author Index

Subject Index